THE GROWTH OF RELIGIOUS DIVERSITY

BRITAIN FROM 1945

A READER

THE GROWTH OF RELIGIOUS DIVERSITY

BRITAIN FROM 1945

A READER

EDITED BY JOHN WOLFFE

Hodder & Stoughton

A MEMBER OF THE HODDER HEADLINE GROUP

This reader is one part of an Open University integrated teaching system and the selection is therefore related to other material available to students. It is designed to evoke the critical understanding of students. Opinions expressed in it are not necessarily those of the course team or of the University.

Orders: please contact Bookpoint Ltd, 39 Milton Park, Abingdon, Oxon OX14 4TD. Telephone: (44) 01235 400414, Fax: (44) 01235 400454. Lines are open from 9.00-6.00, Monday to Saturday, with a 24 hour message answering service. Email address: orders@bookpoint.co.uk

British Library Cataloguing in Publication Data
Growth of Religious Diversity in Britain
from 1945: Reader
 I. Wolffe, John
 306.60941

ISBN 0-340-60066-7

First published 1993
Impression number   10 9 8 7 6 5 4
Year   2005 2004 2003 2002 2001 2000

Typeset by Rowland Phototypesetting Ltd, Bury St. Edmunds, Suffolk
Printed in Great Britain for Hodder & Stoughton Educational,
a division of Hodder Headline Plc, 338 Euston Road, London NW1 3BH
by Athenæum Press Ltd, Gateshead, Tyne & Wear.

CONTENTS

Introduction

1 CHRISTIANITY

2 JUDAISM

3 MUSLIMS

8 POPULAR ATTITUDES TO RELIGION

9 INTER-RELIGIOUS RELATIONS

10 CHURCH, STATE AND POLITICS

11 EDUCATION

12 WOMEN

13 CHRISTIANS AND SEXUAL MORALITY

14 BROADCASTING: THREE REPORTS

INTRODUCTION

This book has been conceived as an integral part of the Open University half-credit course *The Growth of Religious Diversity: Britain from 1945*, but should also be of service to many others needing a compilation of material on this subject. The aim is to provide a selection of sources which illuminate historical developments during the last four and a half decades, designed to convey something of the nature and significance of the increase in religious pluralism during the period. There is, however, no pretension to comprehensiveness: it would be quite impossible within a single volume of moderate size to represent all the groups and tendencies now present in Britain, and so selection has sometimes had to be ruthless. In relation to such a recent period, it is difficult to apply satisfactorily the conventional distinction between primary and secondary sources, but the reader will find here a full range of approaches from the passionately engaged to the analytically detached. Balance is sought not through the representation of every perspective, but through the selection of items that taken as a whole are complementary in their subject matter and point of view.

In making my choice I have been guided particularly by an endeavour to document processes of survival, renewal and adaptation. Although there is ample evidence in this book that rumours of the death of God were much exaggerated, there were still significant ways in which religion struggled for survival. The Christian churches were faced with the erosion of their influence in society and culture, and with profound doubts as to the validity of their traditional teaching. 'Minority' religions – including the long-standing Jewish community as well as the faiths of more recent settlers from South Asia and elsewhere – wrestled with how to define their identity and maintain their beliefs and practices in the face of coldness and lack of understanding of the majority of the population. Some new religious movements stirred outright hostility, leading to legal and political challenges to their very existence.

The potential of religion to survive in the second half of the twentieth century derived not so much from dogged resistance to change, as from an often underestimated capacity for renewal and adaptation. Among the Christian churches, the 1960s and 1970s saw not only fundamental questioning, but evangelical and charismatic resurgence, while many Afro-Caribbean people responded to the coldness of 'white' churches not with religious indifference, but with the fervent development of their own distinctive brand of Christianity. Among Sikhs attacks on their co-religionists in the Punjab strengthened devotion in Britain; while for Muslims the controversy over Salman Rushdie's novel *The Satanic Verses* had a similarly cathartic effect. The very proliferation of new religious movements was a sign of a widespread spiritual searching and restlessness.

Meanwhile, there were numerous endeavours to adapt to changing circumstances, varying perhaps in their effectiveness, but all signs of creativity and engagement. Christians and Jews sought to apply their teachings to a secular society; Hindus, Muslims and others modified their rituals and religious practice in an initially unfamiliar social and cultural setting. In the background was the continuing broad, sometimes rather shallow, stream of diffuse belief among the majority of the population. While its continuities were significant, it too had a potential for regeneration and re-formation which helped to ensure its continuance.

In the later sections of the book the organizing principle shifts from particular religious categories to issues that cut across a range of traditions. Growing attention to inter-religious relations was an illustration of how the different faiths were adapting to the reality of coexistence, but also heightened awareness of the challenges that remained. The sections on politics and on education illustrate how during the 1980s religious questions were regaining a prominent role in national and community life. Vitality too was evident in the aspirations of women for self-fulfilment, freedom and equality in the religious sphere. Sharp debates on sexual morality and abortion were a symptom of restlessness but hardly of complacency. Broadcasters struggled to reflect the complexity and range of religious viewpoints. The underlying impression that emerges of religion in Britain in the second half of the twentieth century is therefore one of dynamism and diversity, often ill-at-ease, sometimes explosive, but seldom stagnant.

I have been greatly assisted in the production of this book by my colleagues in the Course Team, particularly George Chryssides, Kim Knott, Gerald Parsons and Terry Thomas, who have suggested items for inclusion, spent laborious hours tracking down texts, and patiently responded to my queries and quibbles. The organizational unflappability of Jenny Cook and the secretarial assistance of Wendy Clark and Cheryl O'Toole have been absolutely invaluable. I also greatly appreciate the trouble taken by the representatives of numerous organizations, who responded generously to my requests for material. Those items included here are more specifically acknowledged elsewhere; it is a matter of regret that constraints of space force the omission of much other fascinating and significant material.

Editorial policy has been to cut footnotes in originals, except where these have been deemed to contain essential explanatory information. Omissions are indicated by an ellipsis and editorial interpolations by square brackets. Obvious misprints have been corrected, and numbering of paragraphs sometimes deleted or amended (using square brackets) but in all other respects texts have been reproduced entirely as found. A full reference to the source is given at the end of each extract.

John Wolffe
Faculty of Arts, The Open University
March 1993

1
CHRISTIANITY

O n 3 November 1946 the Archbishop of Canterbury, Geoffrey Fisher, preaching in Cambridge, set out a vision of closer ties between Christian denominations (a). His words reflected a post-war sense of new beginnings, but in the event fresh ideas were to be expressed against a backdrop of seemingly inexorable weakening in the social influence of the churches (b). By the 1960s there was a widespread sense of crisis, which found varied expression. Two notable examples are given here: Bishop John Robinson's call for a 'radical recasting' of Christian belief (c); and the controversy in the Roman Catholic Church stirred by Charles Davis's resignation from the priesthood in 1966. This had been precipitated by his questioning of papal authority over the matter of contraception, an issue which was still troubling the Church in 1980 (d).

At the same time more counter-cultural forces were apparent. The 1960s saw evangelicalism gaining renewed confidence and influence, and growing closer to other strands of Christianity, trends evident in the National Evangelical Anglican Congress at Keele in 1967 (e). Charismatic renewal linked theological traditionalism to organizational and liturgical innovation, transforming modes of worship and opening up new spiritual and pastoral possibilities. This is illustrated by Colin Urquhart's account of his ministry in the Church of England parish of St Hugh's, Luton, in the early 1970s (f). Elsewhere, meanwhile, liturgical conservatives staunchly resisted changes in worship (g).

Circumstances by the 1980s gave some credence to the view of John Hick that there were now two very different but ultimately complementary varieties of Christianity (h). His assessment should be read alongside a robust statement of evangelical convictions from Clive Calver, General Director of the Evangelical Alliance (i). It was increasingly apparent that such profound theological divergencies cut across denominational lines, while the significance of historic institutional divisions had diminished. At Swanwick in Derbyshire in 1987 representatives of all the mainstream churches joined in affirming the common ground between them (j).

Finally, three documents from the last decade of this period hint at the continuing challenges facing the churches. When the Archbishop's Commission on Urban Priority Areas reported in 1985, it struggled to find faith and hope amidst the harsh realities of inner-city decay (k). In Wales continuing widespread interest in religion continued, but organizational commitment declined (l). In Ireland, participation in organized Christianity remained much higher, but even there the Roman Catholic Church detected some worrying trends (m).

(a) An archbishop looks forward

I sense a certain reluctance to begin at all. A distinguished theologian has recently expressed the opinion that all schemes of reunion should be postponed until further study, theological thinking and prayer in all Christian communions have led them to a recovered apprehension of the integrity and balance of Christian truth, alike in the sphere of Faith and in that of Order, based on a renewed understanding of the Scriptures of the Old and New Testaments, and of the witness of Christian antiquity. That is to suggest that nothing should be done until the theologians have begun all over again and reached agreed conclusions; the past does not suggest that such theological unanimity will come in any foreseeable future. . .

There is a suggestion which I should like, in all humility, to make to my brethren of other denominations. We do not desire a federation; that does not restore the circulation. As I have suggested, the road is not yet open, we are not yet ready for organic or constitutional union. But there can be a process of assimilation, of growing alike. What we need is that while the folds remain distinct, there should be a movement towards a free and unfettered exchange of life in worship and sacrament between them, as there is already of prayer and thought and Christian fellowship – in short, that they should grow towards that full communion with one another, which already in their separation they have with Christ. . .

My longing is not yet that we should be *united* with other churches in this country; but that we should grow to *full communion* with them. As I have said, and as negotiations have shown, no insuperable barrier to that remains, until we come to questions of the ministry and government of the Church. Full communion between Churches means not that they are identical in all ways, but that there is no barrier to exchange of their ministers and ministries. Every Church's ministry is effective as a means by which the life of Christ reaches his people. Every Church's ministry is ineffective because it is prevented from operating in all the folds of his flock. For full communion between Churches, there is needed a ministry mutually acknowledged by all as possessing not only the inward call of the spirit but also the authority which each Church in conscience requires. . . .

The non-episcopal Churches have accepted the principle that episcopacy must exist along with the other elements in a re-united Church. For reasons obvious enough in Church History, they fear what may be made of episcopacy. But they accept the fact of it. If they do so for a re-united Church, why not also and earlier for the process of assimilation, as a step towards full communion? It may be said that in a re-united Church they could guard themselves, in the constitution, against abuses of episcopacy. But they could do so far more effectively by taking it into their own system. . . .

It is because I fear a stalemate, that I venture to put this suggestion forward for examination. I love the Church of England as the Presbyterian and the Methodist love their Churches. It is, I think, not possible yet nor desirable that any Church should merge its identity in a newly-constituted union. What I desire is that I should freely be able to enter their churches, and they mine, in the sacraments of the Lord and in the full fellowship of worship, that his life may freely circulate between us. Cannot we grow to full communion with each other before we start to write a constitution? Have we the wisdom, the humility, the love and the spirit of Christ sufficient for such a venture as I have suggested? If there were agreement on it, I would thankfully receive, at the hands of others, their commission in their accustomed form, and in the same way confer our own; . . .

William Purcell, *Fisher of Lambeth: A Portrait from Life*, London, Hodder & Stoughton, 1969, pp. 155, 156, 157.

(b) The Scottish churches and social change

[T]he most popular and well-supported church occasions of the post-war period have been glittering grand events: most notably for Protestants the Billy Graham crusade in 1955 and for Catholics the visit of Pope John Paul II in 1982. The first was preceded by some eight years' evangelistic campaigning by 'Christian Commandos' and by the 'Tell Scotland' movement led by a few energetic Church of Scotland ministers and to which BBC radio in Scotland lent a degree of air-time and co-operation that would doubtless be prohibited today. The efforts of these campaigns probably appeared more successful than they really were because of what followed. For six weeks around Easter 1955 nightly mass rallies of some 10,000 people packed the Kelvin Hall in Glasgow, and for two of those weeks others attended churches and halls around the country to participate in the services via relay television. The concluding Good Friday service at Hampden Park attracted just short of 100,000 people, and throughout the crusade both the BBC and especially the Scottish press were carefully and successfully manipulated by the inter-denominational organizing committees. But it would be a misnomer to call the crusade a 'revival'. Only 20,000 (or under 3 per cent) of the 830,000 who attended the principal rallies in Glasgow came forward to 'make decisions for Christ': of these 70 per cent were women, 73 per cent were under thirty years of age (11 per cent under twelve), and 62 per cent were already regular church attenders. The occasions were visual spectacles, carefully orchestrated and designed, but not emotional outpourings. The audiences seem to have been composed overwhelmingly of the middle-aged and the elderly, mostly middle class, sitting stiffly erect and defensively muffled in sturdy overcoats with many of the women in their finest fur hats, coats and tippets. The 'enquirers' were the young, often the very young, and the lasting effects were slight. The bulk of the Protestant clergy were faintly hostile to the crusade and to the 'Tell Scotland' movement with which it was connected. Nearly 70 per cent of Church of Scotland ministers reported that all forms of evangelization in 1954–6 had 'little or no effect' on their congregations, and from 1956 the communicants' roll started its inexorable decline.

The papal visit twenty-seven years later generated a greater show of enthusiasm, predominantly amongst the young – especially schoolchildren – at rallies in Edinburgh's Murrayfield stadium and Glasgow's Bellahouston Park. The visit to Presbyterian Scotland was of enormous symbolic importance, but like the Billy Graham crusade it seems to have had little effect on long-term trends in Catholic adherence. It was significant that the vigorous and irrepressible children's chanting, which nearly overwhelmed John Paul's addresses, was not delivered in any available religious vocabulary but in the tunes and rhythms of the pop world and the football terracing. In terms of church connection, the papal visit does not seem to have stemmed the outflow which set in during the late 1970s in west central Scotland. Whilst the Catholic population of the country grew from 446,400 in 1901 to 823,500 in 1977, it then fell by just under 10,000 in the next six years with the losses occurring entirely in the archdiocese of Glasgow and the dioceses of Motherwell and Paisley. Although twentieth-century statistics are probably not responsive to year-by-year fluctuations in church adherence, it seems clear that religious 'spectaculars' made no impression on established downward trends.

The inability to maintain religious or church-based leisure in the weekly life of the people has been a major cause of the declining role of the church as a focus in urban community life. This change has been more slow and more uneven in rural districts. . . Whilst a few rural parishes maintained very vigorous community religion – as in the village of Craigie in Angus where it was claimed in the late 1960s that every child was a member of the United Free Church Band of Hope – in general the arrival of improved bus services to nearby towns distracted the attention of the young from the local church, and with its decline the heart of many rural parishes was torn out. The fate of the rural kirk in large measure reflects the fate of Lowland rural society as a whole. Where town–country commuters have moved in since the late 1960s, the churches become imprisoned by suburbia; where they don't, paths to churches become overgrown, rights-of-way lapse, and many attend church only for marriage, baptism, and funerals, and perhaps also for annual communion after which a herdsman in the south of Scotland was heard to exclaim around 1960: 'Ah well, that's it by for another year.'

At the beginning of the century, the slowing down of church growth to a level which barely kept pace with population growth was due to the failure in recruiting from children of those who were not church members. A key element in the fall in church membership which started in the 1950s was an alarming failure to recruit even the offspring of adherents. . . . Between the mid-1950s and 1980, the number of Church of Scotland Sunday-school pupils almost halved, and a spectacular fall in church baptisms followed; between 1967 and 1982, they fell by half in the Church of Scotland and by almost 40 per cent in the Catholic Church. This rate of decline is higher than the fall in the birth rate, and would seem to indicate a considerable loss of church connection amongst young married couples.

The origins of this alienation lay at a younger age. A Falkirk survey of over 200 schoolchildren in the 1960s found that 27 per cent stopped attending church before the age of ten, and that by the age of thirteen two-thirds had given up church connection. The crisis of the young reached its peak in the Church of Scotland between 1967 and 1974. The Church's preoccupations with promoting the temperance movement and opposing gambling virtually disappeared to make way for agonizing over the revolution in youth culture. In abandoning the temperance cause, the Church also tried to move with the times by seeking compromises with the hippy-inspired culture of love and opposition to war. There was much in the young's hostility to the Biafran and Vietnam wars, and in their humane and liberal outlook, with which the younger clergy could sympathize. The general assembly was clearly affected by the mood of the times, and for example was remarkably uncritical of the legalization of abortion, the decriminalization of homosexuality, and the liberalization of divorce. In a more profound way, the Church was affected at all levels by the 'moral metamorphosis'. The committee on moral welfare advised the assembly in 1970:

> Need the Church always deplore this new 'permissiveness' as an unalloyed disaster? If the sanctions of commandment and convention are gone, people are set free to respond to goodness for its own sake, under no compulsion, constrained and sustained by the love of Christ and not by the fear of a lost respectability.

And the Church tried to envelop this conventionless morality of western youth within its pale. Energetic youth leaders started church dances and discos in 1966–9, but kirk sessions quickly became concerned with the frequency with which the police visited their premises late on Saturday nights to sort out minor gang fights and complaints from neighbours. The problem became, as one Angus church put it in 1970, to put youth activities on an 'acceptable footing'. It became clear by the early seventies that the Church could not pursue and court youth culture whilst retaining its traditional public standing. The Moral Welfare Committee changed its approach radically between 1970 and 1972. In the first year it found 'the spirit of the age with its new found freedom' providing a healthy challenge to Christians 'to re-think the implications of Christian morality', though in an arch piece of sexism it considered that 'it is the promiscuous girl who is the real problem'. But by 1972, the committee was quite exasperated with 'the turbulent continent of morality' and virtually ceased trying to construct responses to the unfolding 'promiscuous age'.

The decay of church connection amongst Scotland's youth seems to be closely connected with the burgeoning prosperity which, despite the economic difficulties of the late 1970s and early 1980s, has continued to dominate the economic experience of the vast majority of the population.

Callum G. Brown, *A Social History of Religion in Scotland since 1730*, London, Methuen, 1987, pp. 225–7, 228, 229–30.

(c) Honest to God

It belongs to the office of a bishop in the Church to be a guardian and defender of its doctrine. I find myself a bishop at a moment when the discharge of this burden can seldom have demanded greater depth of divinity and quality of discernment.

For I suspect that we stand on the brink of a period in which it is going to become increasingly difficult to know what the true defence of Christian truth requires. There are always those (and doubtless rightly they will be in the majority) who see the best, and indeed the only, defence of doctrine to lie in the firm reiteration, in fresh and intelligent contemporary language, of 'the faith once delivered to the saints'. And the Church has not lacked in recent years theologians and apologists who have given themselves to this task. Their work has been rewarded by a hungry following, and there will always be need of more of them. Nothing that I go on to say should be taken to deny their indispensable vocation.

At the same time, I believe we are being called, over the years ahead, to far more than a restating of traditional orthodoxy in modern terms. Indeed, if our defence of the Faith is limited to this, we shall find in all likelihood that we have lost out to all but a tiny religious remnant. A much more radical recasting, I would judge, is demanded, in the process of which the most fundamental categories of our theology – of God, of the supernatural, and of religion itself – must go into the melting. Indeed, though we shall not of course be able to do it, I can at least understand what those mean who urge that we should do well to give up using the word 'God' for a generation, so impregnated has it become with a way of thinking we may have to discard if the Gospel is to signify anything.

For I am convinced that there is a growing gulf between the traditional orthodox supernaturalism in which our Faith has been framed and the categories which the 'lay' world (for want of a better term) finds meaningful today. And by that I do not mean there is an increasing gap between Christianity and pagan society. That may well be so, but this is not the divide of which I am speaking. For it is not a division on the truth of the Gospel itself. Indeed, many who are Christians find themselves on the same side as those who are not. And among one's intelligent non-Christian friends one discovers many who are far nearer to the Kingdom of Heaven than they themselves can credit. For while they imagine they have rejected the Gospel, they have in fact largely been put off by a particular way of thinking about the world which quite legitimately they find incredible.

Moreover, the line to which I am referring runs right through the middle of myself, although as time goes on I find there is less and less of me left, as it were, to the right of it. Thus, not infrequently, as I watch or listen to a broadcast discussion between a Christian and a humanist, I catch myself realizing that most of my sympathies are on the humanist's side. This is not in the least because my faith or commitment is in doubt, but because I share instinctively with him his inability to accept the scheme of thought and mould of religion within which alone that Faith is being offered to him. I feel he is *right* to rebel against it, and I am increasingly uncomfortable that 'orthodoxy' should be identified with it.

What this structure is must be left for further designation to the body of the book. My only concern here is to plead for the recognition that those who believe their share in the total apologetic task of the Church to be a radical questioning of the established 'religious frame' should be accepted no less as genuine and, in the long run, equally necessary defenders of the Faith.

But I am not sanguine. I am inclined to think that the gulf must grow wider before it is bridged and that there will be an increasing alienation, both within the ranks of the Church and outside it, between those whose basic recipe is the mixture as before (however revitalized) and those who feel compelled above all to be honest *wherever* it may lead them. . . . I am not in the least accusing of dishonesty those who find the traditional framework of metaphysics and morals entirely acceptable (I do so with a large part of myself). What dismays me is the vehemence – and at bottom the insecurity – of those who feel that the Faith can only be defended by branding as enemies within the camp those who do not. . . .

What I have tried to say, in a tentative and exploratory way, may seem to be radical, and doubtless to many heretical. The one thing of which I am fairly sure is that, in retrospect, it will be seen to have erred in not being nearly radical enough.

John A. T. Robinson, *Honest to God*, London, SCM Press, 1963, pp. 7–10.

(d) Authority and dissent in the Roman Catholic Church

To most of our contributors and many of our readers Charles Davis' decision to leave the Catholic Church must have come primarily as a personal shock. He is known and loved by so many of us that it seems almost unseemly to discuss the event in public rather than by private letter. However, his own dignified and candid public statements . . . have, as it were, given his friends permission to discuss, if not his choice, at least the reasons which seem to him to justify it. It could not, in any case, have been a private event: it is the most important thing that has happened in the Catholic Church in England for half a century. If this Church cannot contain her foremost theologian (and only a quite special theological ignorance and frivolity could see him as 'lightweight') then we must look again very hard both at the Church and at the theology.

First of all, though, it is worth thinking about the probable effects of his action. There are likely to be two opposite reactions, neither of which need become fully articulate and both of which may co-exist in the minds of many Catholics. The first is to feel that there must be something wrong with 'progressive' theology if it leads such a man to leave the Church. The second is to feel that there must be something wrong with the Church if he cannot stay in. Because of the first, progressive theologians are liable once more to come under suspicion, but the second might just possibly lead to a real examination of conscience in the Church. If this latter effect should come about we need not be unduly worried about the first. There was in any case something a little unnatural in the respectability that progressive and original theologians suddenly acquired during and immediately after the Council. A new élite of 'right-thinking people' was gradually forming, and the need to be in tune with this orthodoxy was beginning to stifle critical judgement. There were signs, even, of a rather brutal and triumphalist radicalism which could be just as indifferent to persons and to truth as could episcopal authority. There are a certain number of people who could jump off the bandwagon without doing the cause of theology any harm. . . .

What does not need to be endured indefinitely is the special irrelevance of so much of the behaviour of Church officials. Alongside the actual agony of growth in the Church there seem to be these men playing a private game amongst themselves in which the moves are directives and prohibitions and the players score points for formally going through the motions of docility or of repeating the orders correctly. It seems to me that we should treat this game as we do the phantasies of adolescence or any of the other ways in which men escape from reality; we should combine a firm determination to get rid of it eventually with a certain tolerance of it while it is being played. While Church authorities are occupied with these domination games they are neglecting their true role. It would be quite unrealistic to expect them to be sources of enthusiasm and original thought but it is their basic task to be the link between such sources, the framework within which they are kept in balance. To maintain this balance they must, of course, speak with authority, the real authority that comes with understanding and concern and listening to others; the authority that sees itself not in terms of power but as a service to the community, the channel of communication by which each part of the community is kept in touch with the whole, a whole that extends through time as well as space. . . .

It is because we believe that the hierarchical institutions of the Roman Catholic Church, with all their decadence, their corruption and their sheer silliness, do in fact link us to areas of Christian truth beyond our own particular experience and ultimately to truths beyond any experience, that we remain, and see our Christian lives in terms of remaining, members of this Church.

Simon Clements and Monica Lawlor, *The McCabe Affair: Evidence and Comment*, London and Melbourne, Sheed and Ward, 1987, pp. 8–9, 12, 13 (first published in *New Blackfriars*).

CONTRACEPTION AND BIRTH CONTROL

Almost every diocesan report raised this question, some rather circuitously and cautiously, but the majority in detail.

The general request was for the Church to reconsider the implications of *Humanae vitae*; and, in the pastoral situation, to clarify what is seen as a confusing and unclear state of affairs in which contraception is forbidden in principle but the 'informed conscience' can find reason for it.

People do not in general understand this, and find it a dishonest situation.

Most reports reject the forbidding of contraception: they find it unacceptable.

Some dioceses, however, ask that the teaching be reaffirmed without equivocation.

Many Catholics have a crisis of conscience about contraception: it is fairly widely practised; scrupulous people leave the sacraments because of this; other people sort out their own attitudes, remain at the sacraments, but feel ill at ease.

The lack of pastoral guidance is keenly felt.

It is frequently remarked that priests are unwilling or unable to discuss the issue, so that individuals are left to their own guidance without help.

The Church seems, to some, to be not a caring mother, but a hard taskmaster, in this matter.

It is stressed in the reports that couples are not irresponsible or selfish in their attitudes to having children.

As one report says: 'couples are not careless in their decision, but want to be faithful to the needs of all parties: their partner, children, church, society'.

Admission to the sacraments of divorced and remarried people

Almost every report makes an urgent plea for a re-examination of present policy on this matter. A new pastoral strategy should come from the bishops, with special consideration of the spiritual needs of divorcees.

People cannot understand the rigidity of the Church in this regard: 'Jesus would not refuse to come to them. The Church forgives anything, even murder, but not remarriage': this feeling is echoed in many reports.

Reports ask for:

- parishes to give special support to divorcees, and special help for the children of divorced marriages; a blessing on the second marriage; and uniformity of pastoral practice throughout the country.

Liverpool 1980: Official Report of the National Pastoral Congress, Slough, St. Paul Publications, 1981, pp. 67–8.

(e) Evangelical restatement

The ministry of the sacraments — Holy Communion

Its centrality

We have failed to do justice in our practice to the twin truths that the Lord's Supper is the main service of the people of God, and that the local church, as such, is the unit within which it is properly administered. This is not to undervalue in any way attendance at other services of the day, but to admit that we have let the sacrament be pushed to the outer fringes of church life, and the ministry of the Word be divorced from it. Small communion services have been held seemingly at random, often more than one a Sunday, and the whole local church seldom or never comes together at the Lord's Table. As individuals we have lacked both a concern that the local church should amend its ways, and also a personal discipline of attendance.

We determine to work towards the practice of a weekly celebration of the sacrament as the central corporate service of the church, and some of us would recommend the use of 'one loaf' (1 Corinthians 10.17) as biblical and symbolic of that corporate unity. . . .

UNITY WITHIN THE CHURCH OF ENGLAND

REFORM NOT SEPARATION

. . . Dialogue and reformation should start at home. The chaos in doctrinal matters in the Church of England today causes us grief and shame. We reject the current tendency towards 'Christian agnosticism' . . . over the fundamentals of the gospel. In the face of this situation, however, it is reform that we desire, not separation. We look beyond Anglicanism as we now know it to a more biblical united church. . . .

THE FREE CHURCHES . . .

OUR FELLOW EVANGELICALS

. . . We value our present fellowship and co-operation with our fellow evangelicals in other Churches, to whom we are specially bound by a common understanding of the faith, and we desire a strengthening of these relations.

OBSTACLES TO UNITY

. . . Because we belong primarily to each other, we should not attach our loyalties to denominations, buildings, organizations, particular ways of worship, or particular ministers. Such attachments betray immaturity in Christ. We recognize that when these loyalties become obstacles to *organic* unity, they must be renounced, and we call upon all Anglican and Free Churchmen alike to recognize this too. . . .

The church of rome

. . . We recognize that the Roman Catholic Church holds many fundamental Christian doctrines in common with ourselves. We rejoice also at signs of biblical reformation. While we could not contemplate any form of reunion with Rome as she is, we welcome the new possibilities of dialogue with her on the basis of Scripture, as exemplified in the recent appointment of a team of evangelical theologians to confer with Roman theologians.

Philip Crowe, ed., *Keele '67: The National Evangelical Anglican Congress Statement*, London, Falcon, 1967, pp. 35, 37, 39.

(f) Charismatic renewal

One of the first visible changes affected our worship.

Our main service had always been the Parish Communion at nine thirty on Sunday morning. A greater sense of worship and praise was growing at this, although the form of the service remained unchanged. Nor did we have any desire to alter it. We were conscious that the Lord wanted the whole church to remain united and that unity was expressed in the Parish Communion. We must love the brethren whose hearts had not yet been filled to overflowing with love and praise for the Lord. They were just as much part of the family as those who had come into the experience of being baptised in the Holy Spirit.

Every Sunday evening we had the Anglican service of Evensong. This is not a form of worship that appeals to new Christians of whom we had many. Attendance was very small – a dozen was a crowd. Those who regularly came often remarked: 'If only more people would come in the evening.'

For months at staff meetings we had been saying, 'We must do something about Evensong.' But there were so many other things to do.

We needed a form of service in which people could feel free to express the praise in their hearts. The Church Council agreed that 'Evening Praise' should begin. We talked about this with the Evensong congregation, and nobody raised any objections.

Thirty-six people arrived for the first Evening Praise. Instead of leaving only the preaching open to the Lord, the entire service was unstructured, so that we could allow the Holy Spirit to lead us.

Needless to say, there was plenty of praise; but there was also opportunity for quiet meditation after the Bible readings. The sermons at Parish Communion were usually short, because of the number of young children present. At Evening Praise there was opportunity to expand our meditation on the Scriptures – and we were beginning to recognise our need for more teaching and revelation through the Word of God.

After four weeks the size of the evening congregation had risen to almost eighty and within six months to about one hundred and fifty.

Each week was different. Sometimes there seemed to be a great emphasis on praise and joy; at other times the service was very quiet. The Lord dealt lovingly with His children every week. God was at work among us.

Evening Praise lasted at least an hour and a half, sometimes two hours. Yet the children loved to come; they enjoyed praising the Lord, particularly in the free time of worship that often ended the service. Choruses were coming into their own and the children (young and old!) loved them.

But then the Lord was beginning to do some very wonderful things in the lives of our children. . .

'Could you come and lay hands on him please?' Rosemary asked.

Christopher, her thirteen-year-old son was in bed with bronchitis and although the doctor had been treating him, he didn't appear to be making any progress.

'I'll be there later this morning,' I replied.

Rosemary and her husband Cliff had been amongst the first to be baptised in the Holy Spirit at St Hugh's. It was nearly lunchtime when I arrived at their home. It was my usual practice now to pray in tongues when on my way to visit someone. I was more open to the leading of the Holy Spirit when I had been allowing Him to pray in me.

As I went up to Chris's room the Lord told me to talk to him about the Holy Spirit. It had never occurred to any of us that the Lord wanted to fill children with the Spirit! They weren't old enough!

I asked Rosemary to wait downstairs.

'Chris, I want to talk to you about the Holy Spirit,' I began. I went on to explain very briefly and simply how Jesus wanted to come into his life and fill him with the Spirit.

'Whether you want Jesus or not, is entirely up to you. You must decide,' I said.

'I do,' replied Christopher. 'I can see what a difference He has made to Mum and Dad.'

'I had better say something about tongues,' I thought – after all you never know what might happen once the Lord is allowed free-dom to work.

I explained that I might speak in tongues and told Christopher not to be frightened if he felt the urge to do the same. He said a very simple prayer, asking Jesus to be Lord in his life, and I laid hands on him praying that Jesus would fill him with the Holy Spirit. 'Now Chris, I want you to pray out loud, and let the Holy Spirit give you the words to say.'

He began to pray a beautiful prayer about the fountains of God's glory, hardly the kind you would expect from a thirteen-year-old boy! It was full of love and praise and was an obvious sign that the Lord was doing something very important in young Christopher.

I explained to Rosemary and Cliff what had happened, wondering what their reaction would be. They were delighted! Together we asked the Lord to heal Christopher's bronchitis. After praying in English I laid hands over his chest and prayed in tongues. Chris looked much better; I left, praising the Lord.

Soon after I had gone, he got up and spent the remainder of the day downstairs. Later that afternoon he asked Rosemary: 'Did you understand what Colin was saying when he spoke in tongues?'

'No,' replied Rosemary.

'I did,' said Christopher. 'The Lord was speaking to me. He kept on saying "Christopher, Christopher, come to me. I am the living

Christ." He said it over and over again until I said, "Yes, Lord, I come." Then He healed me.'

Later that evening, Christopher praised the Lord in tongues for the first time. For years Christopher had suffered from asthma, but since that time he has never suffered an asthmatic attack.

Colin Urquhart, *When the Spirit Comes*, London, Hodder & Stoughton, 1974, pp. 57–60.

(g) Liturgy and language

A PETITION

To the Right Reverend Fathers-in-God, the Clergy, and Laity of the General Synod of the Church of England.

FATHERS AND BRETHREN

We, the undersigned, are deeply concerned by the policies and tendencies which decree the loss of both the Authorised Version of the English Bible and the Book of Common Prayer. This great act of forgetting, now under way, is a tragic loss to our historic memory and an impoverishment of present awareness. For centuries these texts have carried forward the freshness and simplicity of our language in its early modern splendour. Without them the resources of expression are reduced, the stock of shared words depleted, and we ourselves diminished. Moreover, they contain nothing which cannot be easily and profitably explained.

We ask for their continued and loving use in churches as part of the mainstream of worship and not as vestiges indulged intermittently. We welcome innovation and experiment, but hope that changes will take place alongside the achievements of the past. The younger generation in particular should be acquainted as far as possible with their inheritance.

Clearly this is not an issue confined only to the churches or communities of faith. Some of us do not claim religious belief. Yet we hope that steps are taken to ensure a lively pleasure in the Authorised Version of the Bible in the nation at large. If humane education means anything it includes access to the great renderings of epic and wisdom, prophecy and poetry, epistle and gospel.

PN Review, Vol. 6, No. 5 (1979), p. 51.

(h) Two kinds of Christianity?

It has become obvious that we are living at a turning point in the history of Christianity. This is mainly because the development of modern science has made incredible much of the content of traditional Christian belief.

Here I have in mind such beliefs as that man was originally created finitely perfect but fell through his own wrong choice into sin and misery; that God intervenes from time to time in history by miraculously suspending the laws of nature; that Christ was born of a virgin mother, lived on earth as a divine being with omnipotent power and omniscient mind, made atonement by his death for human sin, and that after his death his corpse came back to life; that the Bible is the infallible, divinely inspired record of all this; that eternal heaven or hell awaits us after death.

The question today is whether such beliefs are of the permanent essence of Christianity; or whether they belong to the history of its interaction with the prescientific culture which has only recently come to an end. If the former, Christianity is doomed to the role of a fading superstition. But if the latter, these mythical concepts can properly be left behind as Christianity advances into the new cultural world of modern science.

In this situation one option for the Christian is to stand by the traditional system of beliefs, regarding it as of the essence of the faith. This is the response of the growing and articulate conservative wing of the churches which today calls itself evangelical. This conservative response has become a major phenomenon. Indeed it is probable that today the main cleavage within Christianity is no longer between the denominations – for their differences are at least in process of being bridged – but between 'evangelicals' and 'radicals' regardless of denomination. Radical Anglicans, Roman Catholics, and, say, Presbyterians have in many ways more in common with one another than with the conservatives within their respective churches; while conservative Presbyterians, Roman Catholics and Anglicans have more in common with one another than with their respective radical brethren. One can only view with dismay the prospect of an increasing polarization along this axis, leading each party to exaggerated self-consciousness over against the other. . . .

Indeed within each of the main denominations today there are, in effect, two Christianities, or two understandings of Christianity, some members adhering to one, some to the other, and some perhaps fluctuating between them. According to one understanding, Christians believe in the verbal inspiration and absolute authority of the Bible, and in Adam and Eve, the virgin birth of Jesus, his unique status as God incarnate, his bodily resurrection, heaven and hell, and the need to evangelize the world because there is salvation only by taking Jesus as one's Lord and Saviour; and Christians give to charity but do not become heavily involved in efforts to change the political and economic structures of the world. According to the other understanding, Christians seek to be disciples of Jesus, whilst interpreting him theologically in a variety of ways, and seek to love God and love their neighbours, both individually and by working for liberation from economic, social and political repression. They see the Bible as a record of vital religious experience within a particular strand of human history; and accept that there are other strands with other experiences and other scriptures.

Conscious that the new contemporary form of Christian understanding differs from the traditional norms enshrined in the great confessions of the past, Christians of the second kind are often tempted to leave the institutional church and to live out their Christian discipleship independently of it. However, the more this happens the more the church will lag behind the ever-changing human consciousness and become ghettoes in which life is lived in terms of an antique mythology. Such extreme polarization could only be disastrous. For each kind of Christianity in fact needs the other. There is a powerful stream of authentic religious devotion within the conservative-evangelical world which seems to require a simplistic conceptuality, and which is upset or confused by theological and political experimentation; and the experimenters need to keep in touch with this great stream, representing so large a part of their own heritage. And within the more experimental forms of Christianity there are immensely important rational and ethical insights whose challenge the conservatives need to hear, and eventually to face, if they are to escape a ghettoed future. Thus dialogue between the two Christianities is quite as important, and might well be both as difficult and as rewarding, as inter-religious dialogue.

John Hick, *The Second Christianity*, London, SCM Press, 1983, pp. 9–10, 73–4.

(i) What is an evangelical?

An evangelical is, at root, someone who first of all holds to the traditional credal doctrinal statements of the Church. He or she believes that Jesus is in fact the Son of God. That he did perform miracles, rose from the dead and through his crucifixion offered an atoning sacrifice for the sins of all who would put their faith and trust in him. A commitment to the Trinity of Father, Son and Holy Spirit as the Godhead apart from all other faiths and beliefs, a recognition of the coming return of Jesus Christ and the fellowship of all believers as the Church of Christ are fundamental to an evangelical position.

Evangelicals are 'people of the book'. They recognise Scripture as truth, and in the words of the Lausanne Covenant, 'without error in all that it affirms'. This divinely given authoritative word from God can be totally trusted. Evangelicals may have some internal differences over the exact meaning of words like 'infallible' and 'inerrant', but have little doubt over the words 'inspired' and 'authoritative'. Indeed, where differences do exist, they are concerned primarily with the exact emphasis of what Scripture means in its context, not with what it claims for itself. For evangelicals the fact that the Bible is God's absolute Word to mankind is beyond dispute. . . .

But evangelicals are not just distinguished by their adherence to doctrinal or biblical truth. They recognise mankind as 'fallen', polluted by sin, given over to practices which are anti-God, and alienated from God by their own actions. Satan is viewed as a personal opponent whose claims on the lives of mankind were over-thrown by Christ on the Cross.

It is to Jesus Christ alone that the evangelical looks for salvation. A 'pluralist' philosophy, which claims there are several routes through different faiths to God, is wholeheartedly rejected. For the evangelical, God is not encountered through Buddha, Confucius, transcendental meditation, or any means other than Jesus – while other faiths may convey good thoughts about God and man, Jesus is the only way to know God as Father and Lord.

We may wonder about the fate of those who have never heard of Jesus, but Paul clearly affirms that conscience and creation point in that self-same direction (Rom. 1:20; 2:15).

To the evangelical the Gospel is 'good news'. Jesus has died and taken on himself in his crucifixion the penalty for the sins of man-kind. To those who ask his forgiveness and receive his life in them by his Holy Spirit come the certainties of rebirth. Guilt and the past are removed. Christ establishes his rule and reign in their lives. Now they are integrated into the family of God – the Church.

The presupposition of 'universalism' – that one day all will be saved – is wholeheartedly dismissed. The truth of the matter is viewed this way. For those who reject Christ's offer of salvation is the tragic expectation of eternity without God. For those who begin a new life in relationship with Christ on earth there is the glorious hope that this is only the beginning of a never-ending story.

Clive Calver, *He Brings us Together: Joining Hands Where Truth and Justice Meet*, London, Hodder & Stoughton, 1987, pp. 9–11.

(j) Pilgrims together

NO LONGER STRANGERS – PILGRIMS!
NID DIEITHRIAID MWYACH – PERERINION!
LUCHD-TURUIS – CONHLA!

Appointed by our churches and under the guidance of the Holy

Spirit we declare that this, the broadest assembly of British and Irish churches ever to meet in these islands has reached a common mind. We are aware that not all Christians are represented amongst us but we look forward to the time when they will share fully with us.

We came with different experiences and traditions, some with long ecumenical service, some for whom this is a new adventure. We are one band of pilgrims. We are old and young, women and men, black and white, lay and ordained and we travelled from the four corners of these islands to meet at Swanwick in Derbyshire. There we met, we listened, we talked, we worshipped, we prayed, we sat in silence, deeper than words. Against the background of so much suffering and sinfulness in our society we were reminded of our call to witness that God was in Christ reconciling the world to himself. We affirmed that this world with all its sin and splendour belongs to God. Young people called on us to be ready to sort out our priorities so that we could travel light and concentrate on our goal. Driven on by a gospel imperative to seek unity that the world may believe, we rejoiced that we are pilgrims together and strangers no longer.

We now declare together our readiness to commit ourselves to each other under God. Our earnest desire is to become more fully, in his own time, the one Church of Christ, united in faith, communion, pastoral care and mission. Such unity is the gift of God. With gratitude we have truly experienced this gift, growing amongst us in these days. We affirm our openness to this growing unity in obedience to the Word of God, so that we may fully share, hold in common and offer to the world those gifts which we have received and still hold in separation. In the unity we seek we recognise that there will not be uniformity but legitimate diversity.

It is our conviction that, as a matter of policy at all levels and in all places, our churches must now move from co-operation to clear commitment to each other, in search of the unity for which Christ prayed, and in common evangelism and service of the world.

We urge church leaders and representatives to take all necessary steps to present, as soon as possible, to our church authorities, assemblies and congregations, the Report of this Conference together with developed proposals for ecumenical instruments to help the churches of these islands to move ahead together.

Continuing to trust in the promised gift of the Holy Spirit, we look forward with confidence to sharing with our own churches the joys of this historic Conference. We thank God for all those who, from Lent '86 and before, have been part of this pilgrimage. We feel their presence with us. We urge our churches to confirm by decision and action the hopes and vision on which we have laid hold, and which we shall not let go.

This is a new beginning. We set out on our further pilgrimage ready to take risks and determined not to be put off by 'dismal stories'. We resolve that no discouragement will make us once relent our avowed intent to be pilgrims together. Leaving behind painful memories and reaching out for what lies ahead, we press on towards the full reconciliation in Christ of all things in heaven and on earth, that God has promised in his Kingdom.

Lord God, we thank you
For calling us into the company
Of those who trust in Christ
And seek to obey his will.
May your Spirit guide and strengthen us
In mission and service to your world;
For we are strangers no longer
But pilgrims together on the way to your Kingdom.
Amen.

Not Strangers but Pilgrims: Report of the Swanwick Conference 31 August to 4 September 1987, London, British Council of Churches and Catholic Truth Society, n.d., pp. 3–4.

(k) *Faith in the city*

To the Most Reverend and Right Hon. R. A. K. Runcie MC, DD, the Lord Archbishop of Canterbury:

Your Grace,

We were appointed in July 1983 with the following terms of reference:

'To examine the strengths, insights, problems and needs of the Church's life and mission in Urban Priority Areas* and, as a result, to reflect on the challenge which God may be making to Church and Nation: and to make recommendations to appropriate bodies.'

(*'The term Urban Priority Areas is used to include inner city districts and many large Corporation estates and other areas of social deprivation.') . . .

15.1   Chapter after chapter of our Report tells the same story: that a growing number of people are excluded by poverty or powerlessness from sharing in the common life of our nation. A substantial minority – perhaps as many as one person in every four or five across the nation, and a much higher proportion in the UPAs – are forced to live on the margins of poverty or below the threshold of an acceptable standard of living.

15.2   The present acute situation of our nation's Urban Priority Areas demands an urgent response from the Church and from government.

15.3   The Archbishops' Commission on 'Church and State' concluded its report in 1970:

'The Church should concern itself first, and indeed second, with the poor and needy, whether in spirit or in body.'

15.4   We echo these words. The Church cannot supplant the market or the state. It can, as we recommend, mobilize its own resources in a way that accords high priority to the poor. It must by its example and its exertions proclaim the ethic of altruism against egotism, of community against self-seeking, and of charity against greed.

15.5   But we are conscious that we have only scratched the surface of some of the major concerns to have emerged from our work. To draw out the implications of some of these, such as the Church's response to the prospect of persistent long-term unemployment, will require more time and resources than have been available to us. There must also be a major national debate on the future of our cities, in which the Church must play a full part.

15.6 Perhaps the most important wider question concerns the structure of our society. One submission to us put it bluntly: 'The exclusion of the poor is pervasive and not accidental. It is organized and imposed by powerful institutions which represent the rest of us.' The critical issue to be faced is whether there is any serious political will to set in motion a process which will enable those who are at present in poverty and powerless to rejoin the life of the nation.

15.7 Here is a challenge indeed. It will call among other things for a clear resolve on the part of Church and government to have faith in the city. We take courage from three realities which are evident to us.

15.8 The first is that changes on a global scale are already upon us, as the era known as the industrial society gives place to something new. The industrial city is one of the focal points of that change. In almost every sphere of life and in a brief span of time the future is being shaped by action or by default. The very assumptions of our culture are now open to debate in new ways. We do not pretend to discern clearly what is to come. We present no comprehensive political or economic analysis. That task goes beyond this Commission. At this time of immense opportunity what we can do is to pledge ourselves as citizens to do our best to engage in the daily moral confrontations of public life and personal relations.

15.9 The second evident reality is the experience of justice, love and hope in human history, focused most clearly for us in our religious tradition. We know that there is a transforming power present in human affairs which can resolve apparently intractable situations and can bring new life into the darkest places. If, as we dare to affirm, the true nature of human life is to be discerned in the life of Jesus Christ, we can take heart and pledge ourselves to a deeper commitment to create a society in which benefits and burdens are shared in a more equitable way. Any attempt to base a society or culture upon other foundations carries with it, we believe, its own nemesis of suffering, bitterness and social disintegration.

15.10   But – and this is our third evident reality – somewhere along the road which we have travelled in the past two years each of us has faced a personal challenge to our lives and life styles: a call to change our thinking and action in such a way as to help us to stand more closely alongside the risen Christ with those who are poor and powerless. We have found faith in the city.

Faith in the City: A Call for Action by Church and Nation: The Report of the Archbishop of Canterbury's Commission on Urban Priority Areas, London, Church House Publishing, 1985, pp. iii, 359–60.

(1) *The view from Wales*

So where does the faith preserved and delivered to the people of Wales by the Celtic saints down the ages stand as we approach the dawn of the third millennium of the Christian era? More particularly, does institutional Christianity in the form of the mainline Churches have a significantly weaker hold on the hearts and minds of the people of Wales today than it has enjoyed in previous centuries?

If this question were to be considered in terms of the numerical strength of the Churches today compared with, say, their strength at the turn of the century, the answer would be clear. By any estimate – for example, a comparison of the statistics produced by the Royal Commission set up to consider the strength of the religious bodies in Wales in the context of the disestablishment debate in 1906 and the results of the MARC Europe Survey *Prospects for Wales* undertaken in 1982 – the percentage of the people of Wales claiming membership of one or other of the mainline Churches as well as the number of those attending a Christian place of worship on a typical Sunday is far lower at the end than it was at the beginning of the century. This is true not only of the percentage (around 40 per cent of the adult population were church members in 1905, compared with 23 per cent in 1982); the same is true of absolute numbers, even though the total population of Wales has increased in the intervening years. In 1905 the total membership of 'Protestant' (i.e. excluding Roman Catholic) Churches was 743,361. The corresponding number in 1982 was 393,500. Interestingly, Roman Catholic membership, which was some 64,800 in 1905, had risen by 1982 to 129,600, i.e. it has doubled over the course of the century. So if we are considering numbers, there is no question but that organized Christianity is considerably weaker in Wales today than it was at the turn of the century. . . .

Having said all that, however, Christianity is far and away the main religion of Wales even today. One in four of the adult population is still formally affiliated to one or other of the mainline Christian Churches. Well over half the children born in Wales are 'christened'; over half the 'first' marriages are solemnized in a Christian place of worship and in excess of 95 per cent of the Welsh dead are laid to rest in a Christian burial ceremony. Christianity is still the official religion of state and civic occasions, notwithstanding the disestablishment of the Church in Wales earlier in the century. One could easily multiply examples. Furthermore, at a deeper and personal level the influence of the revivals and of puritanical Nonconformity still has a residual hold on the Welsh subconscious and results in the odd pang of guilt in a son of Wales who finds himself playing cricket on Sunday or enjoying a pint of beer. However, the truth is that secularism has had its impact, as the statistics for church membership and church attendance as well as the enormous changes in public and private morality and social mores ruthlessly reveal.

And yet, paradoxically, alongside all this, there is an enormous interest in religion in Wales. The departments of philosophy of the University of Wales are stiff with philosophers of religion. Ecclesiastical history is one of the favourite preoccupations of professional and amateur historians alike. Many schoolchildren opt of their own free will to study religion, as do a significant number of students both in the University and in other institutions of higher education. Nor are all these students of religion committed adherents of the Christian faith. Now, as never before, secular educational principles with their deliberate rejection of religious tests reign supreme. Again the prominent place given to religion, predominantly Christianity, by the broadcasting media in Wales is a commercial response to public demand. As many, if not more, people listen to or watch an act of worship on radio or television on a Sunday as attend a place of worship, while religious 'entertainment' programmes such as *Highway* (ITV), *Songs of Praise* (BBC) or *Dechrau Canu Dechrau Canmol* (S4C) have an enormous following. Furthermore, 'hymns and arias', to quote Max Boyce, are still the staple diet of spontaneous choirs at Welsh rugby internationals.

The paradox of Wales at the end of the twentieth century, therefore, seems to be that religion as a phenomenon, and indeed Christianity in particular, arouses widespread public interest at all levels in society, from philosophy seminars to community singing on the terraces, and yet there is a serious decline in the numbers of those committed to one or other of the main Christian denominations, with the exception of the Roman Catholic Church and some of the evangelical Protestant Churches.

D. P. Davies, 'A Time of Paradoxes among the Faiths', in David Cole, ed., *The New Wales*, Cardiff, University of Wales Press, 1990, pp. 210–12.

(m) Irish Catholicism

The Catholic Church in Ireland faces immense challenges as it approaches the end of the second millennium. The rate of religious practice is still one of the highest in the world (around 91 per cent of the Catholics in the Republic were found to attend Mass at least weekly in a major survey carried out for the bishops in 1973–74, partly as an aid to pastoral planning for the future). While the survey revealed many encouraging features about the Church in Ireland, it showed that there are many areas where the task of the Church is urgent. For example, it revealed that of the 91 per cent who attended Mass weekly only 28 per cent received Holy Communion each week, and this raises questions about the quality of people's participation at Mass.

A similar survey of university students conducted in 1976 showed that 70 per cent of students brought up as Catholics go to Mass once a week and 20 per cent go more often. But it also revealed that 14 per cent no longer regarded themselves as Catholics.

The number of religious in Ireland is relatively large, with around 13,700 nuns. However, both the nuns and the brothers (now around 2,000) have been affected by a gradual decline during the sixties and seventies in the numbers of those offering themselves for the religious life. But recent figures indicate that the numbers are on the increase again.

The visit of Pope John Paul II to Ireland from 29 September–1 October 1979 was an occasion of joy and celebration. There is evidence that his visit has been followed by spiritual renewal in many parishes.

In a series of important joint pastoral letters in the seventies – *Human Life is Sacred, The Work of Justice, Ireland Responds to Pope John Paul II* – the Irish bishops challenged members of the Church to take a critical look at their behaviour and lifestyle to see if the demands of the gospel were being [met] in terms of social justice in the home and in society. It was a conference in Kilkenny in 1971 sponsored by the Council for Social Welfare, one of the Church's official advisory bodies, which first threw the focus on the prevalence of poverty in an Ireland then undergoing rapid economic development. A paper read at that conference estimated that about 25 per cent of the Irish people were living at or below subsistence level.

The Catholic Church in Ireland: Information and Documentation, Dublin, Catholic Press and Information Office of Ireland, 1981, pp. 10–11.

2
JUDAISM

*I*n the 1950s, the Jewish community in Britain had already long been
wrestling with problems of identity and definition of the kind that, as the
period went on, were to become increasingly pressing for other minority
religious groups (a). The internal diversity of English Jewry is also well
illustrated by Louis Jacobs's reminiscences of the synagogues in Manchester
and London where he had been a rabbi during the decade immediately after
the Second World War (b). Jacobs was later to be the subject of major
controversy because of his allegedly heterodox theology, an indication that
Judaism, like Christianity, could not insulate itself from the intellectual and
cultural stirrings of the secular world. At the end of the period, however,
Progressive Judaism at least offered hope of an accommodation that preserved
religious integrity (c). Meanwhile Jews took an active part in wider religious
and political debates, as illustrated here by the robust response of the Chief
Rabbi, Sir Immanuel (later Lord) Jacobovits, to the Anglican report on
Faith in the City, in which he drew lessons from the Jewish experience in
Britain, as well as from the application of theological teachings of Judaism.
His interpretations provoked disagreement from some of his coreligionists,
including Edie Friedman, of the Jewish Council for Community
Relations (d).

(a) Who is a Jew?
THE DEFINITION OF A JEW

By what criteria does one Jew define another as a Jew? Certainly a
great deal of intellectual energy among Jews is taken up with this
question. In informal conversation, organised lectures and discussion groups, and in print, themes related to this question frequently arise – 'Are the Jews a nation, race, or a religious group?'
In particular, the impact of Zionism and the foundation of the State

of Israel has resulted in a flood of self-examination and definition of 'positions', much of it in controversial terms.

At one extreme are those Jews who hold the view that they are simply one of a multiplicity of religious denominations in a religiously heterogeneous society, comparable to any of the non-conformist groups; at the other are those to whom the Jews are a nationality, and who at the final extreme advocate the 'liquidation of the exile'.

The stand which individual Jews take in these controversies may bear a certain loose relation to the length of time the individual's forebears have been resident in England. Just as those who hold the former view tend, in the vast majority of cases, to be from Anglo-Jewish families, so those who take the latter standpoint are generally closer to the immigrant generation.

We do not regard ourselves as Englishmen of the Jewish faith. Englishman to us is almost synonymous with Christian. I am a Jew living in Britain or, if you like, a British Jew.

But there are foreign-born Jews, let alone the mass of British-born Jewry of the first and second generations, who simultaneously are identified with Israel and call themselves Englishmen in a more or less untroubled way, yet when they begin to reflect about their status are somewhat puzzled. For example:

The Jewish upper-class are not my type of Jew. I wouldn't feel comfortable with them, feel more as if I'm with an English peer than with my type of Jew. They don't have the homely Jewish traits, are not natural and spontaneous. . . . I consider myself an Englishman of the Jewish persuasion. But still, as long as I think about it, we have a dual obligation. To England, for which we have, if necessary, to lay down our lives, as the country which has taken us in and received us, and to the Jewish nationality – if there is such a thing.

Q. *Do you call yourself an Englishman of the Jewish persuasion, a British Jews, etc.?*
A. (husband): *Me, I'm a Yid [Jew].*

A. (wife): *No, I wouldn't say it quite that way. After all, we're English too, aren't we?*

This unclarity is an indication of their new marginal position, their straddling of two worlds, as contrasted with the outlook of the Jew in the ghetto of the past. He knew, somewhat in the manner of the husband cited above, quite simply what he was. He was a Jew.

As soon as one leaves the world of ideology to examine the norms that actually are operative below the level of explicitness, one discovers the widest agreement on a belief that is essentially by-passed by those preoccupied with defining Jewry as a religious *or* a political entity. This is that Jews are a people between whom there is a biological bond. As such, the only true Jew is one born into the group.

Agreement on this belief is revealed in manifold ways. Jews, wishing to adopt children, want them to be of Jewish birth; and organised adoption societies have for a long time existed to fulfil this need.[1] . . .

Secondly, from the point of view of the born Jew the rôle of the convert to Judaism is eccentric. He would feel restrained, for example, from exhibiting in the latter's presence hostility towards the non-Jewish world. Though it is more difficult to be converted to Orthodox than to Liberal Judaism, both groups place obstacles in the path of the potential convert, pointing out to him the difficulties of being a Jew and the rigour of the training process. In fact it is socially easier for a non-Jew, retaining his identity, to form profound and enduring ties with Jews than to be converted.

The obverse of the above is that to the born Jew persons of Jewish ancestry who no longer regard themselves as Jews are similarly eccentric or marginal because they are in some sense still Jews. Certainly, individuals of this sort who have achieved eminence are liberally identified as Jews within the community. . . .

Related to this is the fact that a Jew who drifts away from Jewish

[1] By Orthodox Jewish Law the child of a Jewish woman is Jewish; thus female parentage is a sufficient criterion for those seeking to adopt a Jewish child.

society, even going so far as to embrace another religion, can return to it. From the point of view of those in the group any person born a Jew has a minimal status as such which except in cases of the most horrifying group disloyalty, he never loses.

A fourth index of the vitality of these ethnic sentiments is the very widespread preference for marriage within the group. In the ghettoes of the past, intermarriage was sadly marked by the same ritual mourning (*shiva*) observed in cases of actual death. Though this is no longer common, survivals of its central symbolism, the writing-off of the transgressor as socially dead, persist. For example:

> Dr A's brother intermarried, you know. And if you happen to ask him about his brother, he'll say, 'I don't have any brother.' . . .

Also of interest is the fascination typically created for Jews by the spectacle of Jews (or so-called Jews) who have obviously different biological characteristics. These would include Negroes, Chinese, Indians, etc. – what are often termed 'exotic' Jews. They arrest attention in the first instance precisely because there is something 'wrong' with their rôle-qualifications. One wonders how they were born into Jewry.

Howard M. Brotz, 'The Outlines of Jewish Society in London', in Maurice Freedman, ed., *A Minority in Britain: Social Studies of the Anglo-Jewish Community*, London, Vallentine Mitchell, 1955, pp. 150–3.

(b) Synagogue life in Manchester and London

The first rabbi of the Central Synagogue was Rabbi Yossele Yoffey, a distinguished Lithuanian scholar who wrote a book long before the Balfour Declaration urging Jews to help settle Palestine as a Jewish homeland. . . .

Rabbi Yoffey . . . died in Alexandria on the way to Palestine, a land he had longed to visit all his life. This was some years before the outbreak of the Second World War and no successor was appointed until well after the end of the war. The reason for the congregation's tardiness in appointing a successor was the strong internal divisions over the type of rabbi they wanted. The older

Yiddish-speaking members wanted someone like Rabbi Yoffey, who could serve as an old-time rabbi, whereas the younger members wanted someone who could speak eloquently in English, had a university degree and could compare with the English ministers in some of the other Manchester synagogues.

My appointment was accepted without dissenting voice by both parties in the congregation. I was, after all, a child of the congregation in a sense. Moreover, it was understood that I would preach regularly in English but would speak in Yiddish whenever this would be required. During my years at the Central I delivered the traditional derashah in Yiddish on Shabbat Ha-Gadol and Shabbat Shuvah, consisting of an Halakhic discourse followed by a homily. I cannot pretend that I was eloquent in Yiddish but I got by, concentrating on the Halakhic part of the derashah with which I could cope fairly easily through my studies at the Yeshivah and the Kolel.

Each night I taught the Blat (a page of the Talmud) in Yiddish for the older members, many of whom used to frequent Rabbi Yoffey's Blat years before. The Blat was taught in the Beth Hamedrash adjacent to the synagogue. This was a large oblong hall with book-lined walls and long wooden tables, around which the participants sat with copies of the Talmud while I expounded the passage we were studying, quite in the old style. A visitor from London, coming in one evening and seeing all this activity, remarked that for a moment he imagined he had wandered into a Lithuanian conventicle, as, indeed, he had. I delivered my weekly sermon in English and in the Western style of preaching though even the younger members liked me to introduce into the sermon an occasional Yiddishism or a Yiddish quote.

This blend of Lithuanian-style rabbinic conduct and English-style formality and decorum took some getting used to. . . .

The New West End Synagogue in St Petersburg Place, Kensington, was the Anglicised synagogue par excellence. It was founded by Sir Samuel Montagu (later the first Lord Swaythling) and other prominent figures in the West End Jewish community who had broken away for some reason from the Bayswater Synagogue, although both the New West End and Bayswater remained constitu-

constituents of the United Synagogue. The services were almost completely traditional in practice except for a few innovations introduced with the approval of Chief Rabbi Hermann Adler, evidently in order to stem the Reform tide which exercised a powerful pull among West End Jewry.

The result was typical Anglo-Jewish compromise. While men and women were seated separately (the latter in the special ladies' gallery) there was a mixed choir, situated in the choir-loft built over the Ark. . . .

After the Chazan and the choir had led the congregation in the Musaf *kedushah*, some of the congregation recited the section dealing with the restoration of sacrifices while others could be observed remaining respectfully silent but clearly determined to demonstrate by that silence, 'You won't catch us praying for the restoration of sacrifices.' . . .

I was inducted into office on 13 February 1954 by Chief Rabbi Brodie. At the *kiddush* after the service I met the congregation, which numbered among its members some of the most illustrious names in Anglo-Jewry.

Chief Rabbi Brodie, I have in honesty to say, could not have been more friendly and encouraging. His induction address welcomed me as a new recruit to the ranks of the London Jewish Ministry and he treated me more as a colleague than a subordinate. . . .

In my introduction sermon I took as my text the prayer of the Reader of the Morning Service on Rosh Hashanah: 'O my Creator, give me understanding that I may transmit thine inheritance; strengthen and uphold me that I may be far from weakness and fear.' Speaking of the Anglo-Jewish tradition represented by the New West End, I said:

This Anglo-Jewish tradition is a great and glorious one, which never falters in spurning the superficial tinsel attractions of the *Zeitgeist* out of loyalty to the perennial ideals of our eternal faith. At its best it is a worthwhile blending of all that is good in the Jewish and British character. It is conservative but not hidebound; firm and consistent but not fanatical; proud of its origins but not insular; sober but not unimaginative; acutely conscious of the significance and importance of Jewish law but not formalistic; it has a love of learning but is not pedantic. The philanthropic achievements, in particular, of those who have followed this tradition have won the admiration of the whole world.

Ephraim Levine, in his few words at the *kiddush*, implied that I was busy buttering up the congregation and I have to admit that I did pile it on a bit. But I really did believe at the time, and still believe today, that the Anglo-Jewish ideal, with all its faults (more than I realised when I gave that sermon), does have the unique blend of which I spoke all that time ago, and it is a pity that there are those in the community who would be only too glad to see it vanish.

Louis Jacobs, *Helping with Inquiries: An Autobiography*, London, Vallentine Mitchell, 1989, pp. 84–5, 104, 105, 108–9.

(c) *Progressive Judaism*

This essay has grown out of a variety of informal discussions over many years among a number of rabbis and community leaders who are active in the British Progressive Jewish world. . . . Our religious qualifications and expertise can be judged by what follows. However, we thought it might be helpful to set out at the beginning some of the factors that we recognise as having shaped both our views and our approach to expressing them. Most of us are British-born Jews, which affects our temperament, our form of self-expression and our particular set of concerns. We are, in the main, middle-class, well educated secularly and professionally trained – all of which both colours and limits our sensitivities to different parts of society. Nevertheless, this background has given us the freedom to get to know different parts of the Jewish world, including the State of Israel. All the people who contributed to this essay carry a degree of responsibility within our particular 'brand' of Judaism, which gives us both an experience of Jewish needs and realities and also a certain caution in our formulation of ideas. We are excited to see the way in which Progressive communities in Britain have grown and accept new challenges. We have a religious commitment that has carried us out of the conventional path that many of us might have been expected to follow – given the part of society into which we were born and the culture that has shaped us.

In what follows, we have tried to affirm our certainties, acknowledge our doubts and question some of the conventions of Jewish life, recognising the strengths and weaknesses of the community to which we belong. This is intended as a position paper but we hope that it has not become so declamatory that the balance between self-affirmation and self-criticism has been lost. Above all, the essay invites response and welcomes discussion.

A. PRELIMINARY PRINCIPLES AND OBSERVATIONS

(1) MODERNITY

Judaism is an ancient yet dynamic tradition which has contributed to the life of humanity quite disproportionately to the number of Jews. Since the enlightenment and emancipation, this tradition has been shaped in a number of different ways. Progressive Judaism is the response our teachers and teaching have made to the ideas of the modern Western world. Such cross-fertilisation is by no means unique in the Jewish experience; it has always occurred and has always revitalised Judaism in each epoch.

There are many aspects of the modern Western world which distress us – its dethronement of God and enthronement of humanity, its uncritical faith in science and scientific knowledge, its abuse of technology as an instrument of human torture and destruction, its excessive materialism, its ruthless exploitation of human and natural resources solely for economic gain, its elevation of self-interest as the main determinant of human relations. There are, however, many aspects which we gladly embrace – its scholarship, its enunciation of individual human rights, its cultural pluralism, its psychological insights, its advances in many scientific and technological areas which offer an enhanced level to the quality of human life. Whatever our ambivalence, the present is with us and we acknowledge that it forms a starting point.

(2) LIVING IN THE WORLD

We recognise that modernity has brought both good and bad to the world. Judaism believes it is essential to live in the world, adopting a stance described as one of 'creative maladjustment'. The meeting between Judaism and the world has not always been positive for Jewish life. Nevertheless, we Progressive Jews do not believe we can fulfil our obligations as Jews by turning our back on it and seeking survival through isolation. We value our difference and distinctiveness but do not wish to preserve it by separating ourselves from the wider community. We choose freely to live simultaneously within two cultures, holding Jerusalem as our highest joy, whilst doing justice to Athens.

(3) TRUTH AND PLURALISM

We understand that truth, which we equate with the divine Reality and the divine will for the world, is multi-faceted and that no single expression of Judaism or of any religion can encompass all truth. . . .

(4) CERTAINTY AND DOUBT

We recognise that a significant level of religious doubt is endemic to modern thinking. The search has been continuous ever since Abraham and Sarah set off on their journey. This emphasis on search is a healthy antidote to the certainties which each generation so frequently holds about truth and a corrective to the plague of fanaticism which defaces the religious world in our time.

Nevertheless, we acknowledge that very many Jews today are less certain than we imagine preceding generations to have been about belief in God. Many others have difficulties with prayer, even though some find the corporate identification of public worship helpful. Such doubt and scepticism are part of a contemporary Jewish reality which it is our duty to face. . . .

D. Israel

(7) Relations with other peoples

Jewish teaching insists that we strive for the most harmonious relationship possible between Jews and others at all levels – spiritual, social and economic.

We share a vision of amity and respect within the greater family of the Abrahamic traditions in which Jews, Christians and Muslims can recognise themselves and each other as inheritors of common spiritual truths.

We have much also to learn from those whose religious tradition belongs outside the Abrahamic family. We approach all with respect and in humility and in the knowledge that salvation is to be found in many different places of worship. The *Ein Sof*[1] gives us a hint of that which unites all faiths. The God of Abraham and Sarah is One, reminding us that chauvinism and unbridled nationalism are a denial of the principle of unity which lies at the heart of the universe.

Jews need a deep sense of Jewish self and a thorough Jewish knowledge so that they may understand and enjoy all insights without having to compromise themselves or in any way minimise or denigrate the teachings of others. The more secure one is in one's own identity, the better one can understand the identity of others. Dialogue with others of different faiths is enriching and working together on matters of mutual concern rewarding.

Our shared aim should be so to frame our respective beliefs and claims that we leave theological space for other faiths and avoid the need to be unnecessarily and hurtfully competitive, condescending, rejecting or denying.

Jews have a particular obligation to other religious and ethnic minorities, since we have played the role of the 'stranger' throughout history. However, Jewish history has made Jews less than open and confident in relation to the world at large. This historical experience is often coupled with a tendency to be so involved in the Jewish 'love affair' with God as to regard what lies beyond the Jewish

[1] The Jewish concept of God as being without end or limit [Ed.].

community as of lesser importance. In some ways, this fearful intro-version is the mirror of the triumphant imperialism of other faiths. Insecurity and suspicion persist and we acknowledge the consider-able amount of work that is required to bring the ideal and the reality closer together in our relations with other faiths.

(8) MISSIONISING, CONVERSION AND OUTMARRIAGE

Progressive Judaism welcomes all those who seek to join our ranks in sincerity. We have only to be satisfied that they are aware of both the opportunities and the difficulties that devolve on all Jews and have the faith, commitment, knowledge and skills to live full Jewish lives. While ours is no longer a missionary religion, it con-tinues to be open to all seekers who wish to find fulfilment of their spiritual quest.

One of the inevitable consequences of living in an open, multi-cultural society is that some Jews may choose non-Jewish partners. Whilst deeply regretting the loss to the Jewish people that this so often represents, we also recognise that there is a challenge which must be faced. We do not believe that ostracism is a helpful response. The Jew within such a relationship is welcome within our communities and we must reach out to the non-Jewish partner. We wish our Judaism to be so attractive that many become Jewish in their own right and others offer willing support to the Jewish part-ner. We are delighted to assist in the upbringing of any children they may have as Jews.

(9) THE JEWISH HOME

Despite the enormity of the social changes which we are witnessing, the Jewish home is still for the great majority a bastion of Jewish life – a place where many of the most important Jewish values are lived. We affirm our commitment to the centrality of the Jewish home as a place of love and study, mutual support and religious celebration, renewal and spirituality. We likewise affirm the essen-tial place of the rituals and observances which characterise the Jewish home – the *mezuzzah*, the biblical passages fixed to the door-post, Sabbath and Festival observances and *kashrut*, dietary practices.

(10) THE SYNAGOGUE

We reaffirm the vital significance of the synagogue. It is the place where Jews come together to worship God in public. It remains our primary educational institution, focused on the rabbi as teacher, minister and local Jewish authority. It serves as a home for the religiously homeless Jew and, increasingly today, as an extended family.

The synagogue establishes patterns of practice both ritual and ethical, from which individuals can learn and make informed choices. It brings together groups of Jews in a democratic, learning and searching community, developing living expressions of Judaism and Jewish life.

Whilst this localised, participatory Judaism is a hallmark of Progressive Judaism, we affirm the need to act responsibly and collectively on matters of Jewish status and fundamental principle. We further recognise synagogal responsibility to the totality of Progressive communities and to the wider Jewish and non-Jewish world through the sharing of resources and the development of services for the benefit of all – for example, in the fields of education, welfare and culture.

(11) CHANGING SOCIAL PATTERNS

Changes in the wider community inevitably affect the Jewish community. Whilst we affirm the continuing vitality of marriage and the family as the primary framework for the living and transmission of Judaism, we also recognise that there are growing numbers of people who do not fit into the traditional pattern – e.g. the unmarried, single-parent families, the childless, the divorced, the widowed, homosexuals. Communal institutions, geared to the needs of conventional families, should be sensitive to the needs of these other groups, approach them in a non-judgemental manner and integrate them into the life of the community at large. Communal institutions are also obliged to make every effort to meet the needs of disabled people and to be sensitive to all manner of handicap.

(12) WOMEN

For many centuries, the role of the Jewish woman was very largely defined for her by Jewish men. Whilst recognising that, in many instances, Jewish women fared better, both legally and socially, than non-Jewish women, nevertheless they still occupied a less than equal position in Jewish life. It is now clear that women must be allowed to define their own role and involvement in Jewish life and the community. Progressive Judaism is unequivocally committed to equality of opportunity for women and men in all aspects of Jewish religious, social and communal leadership and life, including the rabbinate. An awareness of past attitudes to women leads naturally to a need to use inclusive language both in prayer and in general discourse.

These changes reflect the considerable and ongoing change in society at large. Much has already been achieved within the Progressive Jewish world in a relatively short space of time, particularly on a formal level. Not only are such changes right and just but the benefits to our community as a whole are incalculable. Nevertheless, we recognise that a process of inner change, of which practice and language are only external manifestations, is far from complete and we are aware that this issue will hold a significant place on our agenda for some time to come.

(13) RELATIONS WITH OTHER SECTIONS OF THE JEWISH WORLD

Jewish life cannot now be encompassed by any single expression of Judaism and we regard the other streams of organised Jewish life with the utmost respect and goodwill.

We seek the fullest co-operation with our fellow Jews and are committed to the search for Jewish unity as distinct from uniformity. Given the particular philosophies and approaches of Orthodox and non-Orthodox Judaism, we recognise that this may present more difficulties for Orthodox Judaism than it does for Progressive Judaism. But we believe that for all Jews of good will, it is readily apparent that what unites us is far more significant than what divides us.

We recognise that differences of approach over matters of Jewish status have special implications for the unity of the Jewish people but believe that, here also, with good will and moderation on either side, such problems can be resolved. All parties have, however, to be prepared to make sacrifices touching upon their power and authority in the interests of the Jewish people as a whole. For our part we recognise the value of preserving forms and rites which have been common to all Jews in status matters for centuries, so long as this is consonant with the achievement of that which is fair and just to individuals who seek our assistance.

We recognise the existence of many 'secular' Jews, Jews for whom faith is far from central to their Jewish identity. We acknowledge the reality they represent, the questions they raise and the values that many espouse and fight for. We commit ourselves to dialogue in the knowledge that each group has the potential to enrich the other and deepen the Jewish inheritance.

A. M. Bayfield, ed., 'Progressive Judaism – a collective theological essay and discussion paper', *Manna* 27 (Spring 1990), supplement (Sternberg Centre for Judaism, 80 East End Road, London N3).

(d) Faith in the Jewish city

THE RIGHT AND DUTY TO SPEAK OUT

(a) Before examining the findings of the Report in any detail, it should be stated, emphatically and without equivocation, that Judaism is in complete agreement with the basic assumption underlying the entire Report that *religious leaders and organisations should address themselves to the grave social problems afflicting society today*, both by arousing the public conscience on widespread suffering and injustice, granting this 'a high place among our theological priorities'

(3.25), and if necessary even by questioning the morality of economic policies in the light of their effects (9.52).

(b) The Jewish insistence on subjecting social issues to religious critical scrutiny and counsel is, if anything, even more pronounced and prominent. A massive proportion of Biblical and rabbinic legislation is designed to promote justice and fairness in social relations. If the whole range of 'politics' – from sweeping exhortations on international relations to stirring calls for social justice at a national and individual level – were to be removed from the Hebrew Prophets, then their writings would shrink to an insignificant assemblage of some ritual and slight theology. The Biblical Prophets were history's supreme leaders of the opposition. Though they commanded no votes, and stood alone in their day, they are immortal today – for the very reason that they set timeless moral imperatives against the transient dealings and decrees of contemporary rulers wielding political power.

(c) The renewed assertion of religious insights and challenges on current problems in the governance of a just and equitable society is therefore to be welcomed without reservation.

DIFFERING PERSPECTIVES AND EXPERIENCES

(a) From here on, our respective religious traditions, and more especially our opportunities for practical involvement, begin to diverge – leading at times to significantly diverse conclusions.

(b) Of the greatest importance is the pragmatic difference in perspective, gained from our totally differing historic experiences. Whereas in the collective Christian stance in Europe, deprived groups in Inner Cities or elsewhere have always represented exceptions to the norm, Jews have never been anything but a small minority which, until quite recent times, was subjected to severe discrimination and disabilities, and for many centuries confined to cramped life in the Inner Cities. It is precisely this Jewish experience which may provide the single most valuable Jewish contribution to many of the problems discussed in the Report. . . .

LESSONS OF THE JEWISH EXPERIENCE

. . . I drew . . . lessons from the Jewish experience in a discussion on community relations convened by the Commissioner of Police of the Metropolis between senior London police officials and a group of religious leaders, all Christian except myself. A black minister of a West Indian community charged the police with 'institutionalised racism', based on an 'ethnocentric' attitude which sought to impose white behavioural patterns on all minority groups, for example by dispersing West Indians congregating in groups on street corners, though this is their normal and accustomed 'street culture', or by white social workers counselling West Indian parents counter to their traditional, strict child-rearing practices. He condemned these attitudes as 'oppressive', exacerbating the relations between ethnic minorities and the police.

(c) I took occasion to explain that before the most recent influx of immigrants, the last minority to come to Britain were Jews. We could well understand the difficulties, problems and tribulations of social integration. We eventually succeeded, but by adopting an entirely different attitude. Although we had escaped from persecution in countries in which government and police were often looked upon as the enemy, *on arriving here we had cultivated trust in and respect for the police, realising that our security as a minority depended on law and order being maintained.*

(d) Moreover, we never demanded that, ourselves being heirs to a distinct culture and tradition, British society at large ought to change its character and assume a new multi-ethnic form, making due *public* allowance for varying ethnic traditions, whether in policing policies or in family counselling under local authority auspices. *We were quite content for Britain to remain 'ethnocentrically' British.* The Jewish community was most anxious to preserve its own identity, but it had done so (the considerable cost of some inroads by assimilation notwithstanding) not by insisting on public help, nor on changes in official policies, but by creating its own educational and social institutions designed to preserve and transmit what was special and singular in the Jewish heritage.

(e) Of course, I did concede the minister's argument that there were some substantial differences, notably that of colour. But I still felt justified in drawing attention to the successful Jewish self-help in achieving social and economic integration in the face of disabilities which, it should not be forgotten, more recent immigrants and other disadvantaged city-dwellers no longer suffered, especially as they enjoyed welfare state benefits which had not been available to earlier arrivals on these shores.

(f) But I submitted as the most crucial difference the fact that *Jews at the time were content to be patient and to wait and struggle for several generations to attain their social objectives, whereas we now lived in an impatient age demanding instant solutions*, and resorting to agitation and social unrest if these were not immediately forthcoming from government and the more advantaged segments of society.

(g) The lessons to be drawn may be imprecise and not without reservations. They are bound to be unpalatable to a generation conditioned upon rights demanded from others rather than duties owed to others. But it may still be *salutary to remind those presently enduring much hardship and despair that others have faced similar trials before them, and that self-reliant efforts and perseverance eventually pay off*, turning humiliation into dignity and depression into hope and fulfilment.

Jewish social teachings: similarities and differences

(a) Moving from the Jewish experience to the teachings of Judaism, we find a broad measure of agreement with the Christian approach on fundamentals. There is a common abhorrence of social injustice, oppression and deprivation. The Christian conscience condemns poverty as utterly demoralising (Report, Chapter 9), just as in Hebrew poverty (*oni*) is identified with affliction (*inui*) as an unmitigated curse. *Both faiths raise the relief of want as a precept of the highest religious virtue*, and both regard the humiliation of worklessness incompatible with the dignity of man created in the Divine image.

(b) Yet there are some important variations in perspectives, even at the theological level. . . .

CONCLUSIONS – POSITIVE

(a) What can be concluded . . . is that from a Jewish point of view the direction of the critique of present policies and the general thrust in the search for solutions would have to differ in some quite substantial respects.

(b) Guided more by moral concerns than by economic theories or suppositions, *a Jewish religious contribution would lay greater emphasis on building up self-respect by encouraging ambition and enterprise through a more demanding and more satisfying work-ethic, which is designed to eliminate idleness and to nurture pride in 'eating of the toil of one's hands' as the first immediate targets.*

(c) In a partnership of service and civic solidarity, the more affluent section of society should provide more social agencies and counselling services as well as more capital for prudent enterprises in the inner cities, whilst out of them should go those otherwise employed, to provide labour for public works and other useful pursuits, even if at first poorly paid, *with a view to the eventual abolition of the soul-destroying dole. Any job is better than paid idleness.*

(d) The social and counselling services should help to bridge the gulf between 'the two nations' by demonstrating care and concern. As a high priority they should be used also to assist in rebuilding solid family life now so widely ravaged by unemployment and permissiveness. Even more important for the recovery of the health of our inner cities than the building and renovation of housing projects is the repair of home life as the inner fortress of love, care, decency and every social virtue. The Jewish experience of the home as the principal haven against the exposure to the bitter realities of life outside does not bear out the Report's scepticism:

> The identification of Christian perspectives with male dominance and female subservience can only serve to reinforce attitudes which encourage the abuse of women in the family, while an

emphasis on the need to put up with suffering, however terrible, makes women in these circumstances feel guilty if they seek to leave home. As a result, pastoral advice is often directed towards exhorting the woman to keep the family together, regardless of the risk to herself. Clergy have little to offer women in this predicament (12.32).

(e) In a Jewish blue-print for the regeneration of the inner cities, the family would feature very much more prominently and positively. For *when the family breaks down, the most essential conditions for raising happy, law-abiding and creatively ambitious citizens are frustrated.*

THE ROLE OF GOVERNMENT AND UNIONS

(a) Obviously the role of government in revitalising the inner cities must be vital and indispensable. But the Report seems to be unduly slanted against present government policies by placing all existing ills exclusively at their door. Some criticisms may be quite justified. But in the aggregate, the sole concentration on government failures may divert attention from other equally important factors.

(b) . . . *The selfishness of workers in attempting to secure better conditions at the cost of rising unemployment and immense public misery can be just as morally indefensible as the rapaciousness of the wealthy in exploiting the working class in order to add even more digits to their astronomical profits, or as unacceptable as a government biased in favour of equating success with virtue rather than need with opportunity and human dignity with supreme merit.*

FROM DOOM TO HOPE

(a) The overall picture presented in the Report is grim, and even the prospects are described as 'bleak' (9.37). *No Jewish contribution could be more valuable than to help turn despair into hope, resignation into confidence that – given determination, patience, perseverance and faith in the infinite capacity of man to prevail over adversity – the new ghettos will be transformed as were the old and the growing wealth of the nation will increasingly be shared by all through shifting the emphasis from rights to duties and from having a good time to making the times good.*

Immanuel Jacobovits, *From Doom to Hope: A Jewish View on Faith in the City,* London, Office of the Chief Rabbi, 1986, pp. 3–4, 6–7, 14–15.

In the Chief Rabbi's analysis we had, to the minds of many – and to the pleasure of 160 Conservative MPs – an interpretation which supports a Conservative view, and a Thatcherite one at that. I am disappointed that in response to this we did not have additional public rabbinic analyses (among other things) drawing on alternative views of Jewish tradition, which might have given more consideration to the concept of justice.

The precise regulations set down for us on how to achieve justice were directed not at providing charity for the poor, nor offering them mere hope, but rather towards removing those barriers which prevented people from living full, dignified lives. Obviously the barriers which existed at the time the tradition was laid down are different from those existing in 1986. But the principle remains the same. So today, when we talk of racial justice, we do not mean giving charity to black people but rather removing those barriers (such as institutional racism) which prevent too many black people from having the same rights and opportunities as other citizens of this country.

In terms of our own experience, there has been much disagreement as to the exact nature of Jewish life in the East End. There are those who emphasize the rags-to-riches phenomenon – a penniless community which through hard work (the Protestant work ethic?!), complete obedience to the law, communal self-discipline and self-help raised itself out of the ghetto. Whilst acknowledging the above, others emphasize a different perspective: intercommunal strife (such as Jewish establishment opposition to Jewish immigrants) and organization of trade union activities, including strikes and fighting the fascists on the streets. The latter often resulted in difficult relations with the police and, at times, in the kind of anti-police ethos now regarded as the particular preserve of the Afro-Caribbean community. It is clear from the debate itself that our community's movement from immigrant to non-immigrant status cannot be represented by any monolithic view, particularly one which ignores the place of conflict in this experience. We do a disservice both to ourselves and to the non-Jewish world when we persist in presenting our history through rose-tinted spectacles. This is true too in the image we try to project of Israeli life and of British Jewry today.

The idealized picture of the Jewish family (strong, close-knit, contented) is one of the myths the outside world seems to have of British Jewry; it is one we like to perpetuate. We do not like to admit to the outside world, or to ourselves, that the stress of life in Britain is taking its toll on Jewish family life too. Hence the increase in divorce, separation and family conflict and the practice of 'alternative lifestyles'. We fail to acknowledge the diversity within British Jewry – in its religious observations, class, colour, culture and geographical location. One of the sad consequences of maintaining this myth is that it leaves out too many individual Jews who feel that there is no place for them within the established community. Although this has had a positive spin-off in the development of 'alternative' Jewish organizations, such as JONAH (Jews Organized for a Nuclear Arms Halt), the Jewish Feminists, the Jewish Socialist Group and the Jewish Council for Community Relations, too many still feel left out altogether.

Edie Friedman, 'Faith in the City: an alternative Jewish view', *Jewish Quarterly*, 33 (1986), p. 21.

3
<u>MUSLIMS</u>

*T*hree *of the entries to an essay competition for school children held in Birmingham in 1983 provide vivid impressions of how some of the younger generation of Muslims in Britain viewed their religion (a). The first two essays come from the 11–14 age group, one conveying something of the human experience associated with Ramadan and Eid el-fitr, the other raising the challenge of adaptation for recent arrivals in Britain. The third essay, from the 16–17 age group, critically explores perceptions of Muslims as a religious community. This last extract also touches on the central place of the mosque in the religious practice of Muslim men, something described more explicitly by Stephen Barton in his account of a back-street mosque in Bradford in the early 1980s (b).*

As Muslims became more settled, their self-appointed leaders increasingly exerted public pressure for the acceptance of their specific religious requirements by the wider society (c). By 1990 some voices at least had become quite assertive and radical (d). This development occurred against the background of the controversy stirred by Salman Rushdie's novel The Satanic Verses, *published in 1989, and sensitively analysed by a leading Hindu, Bhikhu Parekh, an academic and deputy chair of the Commission for Racial Equality (e).*

(a) *Muslim children present their faith*

Shaheen Akhtar
Eid el-fitr and *Eid el-bakar* are celebrated by Muslims. *Eid el-fitr* comes after thirty days of fasting, which is known as the month of Ramadan. For me *Eid el-fitr* is the best because when you're fasting you look forward to it. In the month of Ramadan my mum wakes me up at three in the morning which is just as hard as the actual fasting. After I managed to get up I have my meal. I try to eat as

much as possible, to last me through the day. When I'm fasting I try to keep occupied to keep my mind off delicious yummy food, then at about nine in the evening you open your fast, the next day you open it 2 minutes earlier and so on. In the evening I try not to eat too much because then I can eat a lot at three. Then after Ramadan comes *Eid el-fitr*. My mum gets up about five in the morning and starts cooking. She cooks savoury rice and sweet rice and English food too. My family and I always go to my uncles and aunts, there we eat and celebrate and give each other gifts. *Eid el-fitr* and *Eid el-bakar* I think should be spent with relatives or grandparents etc. I know the most important thing is for me to spend *Eid el-fitr* and *Eid el-bakar* with my family, relatives and friends, that is one of the reasons we have a great time together.

Moin Uddin
Bismillāhir Rahmānir Rahīm (In the name of Allah, the most merciful, the most kind)

When I was ten, I was in my country. When we celebrated *'Idul Adhā* every single person from my family had new clothes and every Muslim people had a bath just after the dawn. After I had my bath, I wore my new clothes and had some special food. When the prayer time came I went to the mosque to pray. There were lots of people crowded on the paths, in the mosque, in everywhere. After the prayers I shook my hands with my friends and we talked politely. We were happy. When I came to my house, we sacrificed a cow to seek Allah's pleasure. The meat of the cow, we shared with the poor; neighbours and with relatives. On that day we had lots of visitors coming to our house. We talked and discussed and then we ate some food all together. When the visitors went they invited our family to go to their houses. On that day I went to my friends' and cousins' houses and we enjoyed ourselves and we stayed happily.

In this country it is absolutely different. Many Muslims don't sacrifice cows because the cows cost too much money. You don't have many relatives. You cannot enjoy yourselves like my country.

In this country most Muslim people sacrifice a lamb except those who can't afford to. Muslims sacrifice a lamb because it's celebrated to commemorate prophet Ibrahim's (Abraham's) (p.b.u.h.) readiness to sacrifice his son on the command of Allah. So Allah accepted Ibrahim's devotion and obedience and asked him to sacrifice a lamb instead of sacrificing his son. So the people who can afford it, they sacrifice a lamb.

This occasion of great importance comes every year during the days of *Hajj* (Pilgrimage to Makkah) and is observed by offering congregational prayer. Islamic festivals are observed according to the Islamic calendar which is based on lunar months. The festival date is determined by the sighting of the moon.

Every Muslim must remember that what Allah wants is not the animal nor its meat or blood, rather He wants Muslims' devotion and submission to His command.

A Muslim's happiest occasion in life is to see the rule of Allah established on the earth.

Araf Jan
In this short essay I would briefly like to explore my relationship incorporating religion, as an individual, to my community. I would also like to thank you for giving me the opportunity to do so.

As a student, in today's world, my horizons are restricted and in my life there are different things upon which importance is placed, schoolwork etc. So it is very difficult for me to physically relate to Islam, i.e. read prayer five times a day – which is practically impossible. To compensate I have my own views, which is why I am writing.

I personally feel that there is a real need for faith, you need fulfilment in life, something apart from examination certificates. My own search for this started early in adolescence and has led me to ultimately believe in a higher being – even though people would say I am scientifically inclined.

Although my parents first expected me to follow the religion – Islam, and sent me trotting to the nearest mosque; as all Asian parents expect their children to, I don't believe I was actually pressured, nor could I have been, as is the case with many children. Hence what I believe is because I believe it.

Living in a large city as Birmingham, you can imagine I am fairly remote from my community, more than, say, I would in Pakistan. I have also the added pressure of living a Western life; conformity to survive, I call it. I know I have to take on a modern way of life by passing examinations.

I have to, clearly, make known my grave doubts of the religiousness of my community – everyone does not wholeheartedly believe in the faith. What is taught goes unheeded because either it is too inconvenient or restrictive – even what you see in a mosque is not wholly true.

There are true and devoted people but they are few and far between. What you do find in such a place are hypocrites or falsities to put it mildly – people come to gain respect in the social structure, word gets around if someone is attending the mosque! I suppose this is true for every religious community – bad and good all together. However I can say there are people who justly command respect, and so they should – who are honest in their dealings both with God and man.

Unfortunately I have to say, for the majority, religion is just a weapon in social fields, to reinforce futile arguments. People have actually changed religion to suit themselves, their customs etc.

I know I have not the right to criticize so intensively fellow brothers, as I myself am far from perfect. As an idealist I am writing what I believe, you would find discrepancies in any people of no matter what religion. Through my present disillusionment I see hope – the new generations of Muslims, born in this country, will demand much more than the mere name of Muslim, a truer way of following the faith and an honest one.

Jørgen S. Nielsen, ed., *Muslim children present their faith (Muslims in Europe Research Papers No. 19)*, Birmingham, Centre for the Study of Islam and Christian–Muslim Relations, 1983, pp. 2, 16–17, 21–2.

(b) *The life of a Bradford mosque*

(i) THE BUILDING

The two houses that have been converted into a mosque stand in what was the middle of a terrace running downhill from Manningham Lane. In 1978 the houses at the lower end of the terrace were demolished, and it is here that the Twaqulia Islamic Society purchased land for its new mosque. The houses are Victorian, with two rooms on the ground floor, two on the first, an attic and a cellar. The wall dividing the two dwellings has been retained, but the partitions within each house have been removed, thus creating two large rooms, with connecting doors, on the ground and first floors of the mosque. The front door of one house is the entrance and immediately inside is a rack for shoes. The ground floor rooms are used for the children's classes and for prayers when there is an overflow from the rooms above. There is no furniture apart from low reading desks for the children's text books and Qurans, and a mat and cushion for the teacher. The first-floor rooms are used daily for prayers: prayer caps and *lungis* are kept there for the convenience of worshippers. The walls are bare apart from one or two calendars, the timetable for daily prayers and a plan of the new mosque. In the corner of the inner room stands a purely symbolic carpeted *minbar*, of three steps, which is also the only indication of the *qibla*, the direction faced in prayer. Here too is a microphone, for a public address system is used to convey the voice of the muezzin and imam to the other rooms of the mosque. A table and chair are used by the imam when he lectures on the Quran. The cellar has been converted into a kitchen and place for performing *wudu*, the ablutions, before the prayers. There is a toilet outside, at the back of the building. The attics, comprising two bed-sitting rooms, and a small kitchen, are used as accommodation for the imam or others. . . .

(ii) THE FUNCTIONS OF THE MOSQUE

Mosques have always fulfilled several functions, the earliest being places for meeting, marketing, eating and residence as well as for prayer. But prayer is the prime function of the mosque. The individual has no need of a special place for prayer, as any clean space will suffice: 'Wherever the hour of prayer overtakes you, you shall perform the *salat*, and that is a *masjid*'. The designation of a special place arose from the need to pray in congregation. Indeed it came to be regarded as meritorious to pray with others in the mosque. There is another *hadith* frequently quoted by preachers: 'The prayer-rite of the man who joins the congregation is more than twenty degrees better than that of him who prays in his place of merchandise or in his house'. The mosque in Cornwall Road is used five times every day for prayers. The daily congregation may comprise only a handful of people, but more attend on Fridays, at weekends and during holidays. The form of prayer is of course identical with that observed throughout the Muslim world. A certain number of *rakas* are stipulated for each time of prayer, some of them being obligatory, others falling into lesser categories. The obligatory *rakas* are performed by the whole congregation in unison, but others individually. The timetable for the prayers gives both the times within which the prayers may be performed and also the time of each congregational prayer.

Some people come to the mosque before the time given for the congregational prayers and perform non-obligatory *rakas* in any part of the mosque. Their concentration, having entered the prayer-rite, remains undisturbed by others who continue to enter the mosque. When the *azan* is given, all form lines behind the imam, each man just touching his neighbour, taking care to ensure that no spaces are left. After the final *raka* of the congregational prayers, the rows break: some remain seated in prayer, some perform additional *rakas*, some leave the mosque and others stay for conversation.

The mosque is used not only for the congregational prayers but as a general meeting place. Its informal use is restricted by the need to keep the building locked against theft, but men often remain in the mosque after the prayers to discuss the affairs of the community.

Consequently, some who would not otherwise attend the prayers go to the mosque so that their voices may be heard in such discussions. Formal meetings of the Twaqulia Islamic Society are also held in the mosque. On account of its function as a meeting place, the mosque is often said to be central to the life of a Muslim community. However, it is important to recall that the women of the Bengali community are never permitted to enter the mosque.

It is at the festivals and during Ramadan that the mosque's functions as a place of prayer and meeting most clearly combine, particularly when the celebration takes place at night. After the formal prayers, people remain in the mosque to hear the imam's sermon, to pray or read, to prepare food in the kitchen, or simply to converse, activities which may all occur simultaneously. In Ramadan men who live some distance from the mosque share the *iftar* meal there, while some do not leave the mosque at all for the last ten days of the month, but keep a form of retreat, *itikaf*.

The mosque is also used as a school. Classes are held every day except Thursday and Friday for the children of the Bengali community. Such schools are common to Muslim communities throughout Europe. But, as we have seen, they are not in themselves a response to the new situation of the migrants: in Pakistan, Bangladesh and all over the Muslim world children attend similar classes in addition to or in lieu of their ordinary schooling. The provision of some Islamic education for the children, the second of the two aims of the Twaqulia Islamic Society, is perhaps the more urgent for migrants in a non-Muslim society, but the form that education takes is much the same as at home.

Stephen William Barton, *The Bengali Muslims of Bradford: A Study of their Observance of Islam with Special Reference to the Function of the Mosque and Work of the Imam*, Leeds, University of Leeds: Department of Theology and Religious Studies: Community Religions Project, 1986, pp. 88–9, 90–2.

(c) A summary of Muslim needs

The following is a brief resumé of the major recommendations . . . :

1 Muslims everywhere, especially those in schools and employment, should be helped and encouraged in practising their religion.

2 Prayer is an obligatory duty for every Muslim. Muslims, therefore, should be given a few minutes off to perform their prayers on the premises. On Fridays, however, they should be given some extra time as their lunch recess. Unlike the other prayers, the Friday prayer cannot be offered individually at the place of work.

3 Muslims have a different concept of hygiene and they usually need water to wash their private parts after attending the toilet and for making ablutions before prayers. Provision of water jugs or bottles in toilets and bathrooms will be very helpful.

4 Arrangements for a small prayer room will be helpful in large establishments where sizeable numbers of Muslim workers are in employment, as well as in schools, airports and service stations. Similarly, praying facilities for Muslim shoppers, especially in new shopping complexes, will be a great help, because they find it difficult to go shopping in the afternoon for fear of missing their prayer.

5 Muslim dietary regulations resemble, to a great extent, the Jewish dietary rules. Canteens in schools, colleges, factories and offices should provide *ḥalāl* Muslim food for Muslims, as it is easily available. Even Kosher meat will be acceptable. If *ḥalāl* food is not possible to arrange on certain days, vegetables, fish and eggs may be made available. Muslim food should be cooked in vegetable oil or butter. Use of lard or other animal fats makes the entire food unlawful and unpalatable for Muslims.

6 Muslim students should not be obliged to attend morning assemblies.

7 Muslim students should not be given any sex education as Islam does not approve of any practical demonstration of sex organs or sex play.

8 Muslim students should be provided with special facilities for religious instruction.

9 Muslim students should not be asked to wear any form of dress which goes against their religion. In particular, grown-up girl students should be allowed to wear *shalwār* or trousers in place of a skirt.

10 Physical training and swimming are encouraged by Islam, provided the religious requirements are first met. The grown-up girls and boys should not be asked to participate in PT and swimming in mixed groups. Grown-up girls are not allowed to uncover any part of their body in front of others, except their faces and hands, whether for PT, swimming or baths.

11 Muslim patients should be examined and treated by doctors and nurses of their own sex. For female patients in particular, greater care should be taken at the time of ante-natal and post-natal examinations. Expectant mothers feel very embarrassed if they have to undress before and be examined by a male doctor or nurse.

12 On the birth of a child, Islam requires the father or a representative of the family to whisper the call to prayer (*adhān*) in the ear of the new-born child. Facilities for *adhān* should, therefore, be provided immediately after the birth of the baby.

13 If the death of a Muslim patient appears to be imminent, it is customary for the family or their representative to recite verses from the Qur'ān and help the dying patient to recite the *Shah-ādah* (declaration of faith). The hospital authorities should, therefore, allow the members of the family to be present on the occasion and perform these last rites.

14 When death has occurred, the dead body should be immediately handed over to the family and/or representatives for washing, shrouding and burial. Post mortem, except in exceptional cases, is not allowed in Islam.

15 Since there is no priesthood in Islam, any representative from the mosque or Islamic organizations can visit a prison and perform the functions of a 'priest', and should be allowed to do so. Arrangements in this regard can be made by consultation with

the Muslim community of the area. The community can also help the authorities in providing Muslim food, give information on the month of fasting (Ramaḍān) and supply Islamic literature to the inmates.

16 The month of Ramaḍān is the month of fasting for every Muslim. Therefore Muslim employees, Muslim students and also prisoners will be fasting as well as carrying out their work responsibilities. Since these employees will not be requiring the lunch and tea breaks, it will be appreciated if employers would consider shortening and adjusting the working hours of their Muslim employees so as to enable them to fulfil this religious obligation without any difficulty.

17 In many situations, Muslims may require special facilities for pre-dawn food (Suḥūr) and late night prayers (tarāwīḥ).

18 The Festival of 'Īd al-Fiṭr (which marks the end of the Ramaḍān fast) and 'Īd al-Aḍḥā, at the time of pilgrimage, are occasions of celebrations for all Muslims. Muslim employees, as well as students, will, therefore, require a day off on these two annual festivals to celebrate the occasion with family, relatives and friends. Muslim patients, if their health permits, should also be given permission to go home and join in the celebration of the festivals. The dates of the two festivals should be marked on calendars as Muslim holidays.

Mustafa Yusuf McDermott and Muhammad Manazir Ahsan, *The Muslim Guide for Teachers, Employers, Community and Social Administrators in Britain*, Leicester, The Islamic Foundation, 1980, pp. 71–4.

(d) A voice of radical Islam

RELATIONSHIP WITH THE BRITISH AUTHORITIES

1 Islam allows Muslims to accept protection of life, property, and liberty from non-Muslim rulers and their political systems. Muslims placed in this situation may also pay taxes and other dues to a non-Muslim State. . .

2 Muslims living under the protection of a non-Muslim State must obey the laws of that State, so long as such obedience does not

conflict with their commitment to Islam and the *Ummah*. Other minorities in Britain, notably Jews and Roman Catholics, do the same.

3 There are laws on the British Statute Book that are in direct conflict with the laws of Allah; these relate to such matters as usury, abortion, homosexuality, gambling, sale and consumption of alcohol, and the abolition of capital punishment; Muslims can neither agree with nor condone any part of a legal and social agenda which so flagrantly violates the laws of nature as well of God.

4 Muslims will cooperate with the appropriate authorities for the maintenance of law and order and the promotion of peaceful and wholesome conditions for all our fellow citizens. . .

5 Muslims will insist, and continue to insist for as long as it may be necessary, that the British State provide them, their religion and culture protection from gratuitous insult, obscenity and abuse. . .

6 Muslims make it clear to the State, and all sections of British society, that they do not expect to be and will not tolerate being insulted and abused on grounds of their religion, culture and traditions.

Maxim: We are Muslims first and last. . .

GENERAL GUIDELINES FOR THE LIFE OF THE MUSLIM INDIVIDUAL IN BRITAIN

1 Every Muslim, man or woman, must practise Islam in all its dimensions in order to achieve the greatest possible degree of *taqwa* in his/her private, personal, family, social and professional life. . .

2 Every Muslim must pursue excellence in all departments of life, especially in the acquisition of all-round knowledge. . .

3 Every Muslim must ensure that his/her and his/her family's private and public life be committed to the pursuit of Allah's good pleasure alone. . .

4 Every Muslim must ensure that his/her lifestyle does not absorb the moral laxity prevalent in the secular culture of modern Britain today. . .

5 Every Muslim must live within the Statute Laws of the United Kingdom. . .

6 Every Muslim should seek to develop an identity in terms of the goals of Islam and participate in the struggle of the global Islamic movement toward these goals. . .

7 *Jihad* is a basic requirement of Islam and living in Britain or having British nationality by birth or naturalization does not absolve the Muslim from his or her duty to participate in *jihad*; this participation can be active service in armed struggle abroad and/or the provision of material and moral support to those engaged in such struggle anywhere in the world. . .

8 Every Muslim must contribute a regular proportion of his or her income to the Islamic movement instead of the habit of giving small or insignificant amounts only when faced with a 'collection box'. . .

9 Every Muslim must pursue his or her personal goals within the framework of the Muslim community in Britain, of the *Ummah*, and of the global Islamic movement. . .

Maxim: Islam is our guide in all situations.

A STRATEGY FOR SURVIVAL

Recent events have made it clear that Muslims in Britain, indeed throughout Europe and North America, will have to make a conscious effort if they are to survive. The time-honoured assumption that the generally liberal, open and tolerant ethos of the west would guarantee the survival of Islam and Muslims is a thesis no longer tenable. Muslims are faced with a vicious assault on their identity. Recent statements by leading figures in British Government and public life have made it clear that they expect, demand and will not be satisfied with anything less than our total 'assimilation'. Essentially their attitude towards Islam has not changed since the Crusades; their strategy remains the same, only their tactics have changed. Muslims living in the west have to adjust to an environment that is far more hostile than had been assumed.

Muslim communities in the west now need a comprehensive strategy for survival. The Council of British Muslims will debate and develop a comprehensive STRATEGY FOR SURVIVAL as a matter of urgency, made more, not less, urgent by every day that passes.

Maxim: Survive we must, live we may.

Kalim Siddiqui and others, *The Muslim Manifesto – a Strategy for Survival*, London, The Muslim Institute, 1990, pp. 11–12, 15–16, 17.

(e) The Satanic Verses *and the situation of Muslims in Britain*

Salman Rushdie's *The Satanic Verses* has become a terrain for many different and interrelated battles. Strange alliances have been formed across different battle lines, and the British cultural, educational and political scene has undergone transformations hardly anyone could have predicted a few weeks ago. *The Satanic Verses* is a dense and highly complex book, articulated at a variety of levels held together by a range of common concerns. It is, therefore, hardly surprising that most of the protesting Muslims haven't read it all, or have not read it with the care it deserves, and throw around passages taken out of context as polemical hand grenades. I wonder how many of the journalists, and even the high-minded literary critics, have understood it either. . . .

The central life experiences of immigrants cast them in a highly ambiguous relationship with the sacred. Lacking roots in an ongoing way of life, unable to feel in their bones the deepest joys and agonies of their adopted home, cut off from the social well-springs of meaning and value, their lives lack depth and richness, the commonest source of the experience of sacredness. Their dignity as human beings is constantly mocked by the hostile 'host' society; their sacred family ties are brutally snapped by evil immigration laws; their children leave home every morning and return speaking a language increasingly unintelligible and even hurtful to them. Thanks to all this, their predominant mood is one of doubt and suspicion, a subdued rage at the hypocrisy of a society that says one thing but does the opposite.

Different immigrants respond to these experiences and moods differently and evolve different strategies of physical and moral survival. Of these, two are relevant to our discussion. At one extreme, there is total cynicism. All people stink, are impostors, ruthless, cheats, predators, manipulators. None can be trusted, not even or rather especially not fellow-immigrants. Everything in this world is superficial and crude, and can be mocked, deflated, perverted, turned upside down. At the other extreme, there is a retreat to the familiar certainties of the past.

The meaning of life is deemed to be permanently and incorrigibly revealed in a sacred text, a body of rituals, or a pool of inherited and inviolable traditions. Even if these are perceived to be irrelevant or inapplicable in the new environment, they are uniquely the immigrant's own in a society that has stripped him or her of all else, the only thing that *distinguishes* them, gives them a past, roots in the present and the confidence to face the future. The holy text or traditions give certainty in a world of moral void; they are a sure protection against the dehumanising impact of cynicism. At one extreme, then, a deep and self-destructive doubt, at the other, an impenetrable and intolerant certainty. One has lost a sense of sacredness, the other has a surfeit of it.

All immigrants, however reflective and introspective they may be, harbour bits of both tendencies (and many others), nervously holding them in a precarious balance, turning to one when the other fails or becomes unbearable. Rushdie is no exception. He writes about the tension between these tendencies without fully appreciating that it lies at the very centre of his being and both enriches and distorts his perception of his subject matter.

This is evident in *The Satanic Verses*. . . .

Rushdie's imaginative explorations of the birth of Islam, Muhammad's 'terrifying singularity', the way his new religion came to terms with the constraints of the contemporary world, and the logic of total submission are bold and penetrating. Though they might and do offend some of the faithful, they form part of a legitimate inquiry. To have called Muhammad Mahound rather than by any other historically less evocative name was unwise, and comes close to a deliberate attempt to offend and provoke. Since only two out of several hundred verses were suspected of being inspired by Satan, the title of the book, too, was unnecessarily provocative. Muhammad is often described as a businessman, constantly bargaining and doing 'deals' with the archangel. He is sometimes referred to as 'the Businessman'; his is a 'revelation of convenience'; 'his God is really a businessman'; the archangel was 'businesslike' and 'obliging', and even reduced the initial quota of 40 prayers a day to five.

Here, as elsewhere, Rushdie's approach is not only irreverent but mocking, dismissive, angry. It is designed to put Muhammad in his place. Not surprisingly, it has deeply offended Muslim sensibilities. However, this is all part of a legitimate literary inquiry. And if a creative writer were to be hamstrung by the feelings and sentiments of over-sensitive readers, the writer's search for truth would be hampered and humankind would suffer a loss. The offence caused to Muslims could therefore be ignored in the larger interests of truth.

Doubts begin to arise with respect to other parts of *The Satanic Verses*. Muhammad is called a 'smart bastard', a debauchee who, after his wife's death, slept with so many women that his beard turned 'half-white' in a year. Muslims deeply respect Bilal, the emancipated black slave who was the first convert to Islam. Here, he is an 'enormous black monster . . . with a voice to match his size.' Muhammad's three revered colleagues, including Bilal, are 'those goons – those fucking clowns', the 'trinity of scum'. Like any great religious text, the Koran is full of rules and injunctions about forms of worship, helping the poor, concern for those in need, moral purity, self-discipline and surrender to the will of God. *The Satanic Verses* mockingly reduces it to a book 'spouting' rules about how to 'fart', 'fuck' and 'clean one's behind', and why only two sexual positions are legitimate, one of them being sodomy (that tired anti-Muslim canard yet again).

These remarks lack artistic justification. For Muslims, these and other such remarks are not only offensive and distressing; they also take on the character of what lawyers call 'fighting words'. Fighting words are verbal equivalents of the first shoves and pushes in a fight. They insult and provoke the devout; they challenge Muslim men to stand up and fight back if they have any self-respect and a sense of honour. They amount to a declaration of hostility. Even as we all feel not just hurt, but *provoked*, when we, our parents and loved ones or ethnic group are insulted and called obscene names, a Muslim man rightly feels challenged to a fight when those whose venerated memories he holds in sacred trust are ridiculed and abused.

Another passage, which rather surprisingly, Muslim leaders have not highlighted, relates to Mahound's 12 wives. When Ayesha, his young and favourite wife, protested against his taking on so many wives, the novel goes on: '*Who* can blame her? *Finally*, he went into – what else? One of his *trances*, and *out he came* with a message from the archangel. Gibreel had recited verses giving him full divine support. *God's own permission to fuck as many women as he liked. So there*: What could poor Ayesha say against the *verses of God? You know* what she did say? This: *Your God* certainly *jumps* to it when you need him to *fix things* up for you.'

Each of the words I have italicised reflects a supercilious and dismissive attitude. The reference to God's permission to fuck is cheap and vulgar. Even if one rejected the Muslim criticism that Muhammad should not have been presented as an impostor and a devious manipulator, they are certainly right to insist that a man whom millions consider holy and who has for centuries given meaning and depth to their lives, deserves to be discussed in a less aggressive manner.

There is also a brothel scene in which twelve whores take the names of Muhammad's wives. Rushdie has argued that it was intended to provide a profane antithesis to (and thus to highlight and accentuate) the holy. But since the holy has been mocked the brothel scene cannot be its antithesis: rather it is a further expression of the same approach.

Unlike Jesus, a divine figure for Christians, Muhammad is a human being chosen as the vehicle of Allah's will. His family is *ahl-al-baith*, the first family, and his wives are invariably referred to as *alwaj-e-mutahire*, the sacred wives of the prophet. The brothel scene represents a gross assault on the tradition. In pretending to be the wives of Muhammad, the prostitutes do not acquire an aura of sacredness; rather the sacred wives are dragged down to the level of prostitutes. They are symbolically violated. Every customer who plays at being a Muhammad vulgarises and reduces him to the status of an indiscriminate debauchee.

It is not difficult to see why the Muslims feel lacerated. Though they have sometimes called the book blasphemous, the term does not at all convey their basic criticisms. They seem to have adopted it largely because of the British law of blasphemy. Barring a few fundamentalists, most Muslims do not seem terribly worried by the irreverent tone, the questioning of the authenticity of the Koran, and the satirical treatment of Allah and the Archangel Gibreel. Nor are they worried that the book will shake their *faith*. They are *distressed* and *outraged* by what, with some exaggeration, their spokesmen have called the 'obscene', 'indecent', 'most filthy' and 'abominably foul language' in reference to the men whose memories they consider sacred and whose persons they consider holy. They also feel belittled and demeaned in their own and others' eyes, provoked and challenged to a fight by both the language and the 'outrageous liberties' taken with their sacred collective heritage.

These feelings are particularly strong among immigrants who cope with their predicament by holding on to traditionally inherited notions of sacredness. That is why the most uncompromising and tenacious reaction against *The Satanic Verses* came from British Muslims, representing the largest Muslim community in the west. This may also explain why the first generation of Muslims who turned to religion to give some meaning and hope to their empty lives (such as those in Bradford) responded more angrily to the book and more enthusiastically to Ayatollah Khomeini's *fatwa* than the others.

Bhikhu Parekh, 'Between holy text and moral void', *New Statesman and Society*, 24 March 1989, pp. 29–33 (with cuts).

4
HINDUISM

T *he introduction to Hinduism contained in the souvenir of a festival held in Milton Keynes in 1989 gives some indications of how the religion was presenting itself in a British context (a). Devotional life is represented by an account of the Arti service in the Leeds* mandir *(b), while the experience of women also points up the centrality of the home in Hinduism (c). These documents indicate the vigour with which Hindus were able to maintain their traditional observances in Britain, a pattern also evident in marriage rituals (d). Here, as in other respects, there may have been some adaptation, but this has been interpreted as simply a continuation of an inclusiveness and toleration that lies at the heart of the religion. This very inclusiveness however could be associated with intriguing ambiguities, as is apparent in discussion of quite where the line between Hindus and Sikhs should be drawn (e).*

(a) A universal religion

Hinduism is the most ancient and the largest living natural religion in the world. Another name of Hinduism is Sanatan Dharma, which means the eternal right path. Hinduism has no origin and therefore has no end either. The name itself reveals the spirit of Hinduism. No other religion and its followers in the world have undergone such ordeals, hardships, invasions, and harassment as Hinduism and Hindus. Yet they have survived and are a living force with the same glory and spirit. The history of Hinduism has proved that it is an eternal religion.

NATURAL RELIGION

Hinduism is a natural way of life. It is not a man-made religion, not founded or created by any prophet and is not preached and brought up by any leader. Hinduism is not a constructed main road. It is a self-formed footpath trodden by the continuous walking of the masses of their own will and choice. Hinduism is never imposed on anybody at anytime and is the only religion in the world which never believes in conversion. It wants anybody to realise the Almighty by own will. Hinduism does not encourage conversions even if the people of other faiths wanted to be Hindus. Hinduism asks them to worship Almighty by following their own faith. The Buddhist who became the worshipper of the Supreme Almighty Siva, by his self-realisation, was not converted into Saivism. He was asked to worship God Siva by remaining as Buddhist himself. He was included among the great Saiva devotees as 'Sakya Nayanar' (Buddhist devotee of Siva) and not as a Saiva Nayanar. This is the remarkable feature and nature of Hinduism which cannot be even imagined by other religions that are always after conversions.

RELIGION OF UNITY

Hinduism is the symbol of unity. It is not a single religion but a composite one where people of various religions were put together under a single shade. All the other religions of the world were diverted, and separated from some other religion. Diversities of rituals, belief, caste, food, dress, social behaviour, languages and politics have not been able to destroy the deeper spirituality of Hinduism. Its tradition has found it possible to accommodate and apprehend within its fold, a variety of doctrines and cults. The Ardhanari aspect of the Supreme Almighty Siva reveals the union of Saivism with Saktam. Shankara Narayan aspect of Siva tells out the mingling of the Saivism with Vaishnavism. The Linga form of Siva speaks out the union of cults of Brahma, Vishnu and Rudra with Saivism. The Ashtamurty aspect of Siva, i.e. Siva in the form of fire, water, air, ether, earth, sun, moon and soul, shows the union of Saivism with the nature worship and human worship. Like this throughout history Hinduism stands for unity.

Since Hinduism has already many names and forms for the Almighty it is not at all difficult for it to welcome any new name or form. It is an ocean where all the rivers run and join. One can find the other religious faiths also accommodable in Hinduism.

RELIGION OF EXPERIENCE

Hinduism is the religion of experience. It is not based on dogmas and creeds to be accepted with blind faith, but is based on self-realization. It has produced numerous sages and saints who had the vision of the Almighty and experienced God in their lives. Their divine experiences and life histories are known to the world from their own spontaneously born sacred hymns on God and not from the stories narrated by others. Even though the basic sacred scriptures of Hindus are Vedas and Agamas, it has evergrowing store of sacred hymns throughout the ages. Only in Hinduism we see sacred scriptures rendered by women saints, whereas in all other religions such scriptures were written by menfolk.

RELIGION OF LIFE

Hinduism has a very close understanding and relation with Almighty. Hindus believe that God is not sitting somewhere very far from the humun and world. He is everything and everywhere. The Tamil name for God is 'KADAVUL' which means one who possesses everything and within everything. God is in [the] whole universe like the ghee in milk, oil in seed, fire in wood and fragrance in flower. God is in daily life. Hinduism is a way of life. It never separates religion from life and life from religion. Hindus take [a] bath by chanting the names of God and eat after offering to God. Thus every movement, each and every art is the mode of worshipping God. Hinduism is an art gallery, a music hall, a cultural heritage and a social institution.

RELIGION OF LOVE AND GRATITUDE

Hinduism is a religion of love and gratitude. It gives due respect to each and every creature and to everything in the world and puts the same in practical life also. The aspects of nature . . . [such as]

earth, sky, mountains, rivers and living beings . . . [such as] animals, plants and things . . . [such as] wealth, education . . . are seen as divine and being connected to God. [The plant] kingdom has a prominent place in the Hindu way of worshipping God. The trees are the shelters of God. Animals and birds are venerated and worshipped as vehicles of God. Siva in his aspect as Pashupati is the protector of non-human living beings. Hinduism considers all the creatures as children of God and the whole world as a single family. Thus it makes the whole universe holy with its philosophy and way of worship.

RELIGION OF FREEDOM

Hinduism is a religion of freedom. It allows absolute freedom in faith and mode of worship. It never insists that God could be obtained only through a particular name, place or path. Hinduism allows [one] to worship God without form, with form and also through symbols. In Hinduism there is only one supreme which is nameless and formless, also known as Brahman or Sivam. It has names and forms suitable to the tastes, maturity, knowledge, and needs of the human beings. God reaches to the devotee in the form chosen by him.

RELIGION OF HUMANISM

Hinduism is the religion of humanism. In many respects it is more than a religion. It contains the universal truth and the fundamental truths are the same for all . . . humans, irrespective of whatever, wherever and however they are. There [are] no manmade restrictions or rules in Hinduism to impose on others. Hinduism has natural laws and [a] natural way of life. One can eat, drink, dress and live as one wishes. There is a place for everybody in Hinduism. It provides for all the greatest varieties found in human nature. Thus God is father, mother, child, friend etc. Man, woman, married, unmarried, child, youth, old all have their choices of path. Hinduism is the synthesis of all types of humans, it is the only religion which gives equal status and respect to womanfolk. The supreme Almighty Siva is worshipped as half-man and half-woman. The Hindu's sacred scriptures, the Vedas and Agamas were given to Parvati and compiled by her. Parvati, Saraswati, and Lakshmi, the female deities are the authorities of power, education and wealth respectively. When all the other societies consider womanfolk as powerless Hindu society worships woman as power. Hinduism has . . . room for even anti-religion people. The concept of anti-religion people are defined as Lokayatam and Hinduism considers this as the first step or primitive knowledge to realise the Supreme Almighty.

RELIGION OF TOLERANCE

Hinduism is the religion of tolerance and patience and gives due respect to all religions. That is why it is possible for Hinduism to be a composite religion by putting together various cults and sects. It accepts all the religions as the steps of the staircase that leads to God. Hinduism never persecuted anybody for his faith. It is not interested in proving its superiority to other religions through debates, disputes and platform lectures. Even when people of other religions were highly critical of Hindu Gods, sacred scriptures, mode of worship etc., Hindu saints always asked the people to be calm and not to get angry.

Hinduism is a tradition of ever-growing knowledge. There has always been a war between science and organised manmade religion. Hinduism has taught scientific truths centuries before the science was born in other countries. In no other religion one can find such a complete synthesis of science with teachings. Hinduism never separates science from religion. It is a scientific way of life. The tantric literature of Hinduism deals with all sorts of science. The rasayana deals with child diseases and cure. There are eight types of tantras that deal with medicine and other fields. The akasa tantra deals with atmosphere. There are several books that describe different forms of electric discharges, energy emission and formation of water by electric discharges during thunder and lightning. . . .

Hinduism takes great care of the sciences of environment, the forest development, welfare of wild life and plants. It believes that killing of any living being is a great sin and is against humanism and God. . . . Hindu science was never based on killing and dissecting the birds and animals. It was based on non-violence. Hinduism does not allow people to kill plants also. Cutting down the growing or green tree is a great sin.

Feeding cows, crows, ants etc. are prescribed as daily duties in Hindu scriptures.

Even after having easy mass communication system, . . . science and technology is struggling to bring unity among the people. But Hinduism did that very easily through Puranams and Sthalapuranams as well creating love for the land. Hinduism held the people by [a] single thread even though they were separated by political power, language, etc.

RELIGION OF THE WORLD

The inscriptions, copper plates, Siva lingam, Siva temples and other archaeological evidence got from Babylonia, Italy, America, Japan, Sumatra, Singapore, Malaysia etc. prove the existence of Hinduism in the entire world. The Sanskrit and Tamil names of many countries show that once all these countries had Hindu influence. . . . Hindus should awake and protect their most valuable religion by proclaiming themselves with great pride.

This Hinduism is the Sanatan Dharma, the eternal religion which has been perfected by countless Rishis and Avatara to uplift humanity. When you go forth speak to your nation always this world, that it is Sanatan Dharma that Indians arise, it is for the world and not for themselves that Indians are rising. When therefore it is said that India shall rise, it is the Sanatan Dharma that shall rise. When it is said that India shall expand and extend herself, it is the Sanatan Dharma that shall expand and extend itself over the world. It is for the Dharma and by the Dharma that India exists. To magnify this Dharma means to . . . magnify the country . . . What is the Hindu religion? What is the religion that we call Sanatan eternal? It is the Hindu religion only because the Hindu nation has kept it, because in this peninsula it grew up in the seclusion of the sea and the Himalayas, because in this sacred and ancient land it was given as a charge to the Aryan race to preserve through the ages. But it is not circumscribed by the confines of a single country, it does not belong peculiarly and for ever to a bounded part of the world. That which we call the Hindu religion is really the eternal religion, a sectarian religion, an exclusive religion can live for a limited time and limited purpose. This Hinduism is the one religion that can triumph over materialism by including and anticipating the discoveries of Science and the Speculations of philosophy. It is the one religion which impresses on mankind the closeness of God to us and embraces in its compass all the possible means by which man can approach God. It is the one religion which insists every moment on the truth which all religions acknowledge that He is in all men and in all things and that in Him we move and have our being. It is the one religion which shows the world what the world is, that it is the Leela or Cosmic Play of Vasudev the Supreme Being. It is the religion which shows us how we can best play our part in that Leela, its subtlest laws and its noblest rules. It is the one religion, which knows what immortality is, and has utterly removed from us reality of death. I say that nationalism is the Sanatan Dharma. The Hindu nation has born with the Sanatan Dharma, with it move and with it, it grows. When the Sanatan Dharma declines, then the Indian nation declines, and if the Sanatan Dharma were capable of perishing with the Sanatan Dharma the Indian nation would perish.

Sri Aurobindo

Sivapriya, 'The Greatness of Hinduism', *Virat Hindu Sammelan Souvenir*, Milton Keynes, 1989, pp. 49–51 (with cuts).

(b) Arti *in a Leeds temple*

The following account described the actions and words that are performed twice daily at the Leeds *mandir* in the *Arti* service.

Unfortunately, such an account is unable to express the variations and deviations that legitimately occur in the context of the changing religious year. On some nights, for example, only two participants will be present, and on others two hundred may attend. On some occasions the service will be led by a devotee in the absence of the *Pandit*. On others the *Arti* prayer will be directed to Shiva or Mataji (Ambamata) rather than Jagdesh, in order to fulfil the requirements of a festival celebration. On no two occasions will the service be identical. This account aims, however, to describe the actions and verses that are generally observed in daily services, festivals, *samskaric* rites, *Vrats*, and the regular weekly fire sacrifice.

On a typical evening participants gather in the *mandir* having removed their shoes and made personal offerings and greetings. They stand facing the *murtis* of Radha and Krishna, and the married women draw their saris over their heads. The *Pandit*, having bathed and dressed in clean clothes, prepares the tray (*thali*) for worship with pure water (*arghya*), lights the incense (*dhupa*) and places *ghee*-soaked cotton wool *divis* in the branches of the *Arti* lamp. These *divis* are lit, and the *Pandit's* wife brings a covered bowl of food from the kitchen and places it by the *murti* as an offering to the deities (*naivedya*). *Arti* is then ready to begin.

The first *prarthana* is addressed by those present to Vishnu (Shan-takaram bhujag shayanam padmanabham suresham . . .). It describes his qualities and pays him homage:

> Homage to Vishnu who is peace personified, who rests on Shesha, from whose navel the lotus issues, who is Lord of all the gods, the support of the universe, who is limitless like the blue sky, whose glory is like the rain clouds, whose limbs are perfection, whose consort is lovely Lakshmi, whose eyes are like lotus flowers, who the sages see in their visions and feel in their meditations, who removes the fear of birth and death, who is the one Lord of all. Homage to Vishnu.

After this the *Arti* prayer is sung (Om jai jagdesh hare . . .), and this is accompanied with bells, tambourines and clapping, all said to help maintain the concentration of the participants.

Victory to the Lord, victory to the Lord,
  who rescues his devotees and servants from distress.
Keep those who worship you from the miseries of the world,
Give them success and happiness.
You are my mother and father, whose protection I seek.
You are without a second.
Without you (I) have no hope.
You are the great Atman, you are the seed within,
You are Brahma, the great Lord, the spiritual
  master of all.
You are the ocean of mercy, the creator.
I am the servant, you are the master.
Be kind, merciful Lord.
You are the unknowable One, the Lord of life-breath.
I am foolish, tell me how I can meet you,
  compassionate and benevolent one,
Friend of the poor, remover of suffering,
  you are my defender.
Give us your hand and raise us up,
  for we have fallen at your door.
Erase our defects and vices,
  and remove our sins, O God.
Increase our faithful devotion and love,
  and guide us to serve the good and pure.

This *prarthana* contains a number of verses and a repeated chorus, and takes approximately ten minutes to sing, during which the *Pandit* or an assistant rotates the *thali* in front of the focus of worship. The prayer itself both praises and petitions the Lord, and the action of rotating the lamp with its lighted *divis* is thought to purify the *murtis* in order for them to be able to receive the divine power of the deities. At the end of this *prarthana* the accompaniment ceases, and participants bow their heads and hail Krishna (vandana). Those present are then silent while the *Pandit* performs an action with purified (*arghya*) water: he places the *thali* near the *murti*, and, with a small spoon, pours water from a vessel or *vadki* around the outside of the *thali*. This symbolises the participant's circumambulation (*pradaksina*) of the focus of worship. In India the *murti* is housed in a *garbhagrha* or closed shrine, and it is generally possible for worshippers to walk in a clockwise direction around it. This is performed in a spirit of homage to the deity, and as an auspicious act. In Leeds the construction and size of the *mandir* does not allow *pradaksina* to take place, and, instead, it is performed symbolically by the *Pandit* who chants the following *mantra* to accompany his action:

> With each step of this circumambulation may the sins of this and the previous life be eliminated.
> (Yani kani ch papani janmanter krtani ch . . .)

This is followed by a series of *prarthanas* petitioning and paying homage to the Lord in his or her various forms. The participants face the *murti* with hands together in the *namaste* position. While these prayers are sung the *Pandit*, turning on the spot in front of the focus of worship, offers light to the deities represented in the pictures and statues around the room. He holds the *thali* in his left hand, and passes his right hand across the flame in the direction of each representation. The *prarthanas* are as follows:

> You are my mother and father, my brother and friend. You are my knowledge and wealth. You are the greatest God of all.
> (Tvamev mata cha pita . . .)

> All the speech, thoughts and actions brought about by my own intellect and disposition are offered to you, Narayana, for purification.
> (Kayen vacha mansa kriyev budhyatma . . .)

> O Gaura (Shiva) who is (as pure as) camphor, who is the avatara of mercy who protects us from transitory life, who is the serpent king, who dwells in the heart of the lotus. I bow to Bhava (Shiva) and Bhavani (Shakti) for mercy.
> (Karpur gauram karunavtaram sansartaram . . .)

To the one whose good is the greatest good of all, who is (the energy of) Shiva, who fulfils all virtuous aims, who shelters the good. Homage to Gauri Narayani.
(Sarva mangal manglaye . . .)

Let all the beings of your creation be happy. Let all experience well-being, and at no time let suffering be the lot of anyone.
(Sarvepi sukhinah santu . . .)

Om, peace, peace, peace.
(Om shantih . . .)

Finally a short *prarthana* is chanted with everyone facing the *murti* with their hands together.

Om, lead me from delusion to truth.
Om, lead me from darkness to light.
Om, lead me from death to immortal life.
Om, peace, peace, peace.
(Om asato ma sad gamaya . . .) (BU; Iiii 28)

All those present then hail the deities represented at the front of the temple, Krishna, Rama, Ganesh, Hanuman, Shiva and Mataji ('Krishna kanhiyalal ki jay' etc.), and terminate this by paying homage to their religion with the phrase 'Sanatana dharma ki jay'. This is the last *upachara* or offering made to the deities in the *Arti* service, and is known as *vandana*, a form of worship combining the elements of *pranama* and *bhajana*.

After this the *thali* and *Arti* lamp are passed amongst the participants who offer money, and wave their hands across the flame and over their foreheads before performing *namaste* to the lamp. It is said this is done in order to purify the eyes which, more than any part of the body, directly experience suffering and impurity. While this is performed one of two *bhajans* is sung. One of these is Gujarati (Hum tari bolavum jay . . .), and petitions the Lord to let the devotee stay by his side in service and the performance of vows, and the other, a Hindi song (Jagh jagh samsarka . . .), tells the

Lord of the devotees desire to submit to his control. During and after this, a part of the food offered to the deity as *naivedya* is distributed amongst the participants. It has now become *prasada*, and is either eaten then and there, or packed up and taken home to share with family and friends. Other *bhajans* may often be sung after *prasada* is shared.

Kim Knott, *Hinduism in Leeds: A Study of Religion Practice in the Indian Hindu Community and in Hindu-related Groups*, Leeds, University of Leeds: Department of Theology and Religious Studies: Community Religions Project, 1986, pp. 120–3.

(c) The role of an orthodox Hindu woman

INTRODUCTION

Hinduism is one of the world's religions practised by millions of people all over the world. The majority of this population is concentrated in India, although many Hindus are now gradually emigrating to other countries where they find themselves adapting to the way of life characteristic of the foreign land.

As with all religions the degree to which Hinduism and its rituals are preserved in each home varies. Often, in this country practicality is the problem, in which case the nearest alternative measure is taken.

For my project I have taken my home as a typical example. Compared with many others I know, our home maintains a very orthodox approach to Hinduism. This may in part be explained by the fact that my family is Brahmin – the Hindu caste of priests.

THE ROLE IN THE HOME

The home bears great importance within Hinduism, the origin and site of most religious customs and laws. A great Hindu belief is that however humble a lodging may be, providing it is thoroughly clean, God will remain constantly present there. Thus the mother daily perseveres to keep the house in order, continually striving to ensure the holiness of a temple in her home.

Early each morning my mother wakes up long before the rest of the family. After washing and dressing, she will perform the daily ritual of *puja*.

Each Hindu family has a shrine in their home where statues and perhaps framed pictures of the gods are kept. It resembles a temple and in the same way as the priest, a member of the family must take on the responsibility of cleaning and augmenting the gods each day, the act of *puja*.

Whilst chanting prayers throughout, mother picks up each individual statue, bathes it in lukewarm scented water and carefully dries it. Using an already prepared sandalwood paste she places a mark on certain features of the statue i.e. on the forehead, hands and feet. During the summer, rose petals and flowers are strewn over the gods. This done, mother lights a *diva* (oil lamp) and incense stick on a plate and waves it around the shrine invoking God's presence.

This daily deed, usually done by the mother for convenience, is carried out on behalf of the whole family. It symbolises our piety and dutifulness towards God, knowing that as we have strewn flowers over God, He will fill our lives with such beautious things.

Mother pours the remaining water around the tulsi, a pure and sacred green plant, once made holy by a goddess. Today it is worshipped by many Hindu women who pray that they too may be of such good qualities. The pot or kero that the tulsi grows in is also marked with sandalwood paste as is the plant itself.

There is very little that can be said of the actual way my mother cleans the house each day. Due to modern convenience the method is basically the same as the majority of women in England. However, there is a lot to explain within the mental aspect of it.

There exists a strong sense of duty as Hindu women tend to know the role that is expected from them by family, friends and society in general, principles set down by the laws of their faith. The woman is responsible for the welfare of her family and home and of their adherence to the Hindu faith.

Cooking takes up a large part of a Hindu woman's day, it being a priority to feed one's family. Mother prepares many varieties of different foods each day, usually favourites for both adults and children. During the lengthy process of cooking, mother never once tastes any of the food being prepared, especially in the evening. This is due to the fact that each day at one mealtime a plate of the prepared food is first offered to God before anyone else. Tasted food is forbidden.

Mother lays the plate on a cloth before the shrine with *dhoop* sticks and *divas*. Often an *arti* hymn may be sung as the family gathers around to pray. We thank the Lord for the food which we receive from Him each day and pray for those not as fortunate as we are.

All the major scriptures of Hinduism lay down some sort of indication as to the diet of its followers. They have all been interpreted in a variety of ways by Hindus all over the world. In our family nobody eats meat, fish or eggs as this is seen as living at the expense of the lives of God's other creatures.

It is the mother's duty to ensure that these dietary laws are conveyed to her children and to help them understand the reasons behind them. By preparing a variety of enjoyable dishes the mother encourages her children to learn that it is NOT essential to kill another being in order to live satisfactorily.

There is a very restricting law in Hinduism which tends to undermine the relevance of a Hindu woman as an equal to men. The religion has no specifically stated rules, yet each generation has taken examples set by predecessors as a built-in way of life.

Once a month, the woman is condemned to isolation while she is menstruating. During the first four to five days of her menstrual period, the woman is literally isolated from the daily running of the house. It is regarded as sin to cook, clean or feed others and certainly to enter the room where the family shrine is kept. Many people even go as far as not to touch the woman and if by accident they do, they will immediately have a bath to cleanse themselves.

As yet, I have never come across one Hindu woman who is able to give me a wholly valid reason for this strange restriction. Most women have just accepted it as a binding law and few ever question it. It may be that it was the only way women would be allowed a rest from daily chores or it may be that if a woman is barred from religious duties once a month they can never be priests and hence leaders of communities.

Certainly the break from the daily housework is appreciated by most women but it is not always convenient. For example it is so distressing to be outcaste during religious ceremonies, festivals and other events.

In order to repent any sins committed, especially when a woman is forced to cook or clean while she is menstruating (due to the absence of any one else to do such daily chores), each year there is a special atonement day called the *Naag Panchum* when all Hindu women fast for a whole day.

The extent of isolation of the woman during her menstruation is variable. Most families keep the family shrine out-of-bounds to the woman during this period, whilst she is allowed to continue normally with her daily housework. In other more orthodox families, all the housework is banned and the woman is forbidden to touch anyone or anything that other members of the family may need.

THE ROLE OF THE WIFE

A Hindu woman's role as a wife is particularly important for she is expected to become the foundation of the home. The Hindu woman has fine examples to follow from the goddesses, Parvati and Lakshmi who sincerely worship their husbands, Lord Shiva and Vishnu respectively. The wife is expected to look up to her husband throughout their married life for guidance, security and support. Each wife endeavours to respect her husband as the essence of their lives in the same way as the goddesses.

As soon as she is married, the Hindu woman's life is completely dominated by her husband's life. On marrying she forsakes her family and friends and adopts her husband's family as her own. She is now required to place her husband's and family's needs before her own. She must respect each member of her in-laws whether they are younger or older than herself, and usually uses respectful forms of address when speaking with them. Each time an elder person such as the father-in-law or brother-in-law enters the same room the

Hindu woman will immediately cover her head with part of her sari to show her respect.

A Hindu wife wears a sari each day which is a long piece of thin cloth cleverly wrapped over a petticoat. The sari is usually colourful with various patterns but it will never be black. Widows wear plain white saris. Apart from the sari there are other accessories which a Hindu wife will *never* be seen without:

1 A *Chandlo*: a coloured (usually red) spot in the middle of the forehead.
2 A *Purello Setho*: literally this means a filled parting. Each morning the Hindu wife fills the parting of her hair with a red powder called *Kunkoo*.
3 *Chudla*: these are the coloured bangles which a Hindu wife will wear often together with gold or silver ones too.
4 *Mangal Sutra*: a gold necklace given to her at marriage by her husband.

These four things signify the colour in a Hindu woman's life i.e. her husband. After the death of her husband, the woman will wear none of these things. All colour is omitted from her dress forever to signify the absence of her husband in her life.

To a Hindu woman her husband is regarded as the light and colour of her life, second in importance only to God. She will know the position of her role relative to him. Despite all the modern aspects of sexual equality, Hindu women still tend to bear in mind the social status handed down by generations and preserved by the goddesses. The husband has always been the dominating partner who works to feed and fend for his family. The wife's role is basically to rear her husband's heirs in his footsteps under her husband's guidance, for after marriage she belongs wholly to him. Each Hindu scripture points out this way of life as what God intended, thus reasoning his purposeful difference between male and female.

The role of the mother

Becoming a mother is usually the emotional zenith of a Hindu woman, the point in her life where she practically has everything a home should need. Then her exhaustive but enjoyable task begins with bringing up her offspring as followers of the Lord God from whom she received them. She will teach them their religion, its laws and how to adhere to them in many interesting ways. My mother often read us stories edited from religious scriptures specially for children's understanding. They usually include a hero or heroine who is a devotee of God and has been helped through some major hardship. The elementary yet exciting storyline ensures that the children remember the moral of it.

The mother–child relationship is usually a casual but loving one. The child is brought up to bear respect towards his mother. Each morning he will bend down to touch his mother's feet for her blessings for the day. Therefore, especially in the early years of a child's life, the mother's role is essential. During that time his parents are the child's gods, friends and in fact represent his whole world.

The mother is always grateful to God for the children He has given her. Each day she prays to Him to lead them in the right path throughout their lives under His loving guidance. She also prays for those barren women who are not as fortunate as herself to be granted children of her own. There are several special days which occur each year on which the mother fasts to show her appreciation for being blessed with her children.

CONCLUSION

The woman is an essential part of a Hindu home. She is the backbone of an efficiently run and happy home. She maintains the religious life intended and displayed by the gods. She is a subservient wife and a loving mother whose importance is often not appreciated until she is absent.

R. Pandya, 'The role of an orthodox Hindu woman', *Shap Mailing 1988: Women and Religion*, pp. 33–5.

(d) Changes in marriage rituals

My fieldwork clearly indicates that the Hindus of Britain continue to be typical Hindus in their flexible use of tradition. Mother India, even in diaspora, is as assertive as ever when it comes to incorporating novel elements into Hindu culture. In this way, in Britain today, Hindu rituals of marriage solemnization continue to be, with few exceptions, crucial and central elements of marriage law and of British Hindu culture. Without them, there is neither a complete marital union in the eyes of the community nor, it appears, an unchallengeably valid marriage in English law.

Thus, far from being phased out gradually, Hindu marriage rituals in Britain have become revitalized by new concerns and considerations. Fascinating evidence of this is now found when the legally required element of registration of the marriage is ritually built into the complex sequence of Hindu marriage rituals. By doing so, Hindus in Britain and their priestly advisors are asserting their religion's claim to universality in a surprisingly vigorous fashion. The old and well-known concept of the inclusivity of Hindu traditions is thus beautifully illustrated in its application in the modern world and, as I hope to have clearly shown here, not even the authoritative force of the British legal system is immune to such a pervasive force.

Werner Menski, 'Change and Continuity in Hindu Marriage Rituals', in Dermot Killingley, ed., *Hindu Ritual and Society*, Newcastle-upon-Tyne, S. Y. Killingley/ Grevatt and Grevatt, 1991, p. 51.

(e) When is a Hindu not a Hindu?

Religious labels, such as Hindu and Sikh, are sometimes assumed to refer to mutually exclusive communities of faith. The relationship may, however, be far more complex, the boundaries more blurred. The nature of the complexity can be better understood if one both listens receptively to people's descriptions of themselves and their religious allegiance, and reads works of historical and social anthropological research.

How children describe their religion

During recent fieldwork in Coventry I interviewed 8–14-year-old children from two Indian Punjabi communities. These are the Valmikis and Ravidasis. Each community is a structurally distinct group in the sense that it is a caste and that marriage is not expected to take place with outsiders. Each also has its own premises in which a distinctive form of congregational worship takes place.

I noted in particular the children's descriptions of their religious identity. One Ravidasi girl told me:

> I'm a Sikh. I pray to Sri Guru Ravidas Ji and all other Sikh gods. I go to Guru Ravidas Sikh temple.

Another said she was a Hindu. Whereas the first girl had learned, from her school teacher, that her religion was 'Sikh' rather than 'Indian', the second girl had been told at home that she was Hindu, and had then been particularly receptive to what she had learned in her Religious Education lessons at school about Hinduism.

> When I heard (about reincarnation) at school I believed in it. It had a great effect on me because it was my own religion and I thought that it was true.

A Valmiki boy described himself as

> Punjabi . . . Sikh, because my grandad, he's got a turban, and I asked my cousin, 'Am I a Sikh or what?', and he goes, 'Yes, because you take after your grandad.'

A Valmiki girl said:

> I say to myself I'm a Sikh, but like really I'm a Hindu. I'm a Hindu Punjabi. I do many things that Sikhs do. We go to a *mandir*, but I call it a *gurdwara*.

Conversation with these girls and boys raised a number of issues, among them how individuals assume religious labels, what they understand by them and why. By listening to individuals from minority 'denominations' one gains new insight into the complex character of the major faith traditions, and perceives the need for some knowledge of their historical development. One questions the basis on which insiders and outsiders attempt to draw inter-religious boundaries, and observes the factors which generate 'new religious movements'.

These questions are pertinent to the whole spectrum of world religions, but I will concentrate upon the complex relationship between Hinduism and Sikhism, with particular reference to the Valmiki and Ravidasi communities.

DEFINING HINDUISM AND SIKHISM

Any definition of Hinduism is particularly difficult, given its diversity and the general absence of statements. Nonetheless, faced with members of other more doctrinally explicit faiths, Hindus have produced definitions and even statements of belief. Informed outsiders often explain the problems besetting any definition. Some then deem it wisest to define Hinduism in terms of what it is not. For example:

> For practical purposes it is best defined as a vast religious tradition comprising all those systems of thought, beliefs and practices which originated in the Indian sub-continent, other than Jainism, Buddhism, Sikhism and tribal religions.

With Sikhism the task initially appears less difficult since the faith is of relatively recent historical origin and its adherents, being almost exclusively Punjabi, lack the regional and linguistic diversity of Hindus. The Sikh scriptures open with a credal statement, the *mul mantra*, composed by Guru Nanak, the first of ten spiritual masters. Guru Gobind Singh, the tenth Guru, provided a rule of conduct. The Rahit Maryada, the code of conduct which is currently in use, was authorized by the Sikhs' most authoritative elected body, the Shiromani Gurdwara Parbandhak Committee, and is based on this. It commences by defining a Sikh as

> . . . a woman or man who has faith in one God (Akal Purakh), the ten Gurus (from Sri Guru Nanak Dev Ji to Sri Guru Gobind Singh Sahib Ji), the Sri Guru Granth Sahib, and the utterances

of the ten Gurus and the amrit of the tenth Guru, and who professes no other religion.

Amrit (ambrosia) is a word for holy water, in particular that used in the initiation ceremony, so 'having faith in the amrit of the tenth Guru' means accepting the importance of initiation into the *Khalsa*. This is the body of 'pure' Sikhs who are committed to observing the rules enunciated by Guru Gobind Singh in 1699. These include the distinguishing uniform known as the *panj kakke* ('five K's').

THE RELIGION OF INDIAN PUNJAB: A HINDU-SIKH BLEND?

Members of the *Khalsa* regard themselves as unquestionably Sikh and are so regarded by others. But many people who have not 'taken amrit', who do not observe all the *panj kakke*, and may well have short hair, also identify themselves as Sikh. They revere the Sikh scripture (the Guru Granth Sahib) and the ten human Gurus. According to their gender, they use the titles 'Kaur' or 'Singh' as their second name, worship corporately in the gurdwara, and celebrate *gurpurbs* (anniversaries of Gurus' births or deaths). Their marriages are solemnised with the rite of *anand karaj*, the ceremony in which the Guru Granth Sahib is central, and hymns composed by the fourth Guru are recited.

At the same time, Sikhs, like their ten Gurus, come from a Punjabi Hindu background and continue to share in the dominant culture. They participate in festivals such as Divali. The feast of Karva Chauth is kept by many Sikh as well as Hindu wives. The diet of the Sikh and the Punjabi Hindu are the same. Many Sikhs, *amritdhari* (initiated) or otherwise, not only avoid beef but are strictly vegetarian. Some Sikhs follow *sants* (spiritual masters) or living gurus, such as the Radhasoami master, Charan Singh, who draw thousands of Hindu and other followers.

Many Punjabi Hindus have devotional pictures of the Sikh Gurus as well as of such popular deities as Sheranvali Ma (the goddess on a tiger). Certainly until recently, if a Hindu woman gave birth to a son, following prayer in a gurdwara, she would bring him up with uncut hair as a Sikh.

In matters of general behaviour the individual fears the disapproval of members of the *zat* (caste) rather than any religious sanctions. In practice marriage between Sikhs of different castes or Hindus of different castes has been far rarer than marriage between a Sikh and a Hindu of the same caste. This has been especially true of certain castes such as Saini and Khatri. . . .

Without going further into detail it is clear that any line drawn between Hinduism and Sikhism will be controversial. Equally clearly, these terms are powerfully meaningful for individuals in their perception of themselves and others. As teachers of Asian children or students of Indian religion we must not expect to classify people too tidily. Religions are not static entities. At one level they are concepts with which we hope to make sense of individual and collective belief and practice. These are infinitely varied and constantly changing. Normative religious statements and the actual ways in which individuals live and understand the world are not identical. The fact that the Valmikis' and Ravidasis' low-caste status was so significant in religious denominations, demonstrates the gap between such normative statements as 'Sikhism abolished the caste system' and a more complex social reality. Individuals who identify with a particular faith may define it very differently from authoritative religious spokesmen or religious educationists. This is clear from the first Ravidasi girl's explanation quoted above, of what being a Sikh means. But, as the second Ravidasi girl's words indicate, Religious Education is one of the influences on young people as they work out their religious identity.

Eleanor Nesbitt, 'Pitfalls in Religious Taxonomy: Hindus and Sikhs, Valmikis and Ravidasis', *Religion Today*, Vol. 6, No. 1 (1990), pp. 9–10, 12.

5
SIKHISM

By the early 1970s the Sikh community was well established in Britain and was offered guidance on worship and conduct in an English translation of a document originally drawn up by the Shiromani Gurdwara Parbandakh Committee, the central Sikh religious advisory body, and initially approved for publication in Punjabi in 1945 (a). The Sikh Cultural Society also disseminated copies of the Ardas, a key devotional text said at the conclusion of the service (b); and explanations of the distinctive appearance of Sikh men (c).

Sikhs in Britain continued to be powerfully concerned by the turbulent events in the religion's original homeland in the Punjab, above all by the massacre carried out by Indian troops at the Golden Temple in Amritsar in June 1984. Consequent outrage and insecurity was especially influential in reinforcing spiritual ardour among younger Sikhs (d), while it also contributed to sharp debate about religious and political identities (e).

(a) The Sikh way of life

What is a sikh?

A Sikh is any person whose faith consists of belief in one God, the Ten Gurus, the *Adi Granth* and other scriptures and teachings of the Ten Gurus. Additionally, he or she must believe in the necessity and importance of 'Amrit' (the Sikh baptism ceremony).

Essential beliefs

Sikhism is concerned both with a person's life as an individual and with his corporate life as a member of the Sikh Community.

The following two sections are devoted to a fuller explanation of both these aspects of Sikhism.

Sikhism and the individual

As regards the individual, Sikhism is concerned with:

    I. Study of the scriptures and meditation on God
    II. Living according to the Gurus' teaching
    III. Active service to the community.

I Study of the scriptures and meditation on God

A Sikh should

Rise early, bathe and meditate on the one true God.

The following scriptures should be read or recited:

(a) *Japji Sahib*
(b) *Jap Sahib* and *Ten Swayas*   } Early morning prayers.
(c) *Sodar, Rehiras*   Evening prayer. . . .

Congregational Devotion

The Gurdwara

(a) Study of and meditation on the scriptures within the congregation is very important, and Sikhs are urged to visit the Gurdwara as often as possible.

(b) The *Adi Granth* should be opened for reading daily, but should not be left in the open position, unless still in use, overnight.

    The *Granth* is usually closed after the *Rehiras* but may be kept open as long as the Granthi or any other bona fide person is present or likely to be present, so that there is no possibility of the *Granth* being irreverently handled.

(c) The *Adi Granth* should be opened, read and closed with reverence. It should be placed in an elevated position on a form or stool in clean well lit surroundings. It should be opened with care with small cushions being used for support and a *Ramala* (cover cloth) used to cover it in between readings whilst in the open position. A canopy should be erected over the area in which the *Adi Granth* is placed.

(d) No articles other than the above mentioned are to be used.

Rituals derived from the other religions, such as the ceremonial lighting of candles, burning of joss sticks, idol worship and the ceremonial ringing of bells are completely forbidden. . . .

[e] After entering the Gurdwara, the Sikh should greet the congregation, the living image of the Guru, with the words:

Waheguru ji ka Khalsa, Siri Waheguru ji ki fateh.
(Hail Khalsa of the wonderful Lord who is always victorious.)

[f] In the congregation, no distinction should be made between Sikh and non-Sikh; between social position or caste.

[g] To sit on special cushions, chairs, couches or sofas whilst in the congregation, or to show any other distinction or superiority, is contrary to Sikhism.

[h] No one should sit bareheaded in the congregation, or while the *Adi Granth* is open. It is contrary to Sikh belief for women to cover their faces or to wear purda. . . .

Kirtan *(Singing of Hymns)*

(a) *Kirtan* consists of the singing of hymns from the scriptures composed in classical Indian musical style.

(b) *Kirtan* performed in the congregation should be sung by Sikhs.

(c) *Kirtan* should consist of musical adaptations of, either hymns by the Gurus, or the explanations of the Gurus' writings by Bhai Nand Lal or Bhai Gurdas. . . .

[d] To bow one's head before the *Adi Granth*, to show reverence to the congregation, to read or hear readings from the *Adi Granth*, is equivalent to being graced by the presence of the true Guru. Simply opening the *Adi Granth* to look at it, is however a superstition and is contrary to Sikhism. . . .

[e] During a service, the person who sits in attendance at the *Adi Granth* should be a Sikh.

[f] Only a Sikh should sing hymns during a service, but all persons are free to sing or read these for themselves outside the assembly.

[g] The *Adi Granth* is often opened to read a lesson or message

from a page chosen completely at random. When this is done, the lesson chosen is the one at the top of the left-hand page, and if it commences on the previous page, the reading should also start there.

If a *Var* (ode) has been selected, then the whole *Pauri* (stanza), including *Saloks* (staves), should be read as far as the sentence that concludes with the words 'Nanak Nam.'

[h] Such random readings as described above should be used to conclude a service after the saying of the *Ardas*.

Sidharan *Path (Normal reading of the Adi Granth)*

(a) Every Sikh should try to keep a separate place in his or her own home for reading and studying the *Adi Granth*.

(b) Every Sikh should learn *Gurmukhi* and read the *Adi Granth*.

(c) Every Sikh should read a lesson (*Hukum*) from the *Adi Granth* before taking a morning meal. If this is not possible for any reason, the reading should be done later in the day. However, one should not have superstitious fears, if one cannot comply with this requirement or if one is unable to see or read the *Granth* at times of difficulty or before undertaking a long journey. . . .

II LIVING ACCORDING TO THE GURUS' TEACHINGS

A Sikh should live and work according to the principles of Sikhism, and should be guided by the following:

(a) He should worship only one God, and should not indulge in any form of idol worship.

(b) Live a life based on the teachings of the ten Gurus, the *Adi Granth*, and other scriptures and teaching of the Gurus.

(c) Sikhs should believe in the 'oneness' of the ten Gurus. That is, that a single soul or entity existed in the lives of the ten Gurus.

(d) A Sikh should have no dealings with caste, black magic, super-stitious practices such as the seeking of auspicious moments, eclipses, the practice of feeding Brahmins in the belief that the food will go to one's ancestors, ancestor worship, fasting at different phases of the moon, the wearing of sacred threads and similar rituals.

(e) The Gurdwara should serve as the Sikh's central place of worship. Although the *Adi Granth* is the centre of Sikh belief, non-Sikh books can be studied for general enlightenment.

(f) Sikhism should be distinct from other religions, but Sikhs must in no way give offence to other faiths.

(g) Knowledge of Sikhism is highly desirable for a Sikh and this should be acquired in addition to his other education.

(h) It is the duty of Sikhs to teach Sikhism to their children.

(i) Sikhs should not cut their children's hair. Boys are to be given the name of Singh and girls the name Kaur.

(j) Sikhs should not partake of alcohol, tobacco, drugs or other intoxicants.

(k) Sikhism strongly condemns infanticide, particularly female infanticide.

(l) Sikhs should only live on money that has been honestly earned.

(m) No Sikh should gamble or commit theft.

(n) Sikhs must not commit adultery.

(o) A Sikh should respect another man's wife as he would his own mother; and another man's daughter as his own daughter.

(p) A man should enjoy his wife's companionship and women should be loyal to their husbands.

(q) A Sikh should live his life from birth to death according to the tenets of his faith.

(r) A Sikh should greet other Sikhs with the salutation 'Waheguru ji ka Khalsa, Siri Waheguru ji ki fateh' (Hail *Khalsa* of the wonderful Lord who is always victorious.)

(s) It is contrary to Sikhism for women to wear purda.

(t) Any clothing may be worn by a Sikh provided it includes a turban (for males) and shorts or similar garment.

Birth

(a) As soon as a mother is well enough after the birth of a child, she, with her husband and family, should go to the Gurdwara, give *Kara Prashad* (the amount is immaterial) for serving to the congregation, and read hymns of thanksgiving and happiness.

Marriage

(a) Caste or birth should be of no account in Sikh marriages.

(b) A Sikh's daughter should marry a Sikh.

(c) The Sikh marriage ceremony should be according to the *Anand Karaj* ceremony.

(d) A girl should marry when she attains physical and mental maturity, and no marriage should take place if either the boy or girl is of tender age. . . .

[e] The seeking of an auspicious day for the marriage by the use of horoscopes is contrary to Sikh belief; any date that is mutually convenient is suitable. . . .

[f] For the wedding ceremony, the congregation sits in the presence of the *Adi Granth* and hear hymns of praise to God. These may be sung either by the congregation or by professional musicians. The bride and groom should be seated in front of the *Adi Granth*, with the bride seated at the left of the groom. The person who officiates at the ceremony (this may be any Sikh approved by the congregation) then asks the bride and groom and their parents to stand while he says the *Ardas*. This is the start of the marriage ceremony proper, and is followed by a short sermon by the officiator, in which he explains the significance of the Sikh marriage ceremony. The love between husband and wife is compared with the love and longing of the human soul for God. The bride and groom are reminded of their respective duties; the love and loyalty they should show to each other, and how they should share both their sorrows and their joys. Both groom and bride are advised to love and respect the other's relatives as they would their own. . . .

Death

(a) No rituals derived from other religions, or from any other source, should be performed when a death occurs. Solace must be found in reading the *Adi Granth* and meditating on God.

(b) Deliberate exhibitions of grief or mourning are contrary to Sikh teachings. The bereaved should seek guidance and comfort in the hymns in the *Adi Granth* and try to accept God's will.

(c) A dead person, even one who dies very young, should be cremated. However if arrangements for cremation do not exist (e.g. at sea), the body may be disposed of by immersion in water.

(d) Cremation may be carried out at any convenient time whether day or night.

(e) The five Ks should be left on the dead body, which should, if possible, be cleansed and clothed in clean garments before being placed in a coffin or on a bier.

(f) Hymns should be said as the body is taken to the place of cremation.

(g) A close relative should light the pyre and those assembled should sing appropriate hymns from the *Adi Granth*.

(h) The cremation ceremony is concluded with the *Kirtan Sohila* prayers and the saying of the *Ardas*.

(i) Prayers for the departed soul should then be commenced at the deceased's home or at a convenient Gurdwara. These prayers should commence with the usual six stanzas of the *Anand Sahib*, the saying of *Ardas* and distribution of *Kara Prashad*, and should be continued for about ten days. The near relatives of the deceased should take as large a personal part in reading and listening to readings from the *Adi Granth* as possible.

(j) The ashes of the deceased may be disposed of by burial or by immersion in water, but it is contrary to Sikh belief to consider any river holy or specially suitable for this purpose.

(k) The erection of a memorial in any shape or form is contrary to Sikh belief.

III ACTIVE SERVICE TO THE COMMUNITY

It is contrary to Sikhism to consider any form of labour to be below one's dignity or station in life. Stress is laid on the virtue of doing such work for the benefit of the community or for humanity at large. Sikhs should readily volunteer to perform such tasks as sweeping the floors of Gurdwaras and serving food and water to the congregation.

The serving of food and water to all, irrespective of caste, creed or race is known as *Langar*, and is a distinctive feature of Sikhism. It is important that no distinction or priorities are allowed in either the seating arrangements or the serving of food. The dual purpose of *Langar*, besides providing food to the needy, is to emphasize the dignity attached to serving others, and the complete equality and brotherhood of all humanity.

Kanwaljit Kaur and Indarjit Singh, trans., *Rehat Maryada: A guide to the Sikh way of life*, Edgware, Sikh Cultural Society, 1971, pp. 1, 3–6, 8–12 (with cuts).

(b) *The* Ardas

Having first remembered God Almighty, think of Guru Nanak;
Then of Angad Guru and Amar Das and Ram Das; may they help us!
Remember Arjun, Havgovind and the holy Hari Rai.
Let us think of the holy Hari Krishan, whose sight dispels all sorrow.
Let us remember Teg Bahadur, and the nine treasures shall come
    hastening to our homes.
May they all assist us everywhere.
May the Tenth King, the holy Guru Gobind Singh, the lord of
    hosts and protector of the faith, assist us everywhere.
Turn your thoughts, O Khalsa, to the teachings of Guru Granth
    Sahib and call on God.
                    Waheguru.
The Five Loved Ones, the Master's four sons, the forty Saved Ones,
    and other righteous, steadfast and long-suffering souls: think of
    their deeds and call on God.
                    Waheguru.
Those men and women who, keeping the name in their hearts,

shared their earnings with others; who plied the sword and practised charity; who saw others' faults but overlooked them, think
of their deeds and call on God.

Waheguru.

Those who for their religion allowed themselves to be cut up limb
by limb, had their scalps scraped off, were broken on the wheel,
were sawn or flayed alive, think of their sweet resignation and
call on God.

Waheguru.

Those who, to purge the temples of long standing evils, suffered
themselves to be ruthlessly beaten or imprisoned, to be shot, cut
up or burnt alive with kerosene oil, but did not make any resistance or utter even a sigh of complaint; think of their patient
faith and call on God.

Waheguru.

Think of all the different temples, thrones of religious authority and
other places hallowed by the touch of the Guru's feet, and call
on God.

Waheguru.

Now the whole Khalsa offers his prayer
Let the whole Khalsa bring to his mind the Name of the wonderful
Lord;
And as he thinks of Him, may he feel completely blessed.
May God's protection and grace extend to all the bodies of the
Khalsa wherever they are.
May the Lord's glory be fulfilled and His dispensation prevail.
May victory attend our Charity and our Arms.
May God's sword help us.
May the Khalsa always triumph.
May the Sikh choirs banners, mansions abide for ever and ever.
The kingdom of justice come.
May the Sikhs be united in love.
May the hearts of the Sikhs be humble, but their wisdom exalted,
their wisdom in the keeping of the Lord, O Khalsa, say the Lord
is wonderful.

Waheguru.

O true King, O loved Father, we have sung Thy sweet hymns, heard Thy life-giving Word, and have discoursed on Thy manifold blessings. May these things find a loving place in our hearts and serve to draw our souls towards Thee.

Save us, O Father, from lust, wrath, greed, undue attachment and pride; and keep us always attached to Thy feet.

Grant to Thy Sikhs the gift of Sikhism, the gift of Thy Name, the gift of faith, the gift of confidence in Thee, and the gift of reading and understanding Thy holy Word.

O kind Father, loving Father, through Thy mercy we have spent our day in peace and happiness; grant that we may, according to Thy will, do what is right.

Give us light, give us understanding, so that we may know what pleases Thee.

We offer this prayer in Thy presence O wonderful Lord:

Forgive us our sins. Help us in keeping ourselves pure.

Bring us into the fellowship of only those men of love, in whose company we may remember Thy name.

Through Nanak may Thy Name forever be on the increase.

And may all men prosper by Thy grace.

Hail Khalsa of the Wonderful Lord who is always victorious.

Hymns for the Conclusion of the Sikh Service, Edgware, Sikh Cultural Society, Publication No. 5, n.d.

(c) *Why do Sikhs wear turbans and beards?*

THE IMPORTANCE OF THE SYMBOLS

The symbols have both a practical and a deep spiritual meaning for the Sikh. The long hair is a symbol of holiness and is associated in India with saintliness. As in the story of Samson and Delilah, the unshorn hair means moral and spiritual strength. The hair is always to be kept clean and tidy since the Sikh is also a soldier and a householder – not a mendicant or an ascetic. For this reason, the Guru ordained that a comb should be worn in the hair.

As it is an essential article of their faith, Sikh history is full of sacrifices which they have made for the proper maintenance of the long hair. People's beliefs are personal; when they decide to join a religious faith, they do so voluntarily and in full comprehension of the requirements. Once someone wants to be a member he must comply with the rules of the Order.

WHY THE TURBAN?

The turban is an ancient and universal form of headgear worn in various forms by Muslims and Hindus as well as Sikhs. Guru Gobind Singh aimed to change his followers into saint-soldiers modelled on himself and his predecessors. The Guru's ideal was expressed in the holy words from the Guru Granth Sahib:

Sabat surat dastar sira
'Only with the turban on is the appearance complete'

and he wanted his Sikhs to adopt this description very rigidly. Thus, the turban has become an essential and complementary adjunct to the unshorn hair. Let alone the shaving off of a Sikh's hair, the knocking off of his turban is a great personal insult and an affront to the Sikh religion.

TURBAN AND BEARD IN BRITAIN

There is a general tendency among individuals of many religions to become lax in the observance of the obligatory forms but that does not imply that laxity is either tolerated or permitted by the religions concerned. In circumstances which are alien to the original thought and practice of the faith, people are bound to experience difficulty in strictly observing the codes; but taking the easy way out is not the proper solution. For the Sikhs, as for some other religious groups before them, there are some hardships to be faced in this country. The basis of these may lie in the ignorance of the general public as to what are the principles involved. The Sikhs are a brave and industrious people; they are friendly and thoroughly human. An understanding approach and tolerance towards the Sikh religion will undoubtedly result in a happy relationship between the Sikhs and the people of Britain.

Why do Sikhs wear Turbans and Beards?, Edgware, Sikh Cultural Society, Publication No. 8, n.d.

(d) The attitudes of the rising generation

SIKH YOUTH IN BRITAIN

In the 60's and 70's, there were two distinct groups of Sikh youth in Britain. The first were the children of largely uneducated Sikhs from Punjab. They were in the main born in this country, and, for this reason and because of the limited religious understanding of their own parents, they often felt more at home in the culture of the West than in the gurdwara.

The second group of children had in the main, spent their formative years in East Africa where Sikh religion and culture had been allowed to flourish. Their parents quickly established new gurdwaras and, though the pull of western culture was strong, these youngsters felt equally at home in the disco and the gurdwara.

THE POLITICS OF THE GURDWARAS

The role of the gurdwara is important in any study of the social and cultural identity of Sikh youth. In the 50's and 60's the number of Sikhs in the country was comparatively few and the religion largely unknown, and the community felt the need to interest non-Sikhs in their faith. For some years, from the mid-50's to the early 70's, the central gurdwara in Shepherd's Bush used to have an English language service once a month for the benefit of non-Sikhs and young Sikhs who knew little Punjabi. Positive efforts were made in some gurdwaras to acquaint young Sikhs with the main principles of their faith using the English medium.

All this was swept aside with the arrival of better-educated Sikh families from East Africa. The isolation of the community was reduced and need for outside contact lessened. Secure in large families and old social friendships, the community became increasingly inward-looking.

The use of English in the gurdwara lessened in the 70's, although many of the younger brothers and sisters of those who came from East Africa, and most of the children of immigrants from the Punjab understood English far better than Punjabi.

The strong pull of Western materialism attracted many of these young Sikhs and undoubtedly induced many of them to move away from the religion and culture of their parents. Another factor that affected young Sikhs as it affects all other cultures was the natural rebellion of teenagers to the views of parents. Young Sikhs in schools and colleges and many seeking employment, ignorant of their own faith and wishing to assert their individuality, adopted many of the traits of British teenage culture notably the addiction to pop music (often Indianised), alcohol and dress designed to shock and underline individuality.

All too often these youngsters who discarded the symbols of their faith in their attempt to gain the acceptance of the native British met continuing prejudice and many Sikhs, like other Asians, moved into the sad twilight world between two cultures.

A majority of young Sikhs, particularly those of East African origin in colleges and universities, were, however, sufficiently confident in their faith to look to their own religion and culture. Sikh societies flourished in many universities and a national Sikh Students Federation organised impressive seminars and social events.

The gurdwaras were increasingly becoming social clubs for the older generation of Sikhs; a place which afforded opportunities to listen to Kirtan (hymns), chat about old times and enjoy langar (a communal meal). Some of the more progressive gurdwaras organised Punjabi classes, but little attempt was made to teach Sikh youngsters about the richness of their heritage. When children complained about lengthy services in a language they couldn't understand, they were told 'Punjabi sikho' (learn Punjabi), and it will all become clear. What they were not told was that the Guru Granth Sahib (Sikh Scriptures) was not in spoken Punjabi as it is understood today, but in numerous dialects of 15th and 16th century India and was almost a language in itself that required separate and dedicated study.

The net result of combination of ordinary teenage rebellion combined with genuine difficulties experienced by young Sikhs in following the service in Punjabi, was that while children up to the age of 8 or 9 were often seen in gurdwaras, their elder sisters and, particularly, brothers were frequently absent. The Punjab, the birthplace of Sikhism, had, by the early 80's, become increasingly distant to young Sikhs born in this country.

The June 1984 attack on the Golden Temple dramatically affected Sikh attitudes, particularly that of young Sikhs to their religion and land of origin. While it is not the purpose of this paper to dwell on the politics of the sub-continent, it is necessary to look briefly at the circumstances surrounding this attack to get an understanding of the explosive reaction of Sikh youth.

The Golden Temple, founded by the 5th Guru of the Sikhs, Guru Arjan Dev, is the most famous Sikh shrine in India, and is considered both the spiritual and temporal centre of Sikhs. Any attack on this temple was bound to cause indignation but when it came, ostensibly to arrest wanted people within, the outcome was far worse. The timing of the attack on the important martyrdom anniversary of Guru Arjan Dev, could not have been worse. The temple was filled to overflowing with thousands of pilgrims from all over India and abroad. More than 2,000 died in the attack. Many had relatives in Britain.

The anger of the Sikh community in India was magnified by stories of atrocities against innocent pilgrims even after capture. As news trickled from Punjab to Britain, it was found that much that had been rumoured was in fact true. It was not only the loss of life that agitated Sikhs but also what seemed deliberate acts of desecration. These, including the burning after capture of the Central Reference Library containing priceless manuscripts, including writings of the Gurus themselves.

Whilst the entire Sikh population of Britain felt a sense of outrage at these events, it was particularly pronounced in young Sikhs, including many who had previously turned their backs on the Sikh religion. Those who had been drifting unhappily between cultures were suddenly reminded of their roots and were fired by a determination to defend a religion – their religion – from brutal attack. Immediate anger was vented in angry processions and demonstrations outside the Indian High Commission and other Indian Government agencies. Inevitably the anger subsided only to find a new focus against those who had allowed it to happen. The Indian High Commission was an obvious target, but Sikh youth also vented their anger on the older generation of Sikhs who had not only failed to safeguard their religion, but had also failed to induct them, the young Sikhs, in the teachings of their faith.

Young Sikhs, many previously clean shaven, grew beards and wore turbans only now, as if in compensation, the turban was larger – usually saffron, the colour of the Sikh flag, and now the colour of protest. Similarly, the 'kera' that Sikhs wear on the wrist was heavier as if to emphasise a new-found allegiance.

Sikh gurdwaras are democratically managed with both the difficulties and opportunities that democracy provides. Now the gurdwaras experienced a massive influx of militant young Sikhs who soon outvoted and out-manoeuvred the old guard Sikh politicians. Within months the International Sikh Youth Federation became the major Sikh organisation in the country. Today, while many young Sikhs have come back to the centre stage of Sikh life, behind the meetings and demonstrations there is a continuing search for an identity. Young Sikhs have identified themselves with the Sikh community but many have still to look closely at the religious teachings of the Gurus.

LOOKING TO THE FUTURE

Although some five and a half years have elapsed since the attack on the Golden Temple the situation in Punjab has not become any easier. Those in India and abroad advocating a separate Sikh state, a tiny minority in 1984, are now far more numerous. At the same time government repression, as Amnesty International acknowledges, has become far more active.

The effect on young Sikhs in Britain has varied with the passage of time. Some of those who came back to the fold in 1984 have already shed the symbols of their new-found allegiance. Many others, on the other hand, have become firmer and less emotional in their beliefs. They are doing valuable work, both in the gurdwara and outside, and are a real credit to the community – overall the proportion of young Sikhs now to be found in the gurdwaras has shown a considerable increase.

One valuable gain from the world-wide reporting of events in Punjab is a heightened interest in Sikhism among non-Sikhs, and this has further increased with the growth of inter-faith dialogue. Sikhs, mindful of Guru Nanak's teachings that no one faith has a monopoly of truth, have always been reluctant to indulge in proselytising activities but real opportunities now exist to show the world, Sikhs themselves and particularly young Sikhs the power and guidance contained in a faith dedicated to an emphasis on the oneness of the human race, the equality of women and the emphasis on service to society. If young Sikhs can make the pursuit of these ideals their *raison d'être*, they can make a major contribution, not only to their own community, but to society at large in today's troubled times.

Indarjit Singh, 'The search for identity by young Sikhs in Great Britain', *The Sikh Messenger*, Autumn/Winter 1989, pp. 13–15.

(e) A nation as well as a religion?

The Sikh leadership, since its emergence has passed through a number of phases due to the turn of historical events. The phase that I am referring to in this article started on November 15, 1920 when a proclamation was issued from Akal Takhat, to the effect that a committee of 175, to be known as the Central Gurdwara Managing Committee was set up for the management of Sikh Gurdwaras, this committee was later given a Punjabi name i.e. Shromani Gurdwara Parbandhak Committee.

A great historical event occurred on December 14, 1920 when a

Semi-Military organisation under the name of Akali Dal was founded. The aim of this body was to raise and train volunteers for 'ACTION' to take over the Gurdwaras from recalcitrant Mahants and to provide a democratic management for them. The Akali Dal achieved the highest glory, during the Gurdwara Reform Movement, as it was the first mass demonstration of the efficacy of passive resistance in which thousands of men and women voluntarily submitted themselves to brutal violence at the hands of the police. This practical example of non-violence brought glowing tribute to the Akali Dal, from National leaders like Mahatma Gandhi, Jawahar Lal Nehru, Rev. C. F. Andrews, the Ali brothers, Sarojani Naidu and many others.

SIKHISM IS NOT A NATION

Sikhism is a religion, and not a Nation by any stretch of imagination, even today there are many families in which some members are Hindus and some are Sikhs. Christianity is a religion which is owned by the largest number of people living in different parts of the world, but Christianity remains a religion and not a Nation. Christians living in England are English and those in France are French National[s]. Some of our own countrymen both Hindus and Sikhs now living in America have surrendered their Indian Nationality to become American Nationals. From all this it becomes abundantly clear that religion and Nationality are two separate things.

SIKHISM HAS AN INTERNATIONAL STATUS?

Recently an All India Sikh Educational Conference was held at Chandigarh, the organisers of the conference invited a person from America to preside over it. The said gentleman is an Indian by birth, who has surrendered his Indian Nationality to become [an] American National. Strange as it may seem that gentleman declared that [the] Sikh Nation had an Inter-National Status. It is true that a large number of Sikhs have gone to America, Canada, [the] United Kingdom, Malaya and some other countries but these people have gone as individuals in search of better economic prospectus. Many of them have got themselves clean shaved, others are living as Sikhs. These Sikhs did not go there either on deputation or as delegates of the Sikh community so they cannot possibly secure International Status to Sikhism.

ASSOCIATE MEMBERSHIP OF UNITED NATION

He further said that on this basis the Sikh Nation could become an Associate member of the United Nation. To give practical shape to this theory Jathedar Jagdev Singh Talwandi is said to have sent two persons of his party to United Nations' headquarters to negotiate for this membership. All this a bundle of mis-statement and fabrication, which is doing more harm than good to the Sikh Community.

KHALISTAN

Last year a group of Sikhs declared that it would set up a Khalistan Government in an annexe of the Akal Takhat Amritsar and asked the people to pay taxes to the Panthic Government and not to any other Government.

Yet another Sikh gentleman proclaimed himself as the Rashtarpati of a non-existent Sikh state, whose boundaries stretched beyond the Haryana, Himachal Pradesh, Rajastan and Jammu and Kashmir. He said that a similar proclamation would be made at UK, France and Canada. It was also said that the Rashtarpati would announce the names of the member of his cabinet, which would function in Exile.

And now another group organised Khalistan March in Amritsar, raising slogans like, we are not the citizens of India, we are the citizens of Khalistan.

I humbly submit that Khalsa Panth was started by Guru Gobind Singh at Anandpur Sahib in 1699. He was born in Bihar at Patna, lived most of his life in Anandpur Sahib and Paonta Sahib in Himachal Pradesh and died at Nanded in Andhare Pradesh. He stayed in Punjab at Damdama only for a few months. The 'PANJ PAY-ARAS' who form the nucleus of Khalsa Panth hailed from different parts of the country. Therefore the whole of India is our country, and we should not waste our energy in such meaningless and provocative activities. The Akalies can regain their past glory if they direct their attention to really vital problems like, Panthic Unity, clarification of their stand on Sikh homeland communal harmony and Dharem Parchar of proper type suitable to the present day needs.

PANTHIC UNITY

Sant Harchand Singh Longowal, President of the largest faction of Akali Dal has issued an open appeal to all dissident members of the party, who had left it earlier, to return to the fold of the Parent body, where they will be received with open arms, and given respect and responsibility due to them. Jathedar Jagdev Singh Talwandi would be doing great service to the panth, if he and his supporters respond to this appeal and join the Main Dal. That would be a great achievement of the Dal.

SIKH HOMELAND

Different sections of Sikh community have been giving different meanings to this demand. One section has been saying that it would have KHALISTAN. Jathedar Jagdev Singh Talwandi gave an ultimatum that if the centre did not divest itself of all authority except external affairs of Defence Communication and Currency by 13th April 1981, his group would launch a morcha to achieve their objective; that morcha has now been launched. Such statements and actions have created great misunderstanding and mistrust among the Hindus of Punjab, and the Central Governments. It is fortunate and timely that Sant Harchand Singh Longowal has clarified the position of Akali Dal by saying that by homeland they meant 'INTERNAL AUTONOMY' for the states and this struggle would continue along with other states in the country. The Hindus in Punjab should now give up their misunderstanding on this subject.

COMMUNAL HARMONY

Among the religious minorities the Sikhs enjoy an advantageous position compared to other minorities. It is true that Sikh religion is separate from Hindu religion, but no community is closer to the Hindus in their social life than the Sikhs for obvious reasons. In Punjab the population of Hindus and Sikhs is more or less equal. Their political and economical problems are the same. If the Hindus and Sikhs of Punjab forge an united front, they will succeed in getting these solved better, than by striving alone. During Akali-Janata coalition Government Sardar Parkash Singh Badal succeeded to some extent in forging this communal harmony.

DHARAM PARCHAR

Sikh religion is different from other religions in many ways. It can only survive and flourish if it is nursed at all times and at all levels.

Shromani Gurdwara Parbandhak Committee has a Dharam Parchar wing which looks after the Dharam Parchar activities. We have got a large number of granthis, Ragi jathas, Dhadi Jathas and lecturers and these are engaged in Dharam Parchar work in a number of ways.

In spite of all this we find that today a large number of young Sikhs trim their beard, some in the villages have taken to smoking, and many young educated Sikh girls bob their hair. The number of those who offer daily prayer is very small, and those of 'AMRITDHARI' is still smaller.

The reason for all this is that we do not nurse the plant from its start by watering its roots, and satisfy ourselves by arranging Diwans, Gurbani Kirtan and lectures on auspicious occasions. These activities are good in their own way, but it is like [the] sprinkling of water on the leaves of grown up plants which look green for a moment, without having any lasting effect.

Two things are very important to make our Dharam Parchan really effective, and these are running of Balwaris for small children, and translation of our daily prayers in Punjabi.

If running of a modern type of Balwari is made a part of the activity of a gurdwara, it can become a fountain head of Dharam Parchar, for small children with impressionable mind. In these

Balwaris the children in addition to their normal teachings may be acquainted with Sikh religion.

Prayer is part of every religion. In Sikhism too we have daily prayers like Japuji, Rehras etc. These prayers contain the teachings of the Gurus which are not only to be recited daily, but these teachings are to be understood and imbibed into day-to-day living and for this it is necessary that our daily prayers are translated into Punjabi, so that one may understand the meaning of what he prays, so that he may try to live up to it and thus become a true Sikh.

Khushdeva Singh, 'Sikh Leadership', *The Sikh Courier International Quarterly*, Vol. 31, No. 72 (Autumn–Winter 1991), pp. 32–4 (with cuts).

6

BLACK CHRISTIANITY AND RASTAFARIANISM

*I*s it valid to distinguish black Christianity from traditionally white expressions of the religion? Extracts from the reflections, recorded in 1982, of Ira Brooks, a Pentecostalist pastor in Hackney, and Ron Farley, an Anglican priest in Stoke Newington, provide considerable food for thought in relation to this emotive issue (a). However Robinson Milward, a Methodist minister in Green Lanes, talking at the same date, recognized the distinctive features of West Indian culture while perceiving the potential for constructive fellowship with whites. His comments also have implications extending well outside the Afro-Caribbean Christian community (b). All these pastors, however, knew something of the pain of rejection by white Christians, which was also powerfully expressed by Sybil Phoenix, herself a courageous worker for better community relations in south-east London (c).

Meanwhile black people sharply questioned white-dominated religion. This found expression in the proceedings of an Anglican consultation at Balsall Heath in 1986, which also offered a timely reminder of the importance of considering Asian as well as Afro-Caribbean perspectives (d). For others spiritual and personal fulfilment was to be found not in Christianity at all, but rather through the teachings of Rastafari (e).

(a) Varieties of Afro-Caribbean Christian experience

PASTOR IRA BROOKS

Why did I become a Pentecostalist? I became a Pentecostalist through conversion. A deep conviction within the mind. It's a new dimension of understanding, of both the scriptures and God. And it is indeed a personal experience. It is not too private to relate, but it is difficult because it is partly a miracle. I had the experience in England, here, in Sheffield. . . .

When I got to Gloucester I quickly sought out the Anglican church. I was a stranger and they offered nothing, absolutely nothing. Not that I was looking for anyone to lift me up but – I mean – a stranger in the country. Arriving with the warmth of the church I had known, I thought the church, especially the church, would have taken me in. Perhaps back home it was my local church where everybody knew everybody. I don't know. But here it was just a blank grey situation, just like the weather. Everything was cold. The people, the atmosphere. One of my first experiences was chilling. I discovered that certain pews in the church were reserved. How did I discover this? I went and took my seat, and then someone came up and politely hustled me away, drawing my attention to some name or number – I don't remember what was on the seat. And not being accustomed to English ways – you understand? – I had to think, I couldn't pick up things as quickly as they were saying them to me. I was partly bewildered. Sometimes it was days before you interpret what happened last week. When I fully realised what this person was saying to me, that the seats were reserved, I went to sit at the back. After the service nobody spoke to me. . . .

Our Christianity is a way of life. It's a living faith. Perhaps other Christians would say the same. But it's a living faith in which we endeavour to portray this faith daily in our deliberations whether at work or at home. But I hate to compare with other faiths. To do it publicly. I know what I am offering, so the other man must know what he is offering. We are offering warmth and concern for other people. I'm not saying that the white person's experience of God is different. I can only say that the white person has every right to express himself or this Godly relationship in his own way, but there should be some compatibility between black and white. Whether a person is going to express his Christianity as a European or as an African, basically they should have something in common, though they won't link up in all cases. You see, it's a responsibility we have, to examine and share the things we have in common.

White and black Christians have principles in common though the way they express their religious experience may and should be different. . . .

You ask me how my Christian beliefs affect my family relations. It's quite difficult to explain the equality between men and women. I see the wife equal in respect, you see. There is no degree of respect differing man from woman. They are one. But if there's any headship it should be displayed by the husband or the man in the role of responsibility. This is where headship comes in: taking the initiative to defend the wife, to protect the wife, to care for the wife and the family. This is where the man is the head. But not a dominating head. And the woman should be seen as the one who is entitled to understanding and love from the husband as long as she remains a woman to comfort the man. Because if the woman overnight becomes masculine she's going to lose her virtue, so to speak. The woman must remain feminine, this is very important. Feminine does not mean being subordinate but complementary. She tries to maintain her beauty, her sense of femininity to constantly attract and woo the husband to her love. This is the role. But decisions and problems should be shared between wife and husband. The husband coming home from work is coming home to a wife, a real woman. And he would like to see something – how should I put it? – to soothe, to attract him, to make him feel welcome and at home. To make the home attractive and beautiful by her mere presence and attitude. That's what the wife's image is about to me. It's a comfort to me and I comfort her in turn. Now let me say this that I am not saying that a woman has no place in the business of the competitive world. Just like men, so there are women who are capable of competing in the world out there. These women should never be inhibited because they must express themselves. And they should never be forgotten, but I don't think that it should be a general thing that every woman should turn away from her role of being a wife.

Children should be brought up with a sense of direction. They should expect parents to give them guidance in some moral code for living. Speaking as a West Indian parent, social workers in

England seem so quick to brand you with the old sergeant-major label, the stick. But people learn to adapt to a new society. They adjust. Now so far as my family is concerned I have found that my children do accept discipline. But it's more effective when I discipline them through respect. For instance, I say to one, 'I am surprised that you do a thing like that.' Saying something like that to them means a lot because they don't want me to lose respect or trust in them. . . .

I feel a sense of responsibility to the young generation in that they are my own offspring, and through my immigration to Britain they have found themselves in this – how do you say? – vacuum, in this dilemma. How can we fill the vacuum? You ask what do I think would happen if black and white went their separate ways. It would be disastrous. Our only hope is to acknowledge the fact that we are now in a multiracial society. Anything other than that is going to be disastrous. And when I say disastrous I mean the volume of hatred is going to increase. Even now unless people like the police, myself, really all of us who are responsible don't start working together, the riots of the last year will not be a thing of the past. They are not over. It's no use kidding ourselves. Most of these people are realising that they have nothing to lose. Their dignity is gone. That is why people like myself are willing to talk to you so that it may help, that it may go in people's ears, and they will hear and act. Because it needs more than word speaking. It needs action. Otherwise there will be action in the wrong direction. And we're all going to feel it. We're all in it. No matter where you live, you're in it, I'm in it. We're all part of each other now. So we've got to face it.

Father ron farley

My history is in the Anglican tradition. I had an African past, they say, but I don't know it. I'm very unpopular with some West Indians for my views. But I see them dressing in African-style clothes – long colourful shirts and things – but they don't wear them in the West Indies, then why here? I wore in the West Indies what I wear here. Then take the whites: they say, 'Look how we've educated you. You would have been swinging from trees if we hadn't.' To them I say, 'Maybe. But I might have been happy swinging from trees.' That's all in the past. I think when people come here they must make some effort to fit into the ways of the country. Perhaps it has been easy for me. I've always been basically moderate. In my religion, for instance, I don't want, like some believers, to say, 'I'm special. I have a direct line to God,' and shake and tremble with the Holy Spirit. For me, Christianity is not a high note but a quiet one. That suits my tradition and my temperament. They say that's why I joined the traditional church. But I didn't join it. I always was a High Anglican, and I will be that here as I was in the West Indies.

I feel more at home in the catholic side of the Church than the evangelical. I feel so much more at ease, you know. There are people on the evangelical side who appear to me to do spiritual uplifts. On the catholic side, people say, 'We're sinners trying to get grace,' and I identify with that. So there are certain obvious differences between forms of Christianity, which I recognise, though I don't understand some approaches – well, not yet at least. But I do not believe in first-class and second-class Christians. I give you an example. I went to a church in Essex, it was a church on the evangelical side of the Anglican Church, and there were some people there who referred to the catholic side as 'those over there', as though they weren't born-again Christians. I found that offensive. . . .

Certainly Christianity means different things to different people. We've already agreed on that. You ask whether I think the white person's experience of Christianity is different from the black person's. If we're talking about white people in this country, then I think they don't see Christianity as people in the West Indies do. At least Christianity as it was in Antigua at the time I lived there. We used to see ourselves as being dependent on God, and we used to see prayer as a very real thing. You prayed for things that you really needed. I don't think people here – because they haven't experienced the same sort of hardship as we have – would see prayer in such a way. I suppose they see their bread as coming from the baker's round the corner. In the West Indies we see our bread as coming from God. . . . When you're poor, when you really have to think where the next meal, where the next pair of shoes, where the next necessity is coming from, then you have an understanding of your weakness; you appreciate that there are things outside of your control. Over here, you appear to be in better control of your affairs. Your Dad is bringing in the money and you're getting food and education, and people seem in command of their destiny. Maybe I am generalising. There must be people here who endure hardship. But I do believe that the poverty in a developed country cannot be compared with the poverty of an undeveloped country.

Anita Jackson, *Catching Both Sides of the Wind: Conversations with Five Black Pastors*, London, The British Council of Churches, 1985, pp. 2, 7–8, 12–13, 19–20, 27, 67, 69.

(b) A multiracial Christianity?

For me Methodism holds a very special place in the apostolic tradition of the church. It is a denomination distinguished by feeling. I like the evangelistic tradition. I like Methodism's socio-religious awareness of life. I like the broadness of scope. It is comprehensive. It can accommodate anyone. There is a place for you in Methodism. You are born again. Methodism emphasises man's place in society, in the same way that it emphasises the spiritual aspects of man's life. Is it the only way to God? I would answer like the Buddhist philosopher on being asked the best way to Nirvana, 'Here is the mountain. There are several ways to the top.' . . .

I went to several churches, all Methodist, before I found they accepted me. You must understand these experiences were over a long period of time. I moved from place to place. Each place had its own particular standard. But the fundamental thing is, and this is what I would underline, I had to say to myself: 'My church is the Methodist Church, and I'm not going to go because of you.' I told them loud and square, I told them my grandfather was a Methodist, I told them I have a place here. . . .

I received enormous help and support from the Methodist Church. I owe a lot, a lot to the church. I have friends and colleagues in the Methodist Church who are living, walking saints. You couldn't desire better people. They have helped me over years, moulding me, training me to become a minister, helping my human development. They set an example and influenced my life. . . .

I think there is a difference between black and white religious experience. In this sense. If you look at the question of survival, you see that we are different. West Indians when they say they find it difficult to explain to white people the experience of black people, that is true in terms of our survival. You will never be able to understand the language of our sufferings, the emotional strain that we have to go through for survival. It's not something we can verbalise, and yet it is something that instantaneously we can identify among ourselves as black people. And that measure of identity is very important for the survival of the group. This is where the uniqueness of our experience comes in. . . .

Sometimes when I exercise my authority in the church here West Indians readily understand that my authority is West Indian ministerial authority. This is very interesting, you know, because though I have a parallel status to any English Methodist minister yet the natural cultural authority I exert in particular situations is characteristic of a West Indian minister, not a white. I know that I am the end of the church. I must rule my church. People don't run me. I lead my church. I am the leader. That is how the ministry operates in the West Indies. I don't know about now but certainly in my day. I love that tradition where, as happened in my childhood, a police officer misbehaved and the minister removed him from the church. When you have a strict discipline people respond to you and respect you more. I believe in that, and I practise it in my church. I don't think a minister can afford to be weak. You must be seen to be leader. I have been accused of being authoritarian. But I don't mind. I put a lot of love in my actions. My authority also extends to the community. If I see someone on the street misbehaving, I'll stop my car, and tell them to go home. I walk into the barber's and people stop swearing, because they wouldn't swear in front of a minister in the West Indies. My ministry is a West Indian ministry. . . .

Let me say what my two churches are endeavouring to do. I'm sure churches in different parishes are doing similar things, perhaps identical things. But I'd like to see us trying to set examples to others to further the work of God. I believe we have a proper ministry of reconciliation. Reconciliation between people of different cultures, different denominations, different faiths and religions. That to me is very important. Especially in this neighbourhood where you have so many different cultures. It is important to maintain a stable ministry of reconciliation. . . .

At Green Lanes we have a mixed congregation, which worships and works in a harmonious way. Our church council is multiracial. I made sure about that myself when I came here. I would never have a church council that is 100% black or 100% white. I don't believe in that at all. We are journeying together. So the mission here is multiracial. From the church into the community: we have West Indian and white groups in the church. There is a white group here that has been going for forty years. They are very supportive of my church. The High Street church when I came there was 100% black. I challenged my congregation there, 'We are evangelists. We are here to serve the community. So we must endeavour to open up our church to accommodate God's people.' I'm very happy to say that our organist at High Street today is white. We also have two white Sunday school teachers in the Sunday School Department. What better area of the church to begin integration than the Sunday School? That is the starting point. In the congregation we have about ten whites now. This is a great success for the church, because we are looking at a church in Stoke Newington that in 1960 was 100% white and within twenty years, even less, became a black church. Now within four to five years it is becoming a multiracial church. That is my vision – a truly multiracial church.

There is no doubt that there are a number of traditional white Methodist churches that are very introspective, very cold. But at the same time there are also a great number of all-white Methodist churches that are as evangelical as a black-led church. Our form of worship at High Street and Green Lanes is typical of a warm Afro-West Indian evangelical church. There is a special enthusiasm. You come empty, you leave full. This is what we believe. You're refreshed for the week ahead. Most definitely the white members have it in them to respond to this. I can talk about this from experience because I have them in my church, where they respond to worship in a spontaneous way, just like the West Indians. They shout Alleluia with us. When you go to church you go to worship, you go to throw your whole being into worship.

You see, to so many white people, especially white Christians, to shout, to jump, to rejoice in worship is a black thing. Not typical of white people. I don't think that ought to be so. I don't believe for one moment that God is a static God. He is a lively God. Look at the Old Testament. He dropped bomb-shells to wake his people up. Read the Book of Psalms. Throughout the Bible, you see that our God is an active God. He is always on the move. He is a dynamic God. He is a powerful force. So each one of us should have the enthusiastic drive to love, to serve people, to rejoice, and to worship. I can't see myself going to church and sitting back in an introspective way. That's not worship to me. I mean how can you be happy and look like you were coming back from the dentist? When you look like that you haven't been to church to worship. When you go to worship, you radiate happiness in your face.

No, I wouldn't say that a person who was sober in church wasn't normal. I wouldn't say that at all. I would never mark them off. But what I'm saying is I don't believe, seriously, that you can be touched by the Lord, that you can really and truly experience God, and keep quiet. . . .

I believe that the young West Indian community will respond to church leadership as much as to secular leadership. People can only respond to what they see and to what they have. I give you an example. At Green Lanes, I have over three hundred young people, mainly Rastas from the locality. When I began the club, they all came to me with the same tales: they had been to secular places for socialisation but had not had a feeling of identity, belongingness, and protection. Above all things, protection. They were looking for security. And when I opened up my place here, they said they found protection here. They feel at home because they feel protected by the church. And I can tell you that they have told me that no police officer crosses the doorway. If any officer were to attempt to, they say, they'd throw him across the street. They're here to socialise among themselves and have a good evening. No pot-smoking, no marijuana, just here to enjoy their music and meet each other. They have told me that they regard the police as a threat, as an encroachment on the privacy. So they are responding to the leadership of the church. Mark you, I must say, to run this centre straight demands firm leadership. I have banned young people from coming here because they failed to comply with the stipulations. You've got to have firm leadership at all times.

If the church as a large family were to share itself, people would ultimately respond. I'll go a bit further: I've discussed this matter of church and community over and over with my Pentecostal friends. They are now beginning to think socially and politically. How can you politicise, how can you sensitise your people unless you are also involved in the struggle? . . .

What is our future together? Let me answer by explaining what I mean by integration. I've read how white people define integration. What I, a black man, living in a white society – I'll go a bit further and say a white man's world – understand by integration is my black cultural independence and identity. And what I mean by my black cultural identity is simply this: that you with your white culture do not try and erode my black culture, do not belittle my black values. Respect my black values, because I in return respect all these things on your side. So it is a reciprocal acceptance. For many white people integration for the black people means that we must try and become white. That is not integration.

Those of us who came here back in the early 60s into the tidal wave of permissiveness had a tremendous shock to see your white values. The greatest failure of this country was, my dear sister, that the Church jumped on the band-wagon. The Church shouldn't have done that. The Church should have condemned it in a firm way. The Church should have maintained its moral principles and values. It failed. And that failure has not just affected Western society but Third World societies too, because you have so many Third World plagiarists who accepted Western changes. And in the Third World we are now suffering from those changes. In my own blessed Jamaica the Church is debating whether to accept gambling on a Sunday. I am very disappointed. The whole of Western Christianity needs an overhaul. My dream is that the Third World will revitalise Christianity. But it will not be a purely imported revitalisation from the Third World. I think it will also come through the Third World who are living in this country. Myself and my older folks. This is why I am so happy to be in this country, and no force will get me to leave it. Because I see my role here as a divine mission. And I'm happy to be a Third World missionary serving God's kingdom and people in this country.

Yes, let me go back and make clearer what I mean by black values. A black value in family life is that the child leaves his family home only for his own home. The system here encourages black youngsters to leave home prematurely. The permissiveness in Western culture now means that little value is placed on respect for elders in this country, and this has been the main reason for the gap between the black young and the parent generation. My pastoral surgery is where I meet the rawness of everyday experience. There is a clear-cut hiatus between black adults and youngsters in this country, and social and community workers are not being sensitive about trying to bridge the gap. They don't try and understand and bring the parents and children back into close contact. They say, 'The state provides the following solutions,' and the child is quick to opt for those things. When I am the counsellor, I listen to the children and then I listen to the parents, and then it's a matter of good timing to bring children and parents together. It's a conciliatory process at all times.

Anita Jackson, *Catching Both Sides of the Wind: Conversations with Five Black Pastors*, London, The British Council of Churches, 1985, pp. 35–7, 38, 40, 42–5, 48–9, 60–1.

(c) The crucifixion of a black Christian British woman

And so here I am in Britain today, only to discover that being British or living in England does not include being black. As a black person growing up in British Guyana you are firmly British, and I am sure for all the other countries like Barbados and Jamaica, growing up there you are Jamaican, you are Bajan, but you are British; blackness was part of your Britishness. What makes you a second-class citizen, what puts the cat among the pigeons, is that once you're black and you arrive in Britain, you're not recognized as British any more. Coming to London you are suddenly faced with your blackness meaning you are not British – you are reclassified as West Indian, immigrant, ethnic, all the different names white society has for you as a black British person.

They say, gentlemen prefer blondes – but that's no reason for them to kick brunettes. As a black woman, I'm kicked because I'm black – purely because I'm black. It is not because I'm an unlovable woman, or because I'm short and fat, that people treat me badly. They treat me badly primarily because I'm black. People still continue to treat anybody that's different, badly. Although I have spent over thirty years in this country, and have given unstintingly of my service to white society, white society refuses to accept me as a person, as an individual in my own right. And that is a pain that I have come to terms with. I'm not proud of it, but I've come to acknowledge that this is my fate in life, and so I have stopped crying about it. I have come to expect that white people will treat me badly, so when they treat me all right, it's a bonus. If I didn't do that, I would be destroyed – I would not be still a human being, loving, caring and giving. . . .

The non-acceptance of my Britishness in church was the worst element of this society, because my upbringing taught me that I was black British, Christian, and accepted world-wide in a British church. Then I came here and tried to take my place in that church society, and found that my blackness was a barrier.

At the same time, white society refuses to treat me with respect and refuses to treat me as an equal human being. Thank God, I've now been able to retrieve my blackness and to come to terms with living with it. I don't try to be white any more. Because I've tried to be white for years, and I have not been accepted. So I've now retrieved by blackness.

It is fact that one is black and belongs to Britain. You belong – you know you belong. No one can take away that fact. You make your niche in it because you know you belong there. But it is not possible to be black and to feel that you belong to Britain. All the same, because of your humanness you go on working, praying and hoping that eventually there will be an acceptance.

There was a time when the National Front was really bad and I was very low. They used to torment us and I was really very frightened. At Deptford the National Front had lost just by a slim margin, simply because they had split. At one stage people had to have police protection because it was so bad for us here. And then on the news Martin Webster said when they win they're going to close all these churches down and put the bishops out to grass. And I got up and I said 'The National Front will never ever come to power in this country.' I was really scared, but when he made that statement I knew that was the day that they had lost. And from that time the National Front started to go down the drain. They're still around, but not with the power that they had in those days. I've seen that. And I feel that he can do it. His ancient power has not lost its touch – it's us that have lost him.

But until we can get more white people to teach other white people the real meaning of the gospel, I don't think it's going to happen. He really will have to come and be crucified again – he is crucified every day in me. In what white Social Services do to me. What just generally white society does.

Sybil Phoenix, 'Land of Hope and Glory', in Roger Hooker and John Sargant, eds., *Belonging to Britain: Christian Perspectives on Religion and Identity in a Plural Society*, London, Council of Churches for Britain and Ireland, 1991, pp. 100–2 (with cuts).

(d) The agenda for black theology

Our task, as we saw it, was the generation of a Theology of Liberation grounded in the experience of Black/Third World people in Britain. We aimed to carve out of the reality of our lives as Black people a method for bringing together our understanding of the God of freedom, life and love and the world about us. Rather than becoming entangled in academic discussions of the meaning of 'Blackness', 'liberation', or 'theology', we chose to wrestle with the challenge made by black people living in our inner cities, in the knowledge that the acid test of Liberation Theology must be that of what it can offer to the neglected, broken, angry and forgotten people of the backstreets. . . .

We tried to develop strategies for handling situations of this kind as Black people, and to link up that perspective with the way we look at the Bible. We approached the Bible from a feeling of pain, of frustration, and of marginalisation. We tried to carve out, from the passages we considered, a theology which makes sense to our situation as oppressed people in this country. . . .

A BLACK THEOLOGY OF LIBERATION: SOME QUESTIONS

1 How, as Christians, are we to respond to, or be involved in, the violence of the powerless against the powers that oppress them/us?
2 Wherein does the power lie in our society/area/church?
3 In what ways are people in our society divided? Are those divisions always bad?
4 What do you think should underlie Black unity and our possible alliances with other oppressed groups?
5 In what ways can our experiences as Black Christians enrich or challenge the established churches in Britain?
6 How have black people been put down in this society?
7 'Black paralysis': how can we break out of it?
8 In what ways do you think that we can identify with and aid our sisters and brothers in South Africa, the Americas and India?
9 Jesus was killed on a cross of wood. Many people are being killed

on crosses of unjust violence, exploitation, degradation and hunger. We worship Jesus: how do we act towards the crucified peoples of the world?

10 What are you going to do?

11 Does our understanding of the work of Christ change if we see the Messiah as a black person living in the ghetto/inner city?

12 Has the experience of the workshop had any effect on your life, for good or bad?

What follows are responses to those questions, and other issues raised by the workshop members themselves:

'Black people who are close to places of influence must verbally attack the system and structures, and must keep doing so at any cost in the knowledge that whoever loves life will lose it, but whoever loses his life for Jesus' sake will find it.' (Matt. 10.39)

'Being a Christian doesn't mean that you become passive, or simply use the old theology and turn the other cheek when one is struck. Jesus certainly fought against the authority of his day and refused to conform in many ways. I think that as a Christian, and especially as a Black Christian, the violence that I'm faced with every day on the street must be fought with violence. The tragedy is that any form of violent relationship breeds violence. . . .'

'I am not a pacifist, but I think that the present strategy of pitched battles with the police in response to their provocation leaves the initiative with them, will lead to increasing bloodshed and will give them an excuse for intensifying repression.' . . .

'I think that it is irresponsible to say that as a Christian I must continue to accept the violence meted out by society to the Black community.' . . .

'I don't think that we can rely on white society for any real change. The power lies within us to a large extent. In the midst of our powerlessness we do have a lot of power to free our minds. That inner process of liberation must begin to take place. And that moment of liberation takes place when we acknowledge our Blackness, when we acknowledge what is happening to us, and when we acknowledge our pain.' . . .

'We ourselves must stop helping in the process of negation which is taking place where the experience of Black people is ignored. We must stop ignoring and instead take that experience on board. All the pain, all the moments of despair, those moments when I turn to God when I fail to understand what role he is playing in my suffering and the suffering of communities throughout the world. That experience is one of the most powerful things that the Black community can get hold of, because as far as I'm concerned, white is going in a totally different and wrong direction. If your interpretation of the Gospel and what it means to be a Christian, by some strange quirk of nature, leaves out one whole group and pretends that they're not there, then I'm afraid that it leaves a lot to be desired. It cannot be acceptable and cannot be a good thing for God's people. This is precisely what has happened. White western theology must be totally barren as it has failed to recognise Black humanity or to see humanity in Blackness.'

'We must relentlessly press for change in the liturgical setting that will incorporate the Black spiritual experience.'

'More Third World theology would have been helpful. In Asia alone there is a vast range of experience: the Philippines, Korea, China and India are all very different. Male and female theologians may have different approaches. The attitude to other faiths is an important issue in some countries. What has been learnt in interacting with Buddhists, Hindus, etc. in South Asia is useful to study here, where so many Black people are not Christians (or even lapsed Christians?)'

'Indian (Asian) theology has a history, veneration and contribution which is unique. Matters concerning the nature of God, the person of Christ, the meaning of the Spirit, are all matters which need to be offered sensitively and attractively in Asian

(Indian) "models" of theology. We need to learn about these "models" of theology, and to cease trying to interpret the Gospel of Jesus Christ only through western "models" of theology.'

'Indian Christians, as migrant workers in Europe, should share and strengthen our fellow Turks, Moroccans, Arabs, Bangladeshis, Pakistanis, Indians, Filipinos, Sri Lankans in their plight in Britain and the rest of Europe. In fighting racism and injustice we may join hands with women and men of other races and faiths or of no faith who fight for the dignity of the human race.'

'We must help white western Christians to re-interpret their theology and begin to be honest with themselves, because what they have created is the God of comfort. A comfortable image of God with the suffering God put neatly to one side. The God who cares for the people of Hyson Green, Handsworth, Toxteth and Brixton is totally foreign to them.'

Anglicans and Racism: The Balsall Heath Consultation 1986: Address, Reports and Recommendations, London, Race, Pluralism and Community Group of the Board for Social Responsibility of the Church of England, 1986, pp. 39, 40–3.

(e) *The Rastafarian vision*

What Rasta has is an inner force of submission, that makes the individual submit to Jah Rastafari, Haile Selassie I, Almighty God. Rasta is nature and its natural force of appeal and attraction have served to make bureaucratic and formal systems of recruitment and membership unnecessary – so far! . . .

Rasta is the totality of a life's experience and the more the experience grows, the more Rasta is enriched. The life of a Rasta is reflected in history and projected into time. Rasta is the spiritual/ material foundation of 'livity' prophetic realisation. Rasta is the result of a search for cultural identity and racial security; a means by which individuals can be redeemed into the heaven or kingdom of a collective togetherness that is seen as an answer to selfish individualism and anarchy of the personality. Rasta is also a socio-religious medium, whereby a people possess the opportunity and ability to enunciate their concepts and to project their images and life-styles onto wider societies and the world at large.

For Rastas worshipping the Almighty Creator is a constant manifestation. There is no set time for rituals or worship, and, therefore, no set ways of giving thanks and praises to Jah Rastafari, Haile Selassie I, King of Kings and Lord of Lords. Certain things like drumming or smoking or 'grounation' (that is, Nyahbinghi session) can and have been done at special times and places, but one should not believe that these are rituals and that they take precedence over anything else that I n I do. I n I know that in Jah sight all acts are 'I-qual'.

Haile Selassie I, Emperor of Ethiopia, is I n I Messiah and Leader. Wherever, he leads I n I follow. He is I n I 'I-ternal' Father, from that time to this and for all times to come.

Rastas want land in Africa for the building of Rasta society, here on earth. Rastas do not expect to die and go to heaven somewhere in the sky. Africa is the place that is most appropriate for the works that Rastas want to do. Rastas want to create plenty works, not least to help I n I brothers and sisters in Africa to regain the strength that was lost. I n I want to achieve, with the aid of I n I brothers and sisters strength and power for Africa, so that its voice can be heard in the affairs of the world. I n I want to achieve peace and love among all people: I n I also want to achieve justice and rights for all people! . . .

Jah is the original Human Power, and He manifests as I n I Father. I n I are His children and I n I enter His Kingman (Kingdom) with plenty thanks and praises. Jah Kingdom is the higher consciousness of words, sounds and power; the untainted vision of pride and ambition; the balanced capacity to cultivate, harbour and dispense justice, truth and rights and the possession of freedom, wisdom and overstanding. Zion, Africa, is I n I Home!

Haille Selassie I, I-lect of Jah, Himself and the Light of earth, is the one and only man who is found worthy to show the way to Jah Kingdom. He lives there so it was easy for him – even in his flesh form. The Book of Revelations revealed Him as the Man. The Man is spirit and flesh. The spiritual aspect of the man is Capital, while the flesh aspect is Common. So, Rastas speak of the higher and lower heights. On the higher or spiritual heights Man is divine (I-vine) and it is the consciousness of this fact that makes a Man realise His own divinity or spirituality. Man, as Capital and Common, is one, because His flesh and His spirit are one. Both properties belong to the same one man. God is Real, Man is Real, God is Spirit, Man is Flesh; both are important in the Real, because that is where creation takes place. I n I, Rastafari deal strictly with Created Reality. Mind and intelligence reveal I n I works. It is said that one is paid according to one's works. That is naturally true, because Jah help those who help themselves.

Jah Rastafari, Haille Selassie I, is good and merciful because he defends and protects the small nations and people of planet earth. That is what a father does until the day his children grow up to be adults. Right now Rastafari children are adults who must live by their father's example in terms of utterances, works and manners. It would be a very good thing if I n I could humble I n I selves as nobles and study the manners and attitudes of H.I.M., I n I Father, and learn decency, culture and uprightness. Righteousness came easy to the Emperor because he was supremely blessed; the grace of the I-ternal Spirit was with him in abundance. So, while each man is free, noble and divine, in order to come to order and balance I n I must look to the Spirit. The Spirit is the beginning and it is the end (even without end); it is now; was, is forever! Man's task is to get the flesh in line with the spirit because the spirit is always moving the flesh towards action and for the very highly conscious being that means creative action.

Since 1930 to now, Rasta people have always been very creative. Of all the various elements of black people that live (from the times of slavery to now) in the Americas and the Caribbean, Rastafari people have, by far, created the most genuine alternative to the system of slavery and colonialism. Rastas have created a true Black identity; a genuine cultural life-style; the rudiments and structure of a genuine alternative language; a bona-fide and international music; an alternative religious theology and practice that excludes nothing, thereby demonstrating the importance of cultural integration and unity, and, not least a creative and revolutionary philosophy of nature and culture. In 50 years, or so, the Rastafari Movement has moved from the 'lowest' of beginnings to international significance and membership. That is no small achievement when one considers that there were no acknowledged intellectuals and monied people in the movement in its first 40, or so years.

The thing which is responsible for driving Rasta along is the inner determination, because of faith, and wisdom, knowledge and overstanding. I n I Rastafari, are blessed with words, sounds and power. And this has helped I n I to reach the people in a convincing and interesting way. The Rastaman uses his common sense a lot; this is done by him taking up natural positions. That which is common is natural, so in a sense I n I could say that the Rastaman uses his natural sense; in effect, this is what he does. The reverse of the natural sense is the artificial sense and Rastas do not indulge in that, because it leads to artificial thoughts and acts.

In I n I book, slavery and colonialism are artificial systems that do societies very little favours. They are systems designed for class benefits and for the benefit of an entire people who happen to share the same social confines, traditions and behaviours. Rasta fight against slavery and colonialism. The people who establish and perpetuate slavery and colonialism must come to an end and that time is not too far away. Already I n I see that plenty a long suffering people have risen from serfdom and exploitation to independence and power. Today former colonies are in a position where they are causing all sorts of problems for those countries that were former colonial masters. Today, the countries that built up their wealth through exploiting other countries, are struggling to maintain that position of wealth. Now, it is much more difficult for the former colonial powers to live off the land and labour of others. Now, the international climate is much more competitive. Freeness and cheapness are harder to come by, costs and prices are the things that have taken over and these in turn give birth to a thing called inflation; which is tantamount to cancer of the industrial economy.

Now that I n I are seeing clearly, I n I must act on that sight that is the only naturally right thing to do. In this time Rastafari is the Light (by that I mean knowledge) that will lead I n I progressively out of darkness (ignorance) and into Jah Rastafari Kingdom. I n I will continue to chant and play nyahbinghi in order to invoke the spirit and power of freedom, justice, truth, rights, love, equality, faith, determination and victory. In this battle, which is reaching its climax, I n I know that victory belong to I n I. Persecution, through imprisonment, beatings and general practices of humiliation will be part of I n I experiences in babylon, but fear not I brothers and sisters for Jah Rastafari, Haille Selassie I, is with I n I always. Persecution has its negative and its positive sides, it turns I n I into heroes and martyars, prophets and creators. From that flows more power which spells doom for babylon.

Rasta can't fail, because he has seen off slavery and colonialism, by participating in their destruction and that is a most significant triumph. In this time I n I stand triumphant, monarch over what I n I are surveying as, if each man is an emperor for his own domain. Rases are lions of the concrete jungle in the urban countries. Rastafari is post slavery-colonial, a new order of civilisation, where that which is natural will and must triumph over that which is artificial. In the new order, the love and respect of man by man and woman by woman is crucial. It has to be an essential requirement if I n I are to get away from the madness of being dominated by human inventions. In Rastafari, I n I inventions and creations must assist I n I, not dominate I n I. It is only through love and respect that man will humble himself and listen to his fellow man and reach inside him to be one with him; Jah know!

Jah Bones, *One Love: Rastafari: History, Doctrine and Livity*, Tottenham, Voice of Rasta, 1985, pp. 1–2, 77–9.

7
NEW RELIGIOUS MOVEMENTS AND BUDDHISM

*I*t is impossible here even to begin to represent the full range of belief and
practice among very diverse organizations, but a statement from the
Unification Church conveys something of the ethos of that small but prominent
group (a). The growth of New Religious Movements (NRMs) in later twentieth
century Britain stirred considerable social and political controversy (b).
Criticism of New Religious Movements was at times very forceful, as
illustrated here by extracts from parliamentary discussion in 1984 (c).

*Two items relating to Buddhism have been included in this section because,
unlike the other ancient religions, its growth in modern Britain came largely
not through migration of adherents from other parts of the world, but by
through its appeal to Western converts and sympathizers (d). In some forms
indeed, Buddhism had a significant affinity to the 'self-help' spirituality of
some New Religious Movements (e). Meanwhile, by the end of the period,
the diffuse but vivid teachings of the 'New Age' were gaining increasing
popularity (f).*

(a) Some beliefs of the Unification Church

The Unification Church is unique in the world in that it is the only
Church based upon the Principles of God. Formed in 1954 by Sun
Myung Moon after revelation from Jesus it comes to serve mankind.
To set new standards, and follow on directly in the evolution of
religion and things spiritual. The Christian Church came to establish the Kingdom of Heaven and Earth. 'Thy will be done on Earth
as it is in Heaven.' It is God's great and lasting desire that we build
a world of harmony, of justice, of love and concern. God's eternal
purpose is fixed and destined and it matters not whether the

religionists of the day accept His will or not. He merely goes out and raises up others who care to build a better society. This is the story of the great revivals, of the great religions, of a God ever seeking to reveal the great spiritual principles on which civilisation is founded. The neglect of these Principles leads us all to disaster. If we have true love in our hearts for our children, and for their children, then we must exert ourselves as never before to build what can surely be the greatest of achievements. A world of peace and beauty. A world of harmony and mutual love and respect. A world of goodwill and spiritual values.

We have inherited untold technical and scientific ability. We could build the greatest golden age that man has ever seen, irrigating the great deserts, providing drainage for backward countries, schools and universities that educate intellect and character. After all does God desire a drug ridden neurotic society or a strong healthy and vigorous civilisation? These are real problems and real questions that we should all ask. The fanatics will continue to argue and many persons whose only contact with religion is with the fanatics will turn away, quietly saying let's not discuss religion. So the godless have their way. Our daughters can have free abortions, or so the state says. Gone is the beauty of innocence, something that we cherished in watching when our children were at school. Even the animals are created with enough natural born intelligence to work things out for themselves. But we have to be educated in sex, so the educationalists tell us. The stark truth remains that if a boy is taught about birds eggs, sooner or later, somehow or other he will play with them when he finds them. It is human nature. So likewise with youth that has increasingly more leisure time – young people will get centred on sexual activity before they have learnt to love and respect the very beings involved. Those are our children. No one appreciates the beauty of innocence until it is lost, and once lost it is never replaced. Those vital character forming years when we learn to handle our hearts, when we deepen our concern for each other and all around, are engulfed frequently before we have had time to appreciate their beauty and quality. . . .

As Sun Myung Moon says 'To enter the Kingdom of Heaven, a

man must with single heart never waver from God's Will, even though the highest position of glory in the world were offered to him.'

Whatever position in society we hold we must never betray our most sacred trust, that of creating The Kingdom of Heaven and Earth. Ultimately God will judge us all not by our beliefs, but by our endeavour in fulfilling His Will on Earth.

'The Path to Peace and Greatness', Thornton Heath, Holy Spirit Association for the Unification of World Christianity, 1973(?), typescript, pp. 4–5, 6.

(b) How should society respond?

1 [T]here are few simple or easy answers to the questions that have been raised by the existence of NRMs in contemporary Western society.

2 Some commonly observed characteristics of some NRMs arise from the fact that the movements are, for the most part, both *new* and (using the word rather widely) *religious*, and that, unlike earlier waves of NRMs in the West, many have emerged from traditions that are still alien to most Westerners.

3 None the less, the differences between the movements are enormous in every area of belief and practice, and it should never be assumed that the characteristics of some movements apply to others.

4 The vast majority of those who become involved in an NRM suffer no serious damage as a result of their involvement. Many will testify that they gain considerable benefit.

5 It is, however, also true that serious problems do arise in a small minority of cases, and less serious, but none the less disturbing, situations can arise in further cases. Among the *potentially* dangerous situations to which the reader has been alerted, are:

    (i) A movement cutting itself off (either geographically or socially) from the rest of society.

    (ii) A convert becoming increasingly dependent on the movement for definitions and the testing of 'reality'.

   (iii) A movement drawing sharp, unnegotiable boundaries between 'them' and 'us', 'godly' and 'satanic', 'good' and 'bad' – and so on.
   (iv) Important decisions about converts' lives being made for them by others.
   (v) Leaders claiming divine authority for their actions and their demands.
   (vi) Leaders or movements pursuing a single goal in a single-minded manner.

6 It is not always easy to distinguish between individuals who have decided to lead their lives in a way others might find incomprehensible or unattractive, and those who have, for some reason or other, abrogated responsibility. It is an assumption of this book that those who allow others to 'show them the way' are not necessarily being irresponsible. At the same time, it is assumed that each individual should, unless clearly suffering from some kind of mental incapacity, be held responsible, and accept responsibility, for every action that he or she takes.

7 A number of suggestions have been made. Some of these arise from the beliefs that:
   (i) An awareness both of the diversity and of the more frequently recurring features of NRMs can alert us not only to some of the causes for worry to which they give rise, but also to some of the attractions that the movements undoubtedly hold for certain people in modern society.
   (ii) The indisputable evidence that the vast majority of people leave NRMs voluntarily suggests that we have to look beyond the movements' evangelising processes if we want to understand why a particular person does *not* leave.
   (iii) Forcible deprogramming is unethical, illegal, and based on an assumption about mind control that has been severely undermined by a considerable body of scholarly research. It is also likely to result in more problems than it solves.
   (iv) It could be unwise to adopt a *laissez faire* attitude before any particular case has been carefully investigated.

(v) But deprogramming and *laissez faire* are by no means the only options.

(vi) Parents and friends of those who join a new religious movement should make every possible effort to keep in touch and to foster a good relationship with the convert.

(vii) Those who want to help should try to get as much accurate and unbiased information as possible about both the movement and the convert in order to decide how best to act in any particular case.

(viii) They should also encourage the convert to assess *practically* (rather than just theoretically or to rehearse as a matter of faith) his or her movement in the light of factual information and in the light of general principles such as honesty, respect for others and personal responsibility for one's own actions.

(ix) It should never be forgotten that, in Western democracies, adult human beings have the right to enjoy religious liberty.

Eileen Barker, *New Religious Movements: A Practical Introduction*, London, HMSO, 1989, pp. 137–8.

(c) *Parliamentary unease*

Mr Richard Needham (Wiltshire, North): This debate follows the death of Mr Doubtfire and would not have been necessary had it not been for the fact that he became involved with the extraordinarily unpleasant organisation called the Exegesis Programme. It would not be wrong to call it a cult. . . .

What are the training techniques that the programme uses on its so-called students? For £240 one can be effectively locked up for two days; windows are blacked out, one's watch is removed and, except for the needs of nature, one cannot leave. The cult uses techniques of deprivation. It induces a sense of fear, and then one is abused and frightened.

A journalist from the *Sunday Telegraph* attended one of these courses. He wrote:

'Jeff marched up to one of the students and flung a pair of shoes on the floor in front of him. "Your integrity stinks", he screamed, staring the hapless and now nervous student in the eye. "You broke an agreement not to leave things in the room during a break. You can't even cope with little things in life, let alone the big ones. Time is running out for you. Do you want to remake the agreement"?

Now began a familiar aspect of many such psychological seminars – the public confessional. Individually, students sat on a stool in front of the group and described their life and problems, losing all reticence as they were provoked by Kim's sneering abuse. There was a moment of extreme tension when an accountant, so nervous he could only whisper, was made to stand against a wall with his arms outstretched while Kim ordered three assistants to "push, push, push".'

This so-called course is designed to attract people who lack self-confidence and want to find leadership, confidence or the ability to do better than they have done previously. Naturally, it attracts the very people who lack self-confidence and do not have strong characters, which is why they attend such a course. They hope that, as a result, their characters will become stronger. Because of the nature of the cult's techniques, they are most likely to be at risk from having to suffer the abuse that I have described.

One person who went on such a course was my late constituent, Mr Ashley Doubtfire. It is true that he had a psychiatric problem when he was 18. It is also true that he seemed to be over it, that he had built a successful career as a hang glider and a manufacturer of hang gliders, that he was recently married to a nurse, and that both of them decided to attend a course. However, having followed this course in this darkened room, Mr Doubtfire became a complete schizophrenic, and for the following 18 months he was in and out of mental hospitals, until finally, at the beginning of last year, he died at the age of 34. . . .

The Parliamentary Under-Secretary of State for the Home Department (Mr David Mellor): . . . Many of us, as constituency

Members of Parliament, have come face to face with the very real personal tragedy that this growing number of cults that now operate in Britain has brought to bear. I see this as a Member of Parliament and as the Minister responsible to the Home Secretary for the work of charities I receive a full postbag of letters about the activities of groups of the sort that my hon. Friend has described, most of them from distressed friends and relatives who are unable to grasp how intelligent young people with everything to live for and a real future, if directed in the right way, can become involved in, and ultimately dominated and sometimes destroyed by such cults. I know that many hon. Members will have received similar letters. I should be surprised if there is a Member who has not.

Nearly all the letters that I receive ask for the Government to do something. The difficulty is to know what that something should be. The course so often proposed is the sort of direct intervention that, on mature reflection, might be thought to constitute too fundamental an attack on civil liberties, having regard to the fact that it is the very essence of a free society that people may often in their free time choose to pursue activities that, on the whole, may not be in their best interests and that many of us may not think desirable.

To say that the Government should stay their hand on some of the firmer action that some correspondents ask to be taken does not mean that we believe that nothing can or should be done. On the contrary, I am firmly convinced that the sinister activities of some of the groups must be exposed by every means possible and most vigorously discouraged. However, given the restraints of the free society, a society which the Government are determined to uphold, there must be a limit to what the Government can do directly.

Let no one be in any doubt about our views on this matter, the importance we attach to it or the extent to which we applaud the work which so many have rightly carried out in exposing to public view the activities of some of these entirely undesirable groups.

I shall take first the specific case of the Exegesis Programme about which my hon. Friend the Member for Wiltshire, North has spoken with such eloquence and contempt. I set on the record my personal view that on the basis of what my hon. Friend has said, on the correspondence that we have had and on the contents of the excel-lent investigation that was carried out by Mr Andrew Duncan in a thorough piece of journalism, which was written up in his article in the *Sunday Telegraph* Sunday magazine, the contents of the Exegesis Programme seem to be puerile, dangerous and profoundly wrong.

It may interest the House to know that we have been keeping the programme's activities under careful scrutiny for some time. We have asked the Metropolitan police and the Avon and Somerset police, in whose area the Exegesis Programme has also been active, to let us know of any evidence that criminal offences have been committed by the organisation, its offshoots or its members. The police have recently updated their reports and they confirm that there is no such evidence. We shall continue to keep a close eye on what it is doing.

This is the nub of the problem. However much we sympathise with the anguish of those who are affected, we owe it not least to them to make them recognise that, and while we are deeply dis-turbed about the way in which cults alienate members of families and clearly exercise an unhealthy impact on many vulnerable and impressionable people, their known activities do not appear, more often than not, to be unlawful. . . .

All too many of those who become involved in cults do so naïvely and in appalling ignorance of the nature and activities of the organ-isations concerned. The more that the media and Members of Parlia-ment can expose the dangers, the less potent they will be.

In that context, I congratulate the *Daily Mail* on its courage in exposing the truth about the Unification Church and taking on appalling financial responsibilities in one of the longest-running actions in the history of the British High Court. The *Daily Mail* did its public duty in exposing the truth about that group, and after such a long trial it took the jury only a few hours to find the essential truth of what it had asserted.

Other publications, too, might be mentioned. *Private Eye* exposed the dubious activities of the Emins group which, I am sad to say, has its headquarters in my constituency where its presence is greatly resented by me and by many other local residents.

The families of those who have become or risk becoming attracted to such cults particularly need advice and support as they are most likely to be able to warn against and, if necessary, resist the influence of those organisations. For that reason, I pay particular tribute to the valuable work of FAIR – Family Action Information and Rescue – a voluntary organisation which aims to help families whose children become enmeshed in cults and which has recently come to prominence as a sure sign of how wide and deep the concern about these matters runs throughout the community. I am sure that the House will welcome the fact that officials from the Home Office, the Department of Health and Social Security and the Department of Education and Science have met representatives of that body, and we intend to keep in close touch with them.

I should also mention the long-running work of the Deo Gloria trust in informing the public about the activities of these sinister groups.

Parliamentary Debates (Hansard), House of Commons, Vol. 60, No. 154, 14 May 1984, cols. 124, 126–9 (with cuts).

(d) The character of Buddhism in England

Already the question was being asked, What has Buddhism to offer the West? As early as 1927 I was trying to find the answers, and in the course of a public meeting in London I described five qualities which Buddhism must have if it was to be applicable to the West.

1 The truths must be presented in a form acceptable to the West. The Buddha's teaching has a universal message but its form must be digestible by those to whom it is given.
2 We must teach principles, and let people apply them for themselves. The West wants food for thought; ideas, principles, laws of life.
3 Religion and science must somehow be harmonised, religion here meaning the yearning of the heart for That which is behind phenomena, and science the laws of nature in their broadest

sense. The West must understand the existence of a unifying principle which includes both.

4 It must be presented as a philosophy, which appeals to the reason and not to the voice of authority. 'Here is a doctrine,' we must say, 'which is not a dogma. Think it out and apply it for yourselves.'

5 Whatever we teach must be proffered with humility and tolerance, yet as provably true, as tested by thousands of years of experience.

Add to these the sense of Brotherhood, as a fact and not mere sentiment; of self-reliance on the Truth which dwells within; and the quality of interdependent independence. People want something which will teach them to stand on their own feet and at the same time show them how they fit in with the common whole. And finally compassion, a deep understanding of the unity of life and a consequent link between each one of us and everything that lives . . . Buddhism can supply all these.

If this was reasonably true in 1927 I would not appreciably change it in 1967. . . .

[A]lthough the schools will, I think, survive as such for many years, with groups of adherents to 'pure' Theravada or Zen or Tibetan Buddhism as the case may be, most English Buddhists are frankly eclectic, choosing and using those principles found to be most helpful in their search for enlightenment. And why should they not choose? All other so-called Buddhist countries have chosen what principles, of those which travelling teachers taught them, were most of service to their spiritual needs. Thus we have Sinhalese Buddhism (the Theravada complete), Tibetan Buddhism (its own rich blend of three 'traditions'), and Japanese Buddhism (a group of widely differing schools working happily side by side). Why should there not be in time a Western Buddhism, a Nava-yana or 'new vehicle' as Captain Ellam called it, not deliberately formed as such but a natural growth from the same roots of Buddhism as all others, that is, the record of the Buddha's Enlightenment? There is no reason why it should not grow happily alongside, and even blend with the best of Western science, psychology and social science, and thus affect the ever-changing field of Western thought. It will not be Theravada or Zen, Prajnaparamita intuitive philosophy or Tibetan ritual. Just what it will be we do not know, nor does it matter at the present time. The Dharma as such is immortal, but its forms must ever change to serve the ever-changing human need.

Christmas Humphreys, *Sixty Years of Buddhism in England: A History and a Survey*, London, The Buddhist Society, 1968, pp. 75–6, 80–1.

(e) *The nature of Nichiren Shoshu Buddhism*

The basic practice of Nichiren Shoshu Buddhism consists of chanting the phrase *Nam-myoho-renge-kyo* to the Gohonzon, a scroll inscribed with many Chinese and two Sanskrit characters. This is supported by the daily practice of morning and evening *gongyo*, the recitation of two key chapters of the Lotus Sutra, followed by chanting *Nam-myoho-renge-kyo* 'to your heart's content'. If you do this, study and teach others the Buddhist view of life to the best of your ability, you will develop a state of life in which your desires are completely fulfilled, which creates the maximum value and good fortune for yourself and your society, and which is powered by unshakeable happiness and confidence, no matter what problems you may be facing. Nichiren Daishonin, the founder of this Buddhism, states: 'A law this easy to embrace and this easy to practise was taught for the sake of all mankind in this evil Latter Day of the Law.'

This may sound incredible – not only in the sense of being too good to be true but, literally, unbelievable. How can chanting a phrase one does not even understand, over and over again to a piece of paper, possibly have such an effect? What does *Nam-myoho-renge-kyo* mean, anyway, and what is so special about this scroll, the Gohonzon? These are good questions, just a few of the many that will doubtless arise, and hopefully be answered, in the course of reading this book. For now, suffice it to say that perhaps the most challenging aspect of Nichiren Shoshu Buddhism is the way that it forces one to re-examine fundamental assumptions about the nature of life in general, and our own lives in particular. These assumptions are probably so deeply rooted that you may not even be aware you hold them. For example, consider the problem of suffering.

No one wants to suffer. But much as we would all like to live a totally happy life, suffering is an inescapable fact of our human existence. The observation that 'Man is born unto trouble, as sparks fly upward' may not have been much consolation to Job but, nevertheless, remains an uncomfortable truth. Generally speaking, sufferings arise through our encounter with problems and difficulties; this is why much of our time is spent trying to avoid them, even though they are inherent in life. In trying to avoid problems, however, we are often simply putting off the inevitable to a future date, by which time the trouble has usually grown much more difficult to resolve. Personal relationships are a good example of this. The failure to tackle a problem between two people – a clash of desires, for instance – usually for fear of not knowing what the consequences will be, or perhaps simply because of a dislike of conflict, can very easily lead to a build-up of resentments which, when finally expressed, can be immensely destructive. . . .

One of the natural consequences of the close link between problems and suffering is that people tend to confuse the one with the other. For example, if you are unemployed, it is very probable that you are also unhappy; you will probably think you are unhappy because you are unemployed. While it might very well be true that you would probably be happier in work than out of it (though this is debatable, in view of the number of people who complain about their jobs), strictly speaking your unhappiness is not because you are unemployed but, rather, because you feel helpless in being unable to find a job. In other words, it is not so much our problems which cause us to suffer as our inability to overcome them.

This may seem like splitting hairs but, in reality, the difference is fundamental. Problems that we feel confident we can solve, even if only after a great deal of time and effort, we label very differently as 'challenges'. In short, whether our problems are sources of suffering or sources of growth depends entirely on our attitude, both to the problem and to ourselves.

Richard Causton, *Nichiren Shoshu Buddhism: An Introduction*, London, Rider, 1988, pp. 13–15.

(f) The New Age

Freud said that the major problem of civilisation was the repression of our sexuality. In my view, the major problem has been the repression of our spirituality, the repression of our instinct freely to explore the inner dimensions of our Universe and of ourselves.

We have been subject to religions and churches which allow only one kind of belief or approach to the divine unknown. We have been victims of insecurity and superstition. And we have been subject to an intellectual worldview which overthrew the power of superstition and organised religion only, in reaction, to replace it with a worldview so mechanical and so limited that it totally denied the invisible realities of existence.

I cannot ignore the fate of individualistic spiritual seekers in the past and I cannot ignore contemporary forces of repression; historical and modern reality demand new clarity when we discuss spiritual freedom.

I see the New Age phenomenon as the visible tip of the iceberg of a mass movement in which humanity is reasserting its right to explore spirituality in total freedom. The constraints of religious and intellectual ideology are falling away.

The New Age movement represents several very different dynamics, but they thread together to communicate the same message: *there is an invisible and inner dimension to all life – cellular, human and cosmic. The most exciting work in the world is to explore this inner reality.*

According to research carried out by the Gallup poll, almost fifty per cent of all people have experiences that are mystical or, at least, not scientifically explicable. The great beauty of the New Age movement is that if someone in it is approached by someone else looking for insight or counselling about the inner or religious dimension, he or she will not be told: *'Believe this! Do this! Don't do that!'* but rather: *'There are a thousand different ways of exploring inner reality. Go where your intelligence and intuition lead you. Trust yourself.'* New Age attitudes are the antithesis of fundamentalism.

Although the different dynamics which form the New Age phenomenon create a common general message, some of them make strange bedfellows. It would be a mistake to assume that all people who might come under the New Age banner get on with each other – either personally or in terms of their ideas. In fact, some who are identified as New Agers actively reject the label for fear of being associated with seemingly incompatible elements. There are divides, for example, between those of a rigorous intellectual bias and those who are dominantly instinctive and intuitive, even though they might share the same spiritual approach or work in the same field.

It seems to me that there are four major fields:

New Paradigm/New Science
Ecology
New Psychology
Spiritual Dynamics

Under *New Paradigm/New Science* come all the new theories which are reworking our intellectual understanding of the structures of life. These include the insights of sub-atomic physics, cosmology and biology. Here the mechanistic Newtonian view of the cosmos, as being made up of tangible bits and pieces following certain reliable laws of interaction, has given way to a more fluid and expanded view of reality. Matter and energy are seen as bound together, connected and formed in invisible ways that we are only just beginning to understand; according to this worldview, matter, energy and consciousness are one continuum and, like the hologram, all aspects of the whole can be contained and enfolded in a single part. All life is intimately interconnected.

Along with the new science, we are also reassessing the nature of the human body and our approaches to medicine and healing. Equally, we are reassessing the values that underpin our social structures and cultural heritage. Technological and scientific achievements appear to have brought with them many attendant ills as well as benefits. What should our priorities be? Have we, in environmental terms, paid too high a price for material progress?

Linked by a new understanding of our Earth as a complete living organism, Gaia, these questions merge with the approaches of *Ecology*, especially of the deep ecologists. The deep ecologist explores the relationship between all forms of life in its profound spiritual and philosophical dimensions. The concept of interdependence and interpenetration across all species expands to include not only our actions as consumers and workers, but also *the total energy effect of our actions and attitudes*. Not only our supermarket purchases but also our moods create our global environment. This is spiritual ecology taking responsibility for the total state of our planet. Situation by situation, moment by moment, we confront our moral and social responsibilities.

The third thread is the *New Psychology*. Freud pointed out the invisible world of the unconscious, but the new psychology demonstrates not only the repressed and primitive areas of the unconscious, but also the extraordinary dynamics of the supraconscious and transpersonal. A core concept of new psychology is that *all* people are capable of becoming integrated, fulfilled and completely loving human beings.

But for me the hallmark of the New Age is the power of its *Spiritual Dynamics*. Certain weights – repression, fear, power interests, materialism – have been holding down this dynamic; but these weights are shifting.

The new science and psychology show the severe limits of apparent scientific logic.

The new psychology demonstrates no limits in human potential.

The ecological crisis has shown the failure of unfettered industrialisation, science and commerce. Technology becomes the servant of ethics.

The vision of our planet from space and the Gaia hypothesis show us our beautiful and inescapable interdependence. The sense of impotent post-industrial isolation and alienation is disappearing.

And the slumbering spiritual mammoth, like Gulliver released from the many strands, is beginning to awake.

In the New Age movement there is an enthusiasm, humour and release. It draws its lessons and inspirations from many sources. One of its major characteristics is its honouring of all the esoteric religious traditions and of the mystic traditions of native peoples. A remarkable renaissance of the wisdom traditions is taking place, both those within the major religions and those of indigenous peoples. Within the major religions, for example, are the gnostic tradition of Christianity, the Qabalah of Judaism, Sufism in Islam, and Zen and meditation techniques of Buddhism. The native traditions include those of Celtic Europe – such as Wiccan and Druidism – north American Indians, Australian Aborigines and African medicine people. And there is a powerful rebirth of the female aspects of deity, as the Goddess resumes her crucial role in our lives.

At the same time, as people use various mystical techniques to explore their own psyches and consciousness, they have tapped great reservoirs of spiritual knowledge and awareness. Much of this has come through in new teachings and much of it has also come through in inspirational and lyrical prose, as well as music, art and movement. But a common theme resonating through all the new inner awareness is that we are entering a New Age and that human consciousness is going through a transformation that is cosmically significant. Perhaps this understanding of the New Age is vainglorious egotism; that is for you to decide. Less glamorous is the notion that we are passing out of 2,000 years of Piscean astrological influence into the influence of Aquarius, which will affect all aspects of our culture as we move away from Piscean structures of hierarchical devotion to more fluid and spontaneous relationships that dance to an Aquarian rhythm. Also less glamorous is the notion that the problems facing our post-industrial global village with its sophisticated electronic awareness on the one hand and its gross social injustices on the other, are forcing humanity into a new consciousness.

William Bloom, ed., *The New Age: An Anthology of Essential Writings*, London, Rider, 1991, pp. xv–xviii.

8

POPULAR ATTITUDES TO RELIGION

I n 1947 Mass-Observation, which had been founded in 1937 'to study *the habits, behaviour and opinions of ordinary people' in Britain, carried out a study of religious attitudes in an unidentified London borough. The conclusions (a) pointed to considerable ambivalence and half-belief. This impression is confirmed by a variety of evidence from other places and dates; from surveys conducted in 1957 and 1982 (b); from accounts of folk beliefs and practices in the 1970s on the northern coast of Yorkshire (c); and from interviews with working-class people in east London in the 1980s (d).*

For much of the period the monarchy was a focus for diffuse religious sentiment, as was illustrated by newspaper comment in 1952 and 1981, and by the tone of Elizabeth II's Christmas broadcasts (e). Remembrance Sunday too touched chords of popular sentiment, although its function became increasingly a matter of debate (f). Meanwhile professedly scientific attempts to explore religious experience yielded interesting results (g). Such perspectives need, however, to be weighed against the argument that the 'rational' pattern of modern life had produced a secularized culture inherently unreceptive to religion (h).

(a) Puzzled People

In their report, *Towards the Conversion of England*, the Commission on Evangelism remark on the results of previous Mass-Observation surveys of the attitude of ordinary men and women towards religion:

It is open to question which is the more alarming feature, the failure of the Church to attract, or its failure to repel.

The present survey documents this superficial attitude of benevolent neutrality, and seeks to describe its basis, implications, and its relation to other current negativisms. The investigation was mainly carried out in one London suburb, which we call Metrop, but much data already on file from other areas and using various techniques was also consulted.

Not more than one person in ten in Metrop is at all closely associated with any of the churches, and about two-thirds never, or practically never, go to Church. The majority, however – four out of five women and two out of three men – give at least verbal assent to the possibility of there being a God, and most of the rest express doubt rather than disbelief. Uncompromising disbelievers in a Deity amount to about one in twenty.

Irrespective of their own religious beliefs, the majority of people in Metrop consider that religion should be taught in schools. Even among those who openly doubt the existence of God, the majority hold this view. Throughout the survey an attitude of 'goodwill' towards the *idea* of religion and religious faith is apparent, frequently in conjunction with a hostile attitude towards the Church, and a personal religious faith of an exceedingly vague and unorthodox kind. Less than a third of Church of England churchgoers, for instance, give definite verbal assent to three basic affirmations of the Apostles' Creed. Over 40 per cent of them express doubt about the possibility of an afterlife.

The nature of this 'goodwill' towards religion is indicated in the attitude of people with no religious beliefs themselves, who favour religious instruction to 'give the children an idea of what's right and wrong', 'to make them civilised', etc. They still feel that some of the ethical principles of Christianity are right, and they know of no other sanction for them, or means of inculcating them, than the religious one.

To very many religion has come to mean little more than being kind and neighbourly, doing good when opportunity arises. Belief in the Golden Rule, common factor of numerous religious and ethical systems, persists, but without the sanction of faith, or any other sanction than habit and vague memories of childhood teaching.

Throughout this survey we find little difference between the out-look of more and less educated people. The main differences are ones of sex and age. Women in all respects show greater interest in religion than men, more personal faith, and in general a greater respect for religion, whether or not they are themselves 'religious'. Anti-religious sentiments, as opposed to anti-Church sentiments, come predominantly from men. Both in regard to formal observances and general attitude, the younger generation show a much more critical outlook, and *much less interest.* Two young people (under forty) express doubt about the existence of God for every older person who does so. It is mostly the younger generation who dismiss religion with apparent disinterest, while the old, whatever their own beliefs or lack of beliefs, usually show respect for it.

Broadly speaking, criticism of religion comes most from those groups who are least interested, least informed.

Criticism and disillusion centres chiefly on *organised* religion, on the Churches and their dignatories, on the ostentatious *practice* of religion, rather than on religion itself.

This scepticism about organised religion, about the established hierarchy and leadership, runs parallel with other growing scepticisms. Thus, while ordinary people today have increasingly positive ideas about politics and political programmes, their generalised attitude towards politicians and political parties is increasingly one of disillusion and cynicism.

A distrust of established leadership pervades people's minds today. While conscious recognition and spontaneous discussion of the problems of the future have perhaps never been so widespread and urgent as they are now; while more people than ever before are aware of what they feel *should* be done; and while these ideas often correspond closely with the expressed ideals of party programme and Christian ethic – still a great gulf of distrust stretches between leaders and people, mass organisation, and disorientated mass.

The potential scope for imaginative, dynamic leadership today is immense. Current loss of faith (in religion, in politics, in progress, in science, and so on) is very largely a loss of faith in the unwieldy, centralised, remote *organisation*, which increasingly monopolises the potential realisation of ideals, and which seems so distant and uncontrollable to ordinary people.

These ordinary people are looking for something to believe in. As the need becomes more urgent, so their capacity for discrimination is likely to diminish. If any one overriding conclusion arises from the present report it is this: Established leadership is becoming increasingly remote from ordinary people. If it does not re-establish contact soon, unattached loyalties and desires may well find a focus in some new leadership, uncritically accepted because it succeeds in establishing direct contact with immediate, long-felt human needs. The decline in religious faith is but one symptom of an all-round decline of faith in the future, accelerated by war, accentuated by the inevitable anxieties of peace. The need for faith, whether religious or secular, is shown to be acute, though only partially articulate as yet.

Whether pre-existing faiths re-establish themselves or new faiths arise, is a matter which seems likely to settle itself within the next few years – for people cannot carry on for long in the profoundly negative frame of mind which characterises the short-term outlook of so many today.

In the political sphere, the election of a Labour Government in 1945 – a change forecast and analysed by Mass-Observation eighteen months before the event – represents for many a last hope within the existing range of political parties and programmes. Much more than immediate considerations of party and country depend on the success or failure of the Labour Party in re-establishing a dynamic relationship with the people of Britain in the next two or three years.

And, if our analysis is correct, the search for a basic faith sanctioning accepted standards of conduct makes the immediate future actions of the established Church of equally vital importance to future stabilities. The persistence of the Christian ethic today rests on extremely flimsy foundations. Majority goodwill remains in the current attitude of benevolent neutrality. But, at present, goodwill persists largely for want of alternative. If alternative offers it may be seized on hungrily, uncritically and irrevocably. 'The Conversion of England', if it is to be accomplished by the Established Church, will have to be accomplished soon.

Mass-Observation, *Puzzled People: A Study in Popular Attitudes to Religion, Ethics, Progress and Politics in a London Borough*, London, Victor Gollancz, 1947, pp. 156–9.

(b) Two surveys

Have you, yourself, a dislike for any particular denomination or creed?

Yes, Church of England	1%
Yes, Non Conformist	2
Yes, Roman Catholic	17
Yes, Scottish Church	1
Yes, other	5
	26%

All saying 'yes'	24%
No	76

Which of these statements comes closest to your belief?

There is a personal god	41%
There is some sort of spirit/god or life force	37
I don't know what to think	16
Don't really think there is any sort of spirit/god or life force	6

Suppose someone asked you to give him a good reason why we should be honest and truthful and kind. Would you be able to answer him or would you be at a loss what to say?

It is the way to get most out of life	22%
I have always been taught to be honest	18
My religion tells me to	11
It is the way I like other people to behave towards me	8
It makes life happier for other people	7
Other replies	1
Would be at a loss	33

Do you believe that Jesus Christ was the Son of God or just a man?

Son of God	71%
Just a man	9
Just a story	6
Don't know	14

Do you believe that there is or is not a devil?

Is	34%
Is not	42
Don't know	24

Do you think that a person can be a Christian even if he doesn't believe that every word of the New Testament is true?

Yes	79%
No	11
Don't know	10

Do you believe there is or is not life after death?

Is	54%
Is not	17
Don't know	29

Do you believe it is or is not possible to exchange messages with the dead?

Is possible	15%
Is not possible	52
Don't know	33

Do you think a person can be a Christian if he doesn't go to church?

Yes	85%
No	11
Don't know	4

*What's your attitude towards divorce:
it should not be allowed at all; it should
be easier than at the present time; it
should be more difficult than at
present?*

Should be easier 20%
Should not be allowed............. 18
Should be more difficult........... 18
Leave as it is......................... 36
Don't know.......................... 8

*Speaking generally, which would you
say has more influence on the way
people live and their circumstances –
religion or politics?*

Religion.............................. 30%
Politics 41
About same.......................... 17
Don't know.......................... 12

*Do you believe that religion can answer
all or most of today's problems, or is it
largely old-fashioned and out-of-date?*

Can answer.......................... 46%
Old-fashioned....................... 27
Don't know.......................... 27

*At the present time, do you think
religion as a whole is increasing its
influence on British life or losing its
influence?*

Increasing........................... 17%
Same................................. 18
Losing influence 52
Don't know.......................... 13

*Which do you think the world is most
in need of today, greater economic
security for the people of all nations, or
more religion?*

Economic security.................. 48%
Religion............................. 36
Don't know.......................... 16

*Should the Church keep out of political
matters or should they express their
views on day-to-day social and political
questions?*

Keep out 53%
Express views....................... 36
Don't know.......................... 11

*Do you think the connection between
the Church of England and the State
should continue or do you think the
Church should be separated from the
State?*

Continue............................. 37%
Separate............................. 37
Don't know.......................... 26

*Do you think it right to christen
or baptise children or not?*

Yes................................... 82%
No 7
Don't know.......................... 11

*Do you believe in teaching children to
say their prayers?*

Yes, do believe..................... 86%
No, don't believe.................. 7
Don't know.......................... 7

Should they go to Sunday school?

Yes, providing they want to	57%
Yes, even if they don't want to ..	35
No	4
Don't know..........................	4

Asked of those with children of 15 or under: Should children go to Sunday school?

Yes, regularly........................	50%
Yes, now and again	25
No, never............................	25

What do you think the schools should do about religion?

Just have scripture lessons.........	30%
Give regular religious instruction	40
Teach them about other religions as well as Christianity.......................	21
Cut out all religion and scripture	6
Don't know..........................	3

George H. Gallup, *The Gallup International Public Opinion Polls: Great Britain 1937–1975*, New York, Random House, 1976, Vol. 1, pp. 405–7

ASK ALL

158 A lot of people today doubt whether God exists. Do you ever think about whether there is a God or not?

1159 (71%)	Yes	1		
451 (28%)	No	2		ASK 159
18 (1%)	DK	3		
O				

159 Do you believe in God?

1173 (72%)	Yes	1		ASK 162
279 (17%)	No	2		ASK 160
176 (11%)	DK	3		
O				

160   Or do you believe in some kind of
spirit or supernatural force?

103 (23%)	Yes	1	ASK 161
305 (67%)	No	2	
48 (10%)	DK	3	ASK 163

O

---

161   Do any of the following come into
your picture of the supernatural, or
not?

PROMPT and code each item

	No	Yes	DK	$
1 Love	50	49	4	
	49%	48%	4%	
2 Creator	60	39	4	
	58%	38%	4%	
3 Spiritual Force	21	76	6	
	20%	74%	6%	
4 Sustainer	70	17	16	ASK 163
	68%	17%	16%	
5 Life force	31	61	11	
	30%	59%	11%	
6 Some other picture	73	21	9	
	71%	20%	9%	

Specify _____

O

---

162   Do any of the following come into
your picture of God, or not?

PROMPT and code each item

	No	Yes	DK	$
1 Judge	632	486	52	
	54%	42%	4%	
2 Love	90	1065	15	
	8%	91%	1%	
3 Creator	111	1027	31	
	9%	88%	3%	

4 Father	268	878	23	
	23%	75%	2%	
5 Mother	835	294	40	
	71%	25%	3%	
6 Master	668	474	27	
	57%	41%	2%	
7 Sustainer	376	691	102	ASK 163
	32%	59%	9%	
8 Protector	214	918	37	
	18%	79%	3%	
9 Redeemer	226	859	84	
	19%	73%	7%	
10 Some other	929	137	103	
picture	79%	12%	9%	

Specify _____

O

ASK ALL

163　What sort of person do you think
Jesus Christ was; do you think he was

READ THROUGH and code one

199 (12%)	˙a prophet, or	1	ASK 200
703 (43%)	˙the Son of God, or	2	ASK 164
482 (30%)	˙an ordinary human being like other men and women, or	3	
133 (8%)	˙do you have some other view?	4	ASK 165

Specify _____

_____

DK　　5

110 (7%)

O

164 Do you think he was someone
specially chosen by God or was he
God himself in human form?

CODE one

362 (51%)	Specially chosen	1	
286 (40%)	God in human form	2	
11 (2%)	Some other	3	ASK 200
53 (7%)	DK	4	
O			

165 Do you think there was anything special
about him; which of these comes *closest*
to your view?

READ THROUGH and CODE one

313 (44%)	˙He was an example to other men and women, or	1	
209 (29%)	˙He was someone with exceptional spiritual powers?	2	
96 (13%)	Some other	3	ASK 200
	Specify ———————————		
97 (14%)	DK		
O			

ASK ALL

200 People think different things about
whether there's a life after death. Have
you ever thought about it, even if only at
moments of crisis?

1230 (76%)	Yes	1	
366 (22%)	No	2	ASK 202
32 (2%)	DK	3	

202 Do you believe in a life after death or not?

644 (40%)	Yes	1	
718 (44%)	No	2	
265 (16%)	DK	3	
O			

ASK ALL

213 Let's leave that subject now and talk about ghosts and things like that. Have you ever thought about such things?

1062 (65%)	Yes	1	
552 (34%)	No	2	ASK 214
12 (1%)	DK	3	

214 Do you believe that there are such things as ghosts or poltergeists or anything like that, or not?

593 (36%)	Yes	1	ASK 215
904 (56%)	No	2	ASK 223
131 (8%)	DK	3	
O			

215 Why do you think there are ghosts?

PROMPT *and* CODE *one*

180 (30%)	1 Personal experience	1	
123 (21%)	2 The reports of those close to me	2	
178 (30%)	3 There must be something in all the reports you hear	3	ASK 216
62 (10%)	4 I just think there are such things	4	

29 (5%)   5 I don't really know why   5

20 (3%)   6 Some other   6   ASK 216

    Specify ＿＿＿＿＿＿＿＿＿

    ＿＿＿＿＿＿＿＿＿＿＿＿

1 (under 1%)   DK   7

O

---

216   There are different views about what ghosts actually are. Which of the following comes close to your view?

PROMPT and CODE one

341 (58%)   1 Ghosts are the souls of people who have died   1

176 (30%)   2 Some spiritual force, but not related to people's souls   2

    Do NOT prompt   ASK 217

52 (9%)   3 I don't know what ghosts are   3

6 (1%)   4 I've never really thought about it   4

18 (3%)   5 Some other   5

    Specify ＿＿＿＿＿＿＿＿＿

    ＿＿＿＿＿＿＿＿＿＿＿＿

O

---

217   Has anyone close to you (as far as you know) ever encountered anything that they thought might be a ghost?

319 (54%)   Yes   1

269 (45%)   No   2   ASK 218

5 (1%)   DK   3

	218 Have you ever encountered anything yourself which you thought might be a ghost?			
227 (38%)	Yes	1		] ASK 219
364 (61%)	No	2		ASK 230
2 (under 1%)	DK	3		

	219 Have you had that experience often, sometimes, occasionally, or just once?		
22 (10%)	Often	1	
9 (4%)	Sometimes	2	
68 (30%)	Occasionally	3	
128 (56%)	Once only	4	
	DK	5	

Helen Krarup, *Conventional Religion and Common Religion in Leeds, Interview Schedule: Basic frequencies by question*, Leeds, University of Leeds: Department of Sociology, Religious Research Papers 12, 1982, pp. 46–9, 56–8.

(c) Hallowe'en and Christmas in Staithes

HALLOWE'EN

A little later in the year, on the night of 31 October/1 November, Hallowe'en is celebrated. Situated at the transitional point between autumn and winter, the period has had religious significance far back into antiquity. For the Celts the present 1 November was the festival of *Samhain* when evil forces were expelled and the powers of fertility renewed. Since that time the festival has taken on other meanings. Victor Turner writes, 'In European folk beliefs, the mid-night of 31 October has become associated with gatherings of the hellish powers of witchcraft and the devil . . . Subsequently a strange alliance has been formed between the innocent and the wicked, children and witches who purge the community by the mock pity and terror of trick and treat.' . . . In Staithes, Hallowe'en sees the streets and alleyways of the village filled with young children who delight in leaping out from behind corners and rushing at unsuspecting adults. Most of these children wear strikingly elaborate masks of multi-coloured papier-mâché and cardboard and carry lanterns made from hollowed-out turnips with holes for eyes, nose and mouth and with a lighted candle inside. For this one night of the year they are permitted to terrorise the adults of the village with their exaggerated howling and terrible movements, and may accost their elders crying,

> The sky is blue, the grass is green
> Can you spare a penny for Hallowe'en?

A monetary contribution is expected and rarely refused. When asked about the meaning of Hallowe'en, children combine a knowledge of the supernatural with a down-to-earth pragmatism; as one boy put it, 'Hallowe'en's the night when witches and toads come out – but we just do it for money.'

Children's activities on Hallowe'en clearly fall into the category of what Gluckman . . . has called 'reversals', or rituals in which customary hierarchies are inverted. The rites symbolise protest against the established order of adult–child relationships so that for a short time children are licensed to wreak revenge for their structural inferiority vis-à-vis the world of adults. The fact that the rites are restricted to one night in the year results in the reaffirmation of existing roles and may indeed serve to strengthen the existing hierarchy. Hallowe'en is also known as 'mischief night' in Staithes, and children get up to all kinds of general mischievousness, such as tapping on the windows of houses to frighten those inside or writing slogans in 'crazy foam'. Most adults indulge this sort of behaviour. For example, on Hallowe'en in 1975 some children tampered with and rearranged a 'fleet' of stacked lobster pots near the harbour. Next morning I saw the owner of the pots rearranging them. He informed me with a grin: 'you expect this sort o' thing on mischief night'. Such an act occurring at another time would have resulted in serious repercussions, leading to some form of punishment for the children concerned.

CHRISTMAS

The religious significance of Christmas in Staithes, as elsewhere, competes in pluralistic fashion with alternative meanings – gift-giving, card-exchange, spending, consumption, holiday-time, and so on. The meaning which Christmas has for the individual may therefore vary from a purely secular holiday to an important religious occasion which is felt to have been adulterated and perhaps devalued in the wider society. In Staithes the representative picture lies somewhere in between and once more a fusion of folk and official items can be shown to coexist. Beliefs and actions relating to Christmas are dispersed into three major institutional settings; the chapels and church, the family and, taken together, the pubs and the club. Christmas is surrounded by a different set of meanings in each, and while these may seem to be in conflict or to be mutually exclusive, research suggests that for most villagers the distinctions are blurred and 'Christmas' manifests itself in the activities of all three institutions.

Within the chapels, preparations for Christmas begin early. Both Primitives and Wesleyans hold their own Christmas fairs, where gifts and home-made products of various kinds are sold. These provide a useful boost to chapel funds and, as many people put it, 'make you feel that Christmas is on its way'. On Christmas Eve, in keeping with long-standing local practice, carol singers from both Methodist chapels tour the village in separate groups. This always brings out a large number of singers and is much appreciated by villagers. As one man put it, 'when I hear those singers coming round on Christmas Eve, then I know Christmas really is here'. Both groups make considerable effort to reproduce the imagery of a traditional English Christmas, eschewing the more recent carols in favour of old Methodist tunes and traditional folk carols. The Wesleyan singers dress in Victorian costume for the occasion, whilst the Primitives accompany their singing with an old portable organ. Both groups make a special point of singing at the houses of other chapel folk.

In recent years it has been the practice to hold a midnight service in one or other of the Methodist chapels, but this has only been poorly supported. The practice was initiated by the present minister but does not, so far, seem to have captured the imagination of local Methodists. Midnight Mass and Communion are held in the Roman Catholic and parish churches and both are well attended. Services are also held on Christmas Day in these churches, though not in the chapels.

Within the private sphere of family life, traditions and customs relating to Christmas are similar to those found elsewhere in our society. Great emphasis is placed upon card- and gift-exchange between friends and relations and considerable expense is incurred thereby. It is interesting to note the extremely large numbers of presents received by many children, since for those who come from long-standing 'Steeas' families, in particular, and who in consequence form part of an extensive kinship network, a large body of kin are represented as potential gift-givers. This became quite apparent during fieldwork whilst visiting various local families on Christmas Day, when the rituals of gift-exchange emerged as powerful agents of community maintenance. . . .

The Christmas activities in the public houses and social club in the village are essentially charitable. Each organises its own Christmas draw, or lottery, and the profits go towards buying hampers and Christmas gifts for the elderly. The pubs are frequently crowded on Christmas Eve and it is also the habit of many men in the village to visit their 'local' at lunchtime on Christmas Day. On both occasions the singing of carols is popular. As in the domestic sphere this is once again a time of intensive conviviality, with much buying of drinks and displays of generous sociability.

SUMMARY

The beliefs, practices and symbols associated with the annual cycle in Staithes indicate the interplay of communal factors with those of both official and folk religion. Emerging from this interplay is a complex pattern of sociability and religiosity in which important religious times are often those when villagers gather to celebrate not, for example, the birth or resurrection of Jesus Christ but rather the founding of the Sunday School or the building of the chapel. Such occasions are typically marked by concerts or special teas and not solely by a religious service; they have, in consequence, the overriding quality of being enjoyable for those taking part. Their importance, therefore, lies in the fact that they are underscored by communal rather than, say, specifically Methodist values; they are occasions for recalling past times and for reconstituting shared sentiments, often expressed in terms of an idealised view of village and chapel life in earlier periods.

David Clark, *Between Pulpit and Pew: Folk Religion in a North Yorkshire Fishing Village*, Cambridge, Cambridge University Press, 1982, pp. 106–9.

(d) Working-class attitudes in east London

Though Protestantism seems to have caused some rooting of individualism in Tower Hamlets (and television is probably topping up the culture with its modern variant, liberal pluralism), emphasis on belief as such in any analytical sense was generally absent. Asked if they believed in God, the interviewees did not (in their own words) distinguish between theism and pantheism, or bring up creation, omnipotence, omniscience, human free will and so on as themes. It was as if 'God' was taken for granted as a word and to *think* about it was strange.

There was more 'belief in God' than in other Christian ultimates, such as the divinity of Jesus and the existence of life after death. Few people denied the existence of God; the greatest disbelief, though more of a 'religious' than a secularist kind, came from some upper working-class men in the . . . sample [of those who had had children baptised in the Church of England]. (Perhaps relatively pious women attracted them.) The consensus was probably doubting belief, an ambiguity closer to experience than to conceptual rigour. Perhaps it was the impact of experience that made a good quarter of the replies develop into less positive statements. 'Well, there's only one God in the world . . . We don't see him.' No reference was made specifically to the Holy Spirit.

Some exceptionally differentiated statements included a reference to free will, and a distinction between 'God' and 'some great power' (in which the lift engineer believed). The Bethnal Green mother said, 'It's all according to what you think God is. You can't imagine a God sitting up there [laughs].' Three outsiders, the crippled man, the Anglo-Burmese, and the unemployed man with seven 'O' levels ('I believe in a power within everybody which I call the sub-conscious . . . The difficulty is in getting hold of it'), were also much more sophisticated than the others.

Their statements included fatalism (hardly predestination): 'I just believe there's a God of some sorts [laughs] I'm not too deeply into it – I just think there's something else that kind of moves us about and guides whatever your destiny. We take a path we don't really want to travel and yet we find ourselves on it . . .' 'God' was affirmed through denying 'atheism' and 'Allah'. A naïve psychological analogy was used: 'I think if you can pray to somebody he must be there.' The 'Almighty' was also 'the only one I'd turn to . . . for the strength to come back again' if 'I'm really down'. Prayer was mentioned by very many, seemingly largely in the context of asking for favours for oneself or others at times of hardship or distress. There was no 'Anglican' wordiness about taking a 'mature' view of an ineffable God.

Doubt was only once scientistic (the lift engineer fascinated by science fiction); and only once expressed through psychological insight (the SDP voter said people only want to believe in God because they would like to believe there is someone who is going to help them). Experience of suffering was much more important. (Here 'God' implicitly seems to be identified with an omnipotent being of love and compassion, not as a God, such as Allah, who transcends good and evil.) At least three-eighths of the interviewees were spontaneous in linking God to the experience of suffering or evil. 'I believe there's somebody there but then he's looking down in funny ways, he's doing things in funny ways.'

'It's hard to believe when you see all this suffering in the world,' said the 'nerve' hospital woman; the lift engineer said, 'I don't believe that if there was a God he could be so mean'; the road sweeper said, 'You've got Ethiopia'; the bingo-loving grandmother mentioned 'child murderers', saying, 'and you say, "Where is God?"' Other people said: 'Our first boy died of leukaemia. If there is a God, why let a child like that suffer?'; and, 'You're supposed to be with God all the time. So if you're with God, why are you suffering now?' The suffering mentioned related more to sympathy with others than to the self, and tended to be natural rather than obviously caused by human agency.

Some referred to pain expressed through religious allegiance. 'I think religion causes a lot of trouble, you know. The Irish and all that.' The Bethnal Green mother spoke of 'India: one lot went into the temple.' The cultural pluralism of television news seems to encourage a pessimistic impartiality.

Evil as an almost numinous force was only mentioned by the woman who said she had defrauded her employer: in prison with a child murderess, 'I had a good look into her eyes. She really looks evil, which I found sad because I thought, "You cannot help that." On the surface she's trying very hard to be good. But it'll beat her in the end, this evilness. She's not mad though.' She wondered if this was the devil, or to be understood psychologically. But generally suffering was not linked with evil to produce a symbiosis with theistic salvationist belief.

A positive link between suffering and the ultimate was suggested by only two people, both outsiders: the crippled man said 'God only gives you the cross to carry that you're able to carry'; and the Anglo-Burmese was the only subject to relate suffering to a Jesus who saves ('Jesus came to suffer what man suffered. He degraded himself'). The only other person to bring up Jesus in the context of suffering saw him 'as a human being really . . . not so much as a God'.

Only about a quarter of the interviewees seem to have believed Jesus was the Son of God. A naturalistic theme emerged: 'I believe-like he was there.' Jesus was 'just an ordinary person'; stories about him 'could be by Enid Blyton' (the Bethnal Green mother); and, 'He might have been a madman for all they know, and they believed in him. It's like that Billy Graham, because everyone believes that he's something really good, don't they?' The retired baker said it is 'only people's imagination that Jesus is the Son of God . . . Virgin Mary a virgin? No, my foot [laughs]. You must be joking. How can she be a virgin if she had a child? [laughs] I've put you on the spot, haven't I?' There was also an ethical theme; and even an ethical analogy: Jesus was God 'for all the good work he's done'.

Both samples seem to have been evenly split on the question of whether or not there is life after death, with roughly a third believing, a third disbelieving and the other third doubting. 'I believe there is a hereafter. But I don't know what it is. I just don't think. I don't puzzle me brains,' said the wife from Spitalfields. Three believed in reincarnation (the Anglo-Burmese, the lift engineer and the man who said he had once owned lorries). The roadsweeper did not believe 'in knocking' life after death because of one of his children's psychic experience. Incertitude was expressed by the bingo-loving grandmother ('Oh, I don't know about that') and the sixteen year old girl ('Well, I've never encountered it'). Down to earth disbelief was expressed thus: 'Once you're dead you're dead. You can't come back again'; and, 'Once you're gone you're gone.'

Geoffrey Ahern and Grace Davie, *Inner City God: The Nature of Belief in the Inner City*, London, Hodder & Stoughton, 1987, pp. 109–12.

(e) Throne, church and nation

All that has passed since the death of the King has caused deep reflections, at their deepest today, on the subtle connexion between the Throne and the faith of Englishmen. Most Englishmen do not go regularly to church. Many who do would find it hard, as recent controversies have shown, to swear belief in every article of the creeds which they there recite. Yet the sentiments evoked by the death and accession of monarchs have a quality which it is no impiety to call religious. They go beyond and beneath the bare externals of the ancient partnership between Church and State which has played so mighty a part in the making of England.

In constitutional theory the reigning Sovereign of the United

Kingdom is 'supreme in all causes both spiritual and temporal'. The spiritual and temporal headships are aspects of the same sovereignty. The established Churches of England and Scotland both acknowledge the royal supremacy; but the numerous nonconforming Churches long ago secured full independence, and the spiritual obedience owed by the Crown's Roman Catholic subjects to a foreign court is no longer regarded as a threat to social order or a derogation from royal authority. . . .

These are the externals; that there is a reality at once more lively and more subtle has been witnessed in the past week. Monarchy expresses more vividly than any other element in the constitution that conception of honour founded on service, of obedience freely given and repaid by diligent protection, which is the distinguishing mark of the Christian view of leadership. The King of England is not raised far above his subjects like a pagan emperor; he is not the object of a worship which sanctifies his caprices into divine commands. He is the liege lord of every one of his people; the honour he is paid is individual and the protection which he gives is personal. It is a remarkable fact that in Britain men honour their King by calling him a friend and find in the fidelity with which he performs routine duties, many of which call neither for heroism nor for extraordinary skill, a special reason for respecting him. Such a conception of sovereignty would be impossible outside the bounds of Christian civilization. It may be that modern theologians, rightly alert against the danger of allowing secular emotion to pass for religious belief, have lost their sense of the value of temporal loyalty as one approach to the understanding of religious truth. In this way, and always in the zealous practice of their faith, the Kings and Queens of England still play an indispensable part in the nation's spiritual life.

The Times, 15 February 1952.

Today Prince Charles and Lady Diana Spencer are married. The day is theirs. The royalty, prelates and dignitaries in St Paul's Cathedral, the horsemen, coachmen, bandsmen, footguards on the processional route and the ubiquitous security men who are their sharp and unsheathed doubles, the cameramen and commentators, the people who fill the streets, all these which make the spectacle are but the supporting cast. Even before the altar of the cathedral at this as at all weddings it is the couple themselves who make the marriage by their vows. However gloriously coped or royally laden, no other person present is more than an assistant, prompter, witness.

The day is theirs, and because it is theirs it belongs to the nation too. The nation is of old stock and new stock, mature, diverse, undrilled. Its people respond in many ways and the day belongs to all of them. It is not only for those who have woken from their bivouacs on the Mall, are crowding in to fill the streets, have been getting up their local revels, or have apportioned their day according to the television schedules. It belongs as well to those who feel that one more wedding picture thrust under their noses will make them scream, to company accountants gloomily reckoning the cost of yet another holiday with pay, and to those so moved by the occasion that they are off on a day-trip to Dublin or Boulogne for a seminar in republican studies. When Shakespeare chronicled the English monarchy he showed it in palaces, abbeys and battlefields. But part of the rich texture of his theme he found in Eastcheap, Gadshill and the orchards of Gloucestershire. The complicated and earthy sentiments their royal house evokes from the British people are comprised of more than awe and admiration.

The marriage of princes has always been the stuff of fairy tales and politics. The fairy tale is undimmed – a most personable prince, heir to a throne the most historic, secure and efficient in the world today, his bride young and beautiful and innocent of pomp – it is this and the spectacle in which it will be set that accounts most of all for the estimated three-quarters of a billion television watchers from Perth to Perigord and from Karachi to Calgary. The politics of the occasion are much changed from the days when the marriage of an heir apparent cemented a dynastic alliance and promised to exclude the disturbance of future rival claimants. The dynastic aspect of Prince Charles's marriage is unimportant, and the numerous and fruitful House of Windsor has already provided amply for uncontested succession. But there is a political significance of another kind in today's events.

The Crown in Parliament is the constitutional focus of unity in the nation; and of those elements it is the Crown that symbolizes unity without alloy. A nation does not, any more than a family, enclose the sum of its members' relationships, or exhaust their obligations and concerns. The world is wider. But like the family the nation is a primary unit in the construction of social order. Without coherence and inner loyalty it cannot function well. Its visible symbols of unity and loyalty are of much more than ceremonial importance.

The shocking and mysterious outbreaks of street violence this summer have shown how fragile civil order is. No one supposes troubles can be charmed away with a royal wand or smothered by royal sentiment. But today's ceremonies, symbolic of the nation's unity and symbolic in the ceremony of marriage of the realization of love, self-dedication and fruitfulness, are capable of refreshing the spirits of a people depressed by persistent economic malfunctioning and with new grounds for self-doubt suddenly presented to them.

The English throne is now identified with exemplary family life. That is one reason for the respect and affection in which it is held. Part of the public gratification in the royal wedding is in the prospect it affords of that character being carried forward into the next generation. The elements are present and the auspices good, but to fulfil its promise the marriage will need room to grow in mutual knowledge and happiness. For this as for all marriages that growth will be easier if external factors are conducive to it. The bride is eleven years younger than the prince. He is accustomed to thrive on a rapid round of public engagements and representative activities. She is not. Long years lie before them near or at the pinnacle of public attention. There is time and much to be said for the prince, when he resumes public duties with the princess at his side, to take an easier pace than he set for himself as a single man. They have a marriage to build and a family to make. They, their advisers, the press and the public should give them room to do it. For which we wish them 'quiet days, fair issue and long life, With such love as 'tis now'.

The Times, 29 July 1981.

The Commonwealth reveals its strength in many different ways. Any of you who attended or watched the events at the Commonwealth Games at Brisbane cannot have failed to notice the unique atmosphere of friendly rivalry and the generous applause for all the competitors.

In a world more concerned with argument, disagreement and violence, the Games stand out as a demonstration of the better side of human nature and of the great value of the Commonwealth as an association of free and independent nations.

The Games also illustrated the consequence of the movement of peoples within the Commonwealth. Colour is no longer an indication of national origin. Until this century most racial and religious groups remained concentrated in their homelands but today almost every country of the Commonwealth has become multi-racial and multi-religious.

This change has not been without its difficulties, but I believe that for those with a sense of tolerance the arrival and proximity of different races and religions have provided a much better chance for each to appreciate the value of the others.

At this time of the year, Christians celebrate the birth of their Saviour, but no longer in an exclusive way. We hope that our greetings at Christmas to all people of religious conviction and goodwill will be received with the same understanding that we try to show in receiving the greetings of other religious groups at their special seasons.

The poet John Donne said, 'No man is an island, entire of itself: every man is a piece of the continent, a part of the main.'

That is the message of the Commonwealth, it is also the Christian message. Christ attached supreme importance to the individual and he amazed the world in which he lived by making it clear that the unfortunate and the under-privileged had an equal Heaven with the rich and powerful.

But he also taught that man must do his best to live in harmony with man and to love his neighbours. In the Commonwealth, we are all neighbours and it is with this thought in mind that I wish you all, wherever you may be, the blessings of a happy and peaceful Christmas.

The Daily Telegraph, 28 December 1982.

(f) The changing face of Remembrance Sunday

Only once more this century after tomorrow will we in the United Kingdom find that we are making the same point on the clock in the same way as other rememberers in the Commonwealth. By calendar coincidence, tomorrow and in 1990 the eleventh hour of the eleventh day of the eleventh month brings a universal acknowledgement of all our war dead.

We dropped this specific time for this homage more than a generation ago, when the dead of the previous generation's world war were being honoured on Armistice Day. In 1946, we adopted the more convenient nearest Sunday as Remembrance Sunday, leaving others to go on in the older way; the Canadians to continue a public holiday on the eleventh, the Australians and New Zealanders to remember more especially Anzac Day but to continue to stop for two minutes on November 11, however inconvenient.

Passing years and fresher conflicts, as well as fresh attitudes to them, have contributed to the change of date, and to a change of form. We no longer refer to Central Powers, Armistice, Empire, Dominions and of course a King. We deleted patriotic hymns like 'I vow to thee my country' in favour of international ones like 'All people that on earth do dwell' and ones of awe like 'Judge eternal throned in splendour' for the more calm 'Blest are the pure in heart.' This year God becomes 'You' instead of 'Thou'.

Having moved the occasion once, and started to think more about our future and less about others' past, how long will we go on remembering the great wars at all? Having changed the content and style so much, how long will we go on saying we are 'remembering' the same thing that we as a nation were first called to remember in 1919? When those questions are asked, as they will be more often with the passing years, we will be reminded that already only one in ten of this country's population was born before the century's first great global conflict, and that well under half were born before the second began.

Whatever individuals' age, the essential national spirit of gratitude is still there in this age; the date and hymns have their place, but do not have the place. The spirit will show in faces at the Cenotaph tomorrow, and at other memorials and services throughout the country. Everyone will reflect on the three facets of remembrance; the acknowledgements of the living, of the dead and of God. The order of priorities may vary, as the date has, and as the elements of ritual have too. No matter. Christians anyway take from the death of a man they did not know personally a spirit of personal commitment. Even if for some tomorrow's event might just as well be at the Tomb of Warriors Unknown to them, many will still feel a call to a commitment through an international ritual. The passing of the years, and the changes of the calendar, do not diminish the call to a commitment, or the opportunity.

The Times, 10 November 1984.

(g) *Personal religious experience*

In most cases these experiences were self-evidently religious to those who reported them. Our question 'Why was your experience religious?', which followed if they had so defined it, was often seen as stupid or irritating. For these people, the very awareness of a presence seemed to carry with it a knowledge of who the presence was. A parallel may be the way that, when we meet a person familiar to us, there is no gap between seeing them and knowing who they are. One person's reply to our question was typical:

Because it was Jesus.

Other people made attempts to qualify their answer, though in effect merely confirming a recognition:

Because it falls within my set idea of religion; to do with Christ.

A thirty-three-year-old working-class woman recognizes where the words which she uses to express her experience come from:

When you're brought up that way, you just see things that way.

The experience itself almost always has the perceptual quality which was noted in the previous chapter. There is, however, a gradation from what is experienced as immediate recognition towards more reflective ways of interpretation. Asked why his experience was religious, one man says,

Probably because religion to me is a way of life which is influenced by a spiritual awareness.

For someone else,

It makes you feel there is a power you can call God or the Life Force.

Uncertainty about the orthodoxy of the experience comes through in the following comment:

When I think of religion, I think of Jesus and the God that you

*TABLE: 'WAS YOUR EXPERIENCE RELIGIOUS?'

The presence of God	100%
Answered prayer	100%
Meaningful patterning of events	73%
Presence of the dead	55%
A presence not named	43%
Premonitions	36%

* Table refers to responses from the Nottingham city survey and records the proportion of people reporting a particular kind of experience who classified it as 'religious'.

read about in the Bible. I don't really know if what is guiding us is that God.

The label 'religious' continues to be used by many whose interpretations would certainly not be considered as Christian orthodoxy, though familiar enough in Indian religion:

You're apparently making contact with something other than yourself, or with a deeper part of your own nature that you don't know about.

A woman who still calls her experience religious says:

In a very very loose definition, yes. Certainly I do believe it's myself, but I don't think it's my ordinary everyday self.

Finally amongst those who called their experiences religious, a very small group did so by elimination: 'It can't be explained in any other way.' The infrequency of this interpretation suggests that criticisms of the 'God of the gaps' have made a very deep impression.

For the group of people who rejected the label 'religious' as a description of their experience, the commonest reason was that it did not fit with what they understood by the word. Several accounts sounded very much as if they fell into the traditional category of religious experience, but not as defined by our informants. For example:

No! (This was personal) To me religion means a Churchianity study.

And,

I've never been very interested in religion. I suppose religion implies belief, and this was pure experience.

Or,

I don't believe in God; I disapprove of religions.

Premonitions, encounters with the dead and encounters with an evil presence were often ruled out of the category 'religious' on the grounds that they did not fit with the Christian picture as it had been taught. A surprisingly small number of people offered an explanation of their experience in naturalistic terms. Telepathy, which has a somewhat dubious status within orthodox science, was drawn upon, or simply 'psychology'. Thus,

> I believe it was a psychological process. At the time possibly I thought it was a god.

And,

> I'm fairly sure it's completely to do with upbringing.

David Hay, *Exploring Inner Space: Scientists and Religious Experience*, Harmondsworth, Penguin, 1982, pp. 149–52.

(h) *Rationality and secularization*

Fundamental to the argument . . . is the idea that cultural movements and ideological systems can become potent agents of secularization without involving conscious 'secularism', or indeed without having any direct bearing on the truth or falsity of religious faith. Any cultural development tending to preoccupy people with ideas, interests and knowledge bereft of supernatural, metaphysical, otherworldly assumptions, tends inevitably towards secularization. Thus to the extent that modern Britain has become a society preoccupied with technical skills, scientific knowledge, mundane goals and humanistic values, the Christian religion has become epiphenomenal within it; and this is true despite the fact that the skills, knowledge, goals and values in question are not, in most cases, inherently counter-religious. . . .

Religion's crisis of plausibility in modern culture, precisely because it reflects more or less unconscious, reflexive orientations of the mind rather than specific intellectual doubts, has more to do with this generalized, subtle assumption of rationality than with any other aspect of the modern world.

Aldous Huxley's 'Elinor Quales', of *Point Counter Point*, who found religious ideas and motives 'oddly incomprehensible', is a paradigm of modern areligious rationality. Able to admire genuine religiosity for its sincerity, she felt that 'it was all rather absurd and superfluous', for

> . . . she never remembered a time, even in her childhood, when she seriously believed what people told her about the other world and its inhabitants. The other world bored her; she was interested only in this. . . . Religion and, along with religion, all transcendental morality, all metaphysical speculation seemed to her 'nonsensical in precisely the same way as the smell of Gorgonzola seemed to her disgusting. There was no getting behind the immediate experience.

The immediate experience was itself complex, something shaped by the subtle realities of life in a modern environment, and the historian of secularization can only generalize about the specific relationship between this environment and religion's crisis of plausibility.

Clearly, however, an important aspect of the relationship has to do with the fact that the modern world is artificial rather than natural. It is a habitat fashioned by the human species for itself, autonomous (in many respects) from non-human influences. A hallmark of modernity is enhanced consciousness of human responsibility. Human self-confidence might wane, but the modern environment seems likely to remain hostile to traditional religious consciousness while ever optimists and pessimists alike share this historically novel sense of human responsibility. In John F. Kennedy's much-quoted words: 'Man holds in his mortal hands the power to destroy all forms of human poverty and all forms of human life.' Either way, the traditional 'salvationism' which seeks supernatural aid at the limits of human knowledge and power is denied authenticity. The old orthodoxy may be true, but in a modern environment it is certainly less plausible than ever before.

For the time is past, in modern societies, when *homo sapiens* was obliged, like other species, to live in direct and immediate harmony with the rhythms of nature, and to adjust both consciousness and behaviour to the unpredictability, bounty and scarcity of the natural world. Modern culture has been fashioned by a different set of adjustments. The modern child is brought up, in many cases, without a feeling of dependence on the tides or the seasons, the vagaries of weather, wind and harvest. The modern equivalents are almost exclusively matters of human contrivance: television programmes and railway timetables, institutionalized forms of entertainment, and the spectacle of an adult world dominated by the artificial rhythms of stock market, interest rates, wages policies, inflation and unemployment. The crises, failures and disasters of such an environment may, potentially, exceed those associated with what insurance brokers and religious believers still call 'acts of God', yet they are so patently human failures, aberrations in an artificial system, that they evoke no obvious metaphysical response or supernatural explanation.

The work processes of the modern age, rooted in the artificiality and man-made complexity of the production line and the machine, are the central pillars of its this-worldly rationality and its consciousness (or false consciousness) of autonomy. . . .

To avoid becoming itself secularized in such an environment, and at the same time to have an impact on its contemporary 'world', the modern Church must accept a prophetic relationship with the dominant culture. It must elaborate an effective critique of modern secular rationality. It must be as much counter-cultural as it is, inescapably, sub-cultural. The world may never be greatly influenced, but there will be accompanying counter-cultural movements supportive in the diagnosis of contemporary ills, if not in the kinds of remedies advocated. Indeed, the greatest of the modern prophets are at present secular in outlook, even although the triumph of their ideas would represent an emphatic reversal of modern secularization. Herbert Marcuse is a case in point. 'Industrial society', he has argued,

> . . . possesses the instrumentalities for transforming the metaphysical into the physical, the inner into the outer, the adventures of the mind into adventures of technology. The terrible phrases (and realities of) 'engineers of the soul', 'head shrinkers', 'scientific management', 'science of consumption', epitomize (in

a miserable form) the progressive rationalization of the irrational, of the 'spiritual' – the denial of the idealistic culture.

But however acute their message, however incisive their critique, it takes a convulsion in the mainstream culture before prophets cease to be mere voices crying in a wilderness. And it is perhaps an index of the extent to which supernatural religion had been relegated to the edges of modern consciousness that even Marcuse, for all his deep misgivings about the sterile rationality of modern Western culture, feels sufficiently uneasy about the traditionally taken-for-granted notion of the 'spiritual' to italicize the word in a stylized admission of diffidence.

Alan D. Gilbert, *The Making of Post-Christian Britain: A History of the Secularization of Modern Society*, London, Longman, 1980, pp. 63–6 (with cuts).

9
INTER-RELIGIOUS RELATIONS

T *he first three extracts illustrate the variety of Christian theological responses to other religions around the middle of the period. The Roman Catholic position received authoritative statement in a declaration by the Second Vatican Council in 1965 (a); conservative Protestantism is represented here by the writing of Sir Norman Anderson, an Evangelical Anglican (b); while John Hick here relates the development of his theologically pluralist position to his encounter with people of other religions in Birmingham (c).*

As the churches groped towards policies on other religions, some of the clearest thinking came from John Taylor, Bishop of Winchester from 1975 to 1985, a former missionary (d). Contact and dialogue gathered momentum in the early 1980s as illustrated by the opening entries from the diary of meetings with Muslims in Birmingham kept by Andrew Wingate, then on the staff of Queen's College (e). By the end of the decade the framework in which encounter was taking place was becoming clearer: guidelines from the Council of Churches for Britain and Ireland (first issued in 1981) were revised in 1991 (f), and can usefully be compared with the non-confessional statement produced by the Inter-Faith Network in the same year (g). Considerable scope for controversy remained however. In December 1991 an open letter expressing concern about inter-faith worship attracted the signatures of numerous Anglican clergy (h); some still emphatically saw people of other religions as a mission field (i).

There is still only a relatively small amount of material on this topic from non-Christian sources, but three examples are given here, a Hindu view of Christianity in the 1970s (j); and Jewish and Muslim reactions to plans for a Christian 'Decade of Evangelism' in the 1990s (k, l).

(a) The Second Vatican Council on Non-Christian religions

1 In our times, when every day men are being drawn closer together and the ties between various peoples are being multiplied, the Church is giving deeper study to her relationship with non-Christian religions. In her task of fostering unity and love among men, and even among nations, she gives primary consideration in this document to what human beings have in common and to what promotes fellowship among them.

For all peoples comprise a single community, and have a single origin, since God made the whole race of men dwell over the entire face of the earth (cf. Acts 17:26). One also is their final goal: God. His providence, His manifestations of goodness, and His saving designs extend to all men (cf. Wis. 8:1; Acts 14:17; Rom. 2:6–7; 1 Tim. 2:4) against the day when the elect will be united in that Holy City ablaze with the splendor of God, where the nations will walk in His light (cf. Apoc. 21:23 f.).

Men look to the various religions for answers to those profound mysteries of the human condition which, today even as in olden times, deeply stir the human heart: What is a man? What is the meaning and the purpose of our life? What is goodness and what is sin? What gives rise to our sorrows and to what intent? Where lies the path to true happiness? What is the truth about death, judgement, and retribution beyond the grave? What, finally, is that ultimate and unutterable mystery which engulfs our being, and whence we take our rise, and whither our journey leads us?

2 From ancient times down to the present, there has existed among diverse peoples a certain perception of that hidden power which hovers over the course of things and over the events of human life; at times, indeed, recognition can be found of a Supreme Divinity and of a Supreme Father too. Such a perception and such a recognition instill the lives of these peoples with a profound religious sense. Religions bound up with cultural advancement have struggled to reply to these same questions with more refined concepts and in more highly developed language.

Thus in Hinduism men contemplate the divine mystery and express it through an unspent fruitfulness of myths and through searching philosophical inquiry. They seek release from the anguish of our condition through ascetical practices or deep meditation or a loving, trusting flight toward God.

Buddhism in its multiple forms acknowledges the radical insufficiency of this shifting world. It teaches a path by which men, in a devout and confident spirit, can either reach a state of absolute freedom or attain supreme enlightenment by their own efforts or by higher assistance.

Likewise, other religions to be found everywhere strive variously to answer the restless searchings of the human heart by proposing 'ways', which consist of teachings, rules of life, and sacred ceremonies.

The Catholic Church rejects nothing which is true and holy in these religions. She looks with sincere respect upon those ways of conduct and of life, those rules and teachings which, though differing in many particulars from what she holds and sets forth, nevertheless often reflect a ray of that Truth which enlightens all men. Indeed, she proclaims and must ever proclaim Christ, 'the way, the truth, and the life' (John 14:6), in whom men find the fullness of religious life, and in whom God has reconciled all things to Himself (cf. 2 Cor. 5:18–19).

The Church therefore has this exhortation for her sons: prudently and lovingly, through dialogue and collaboration with the followers of other religions, and in witness of Christian faith and life, acknowledge, preserve, and promote the spiritual and moral goods found among these men, as well as the values in their society and culture.

3 Upon the Moslems, too, the Church looks with esteem. They adore one God, living and enduring, merciful and all-powerful, Maker of heaven and earth and Speaker to men. They strive to submit wholeheartedly even to His inscrutable decrees, just as did Abraham, with whom the Islamic faith is pleased to associate itself. Though they do not acknowledge Jesus as God, they revere Him as

a prophet. They also honor Mary, His virgin mother; at times they call on her, too, with devotion. In addition they await the day of judgement when God will give each man his due after raising him up. Consequently, they prize the moral life, and give worship to God especially through prayer, almsgiving, and fasting.

Although in the course of the centuries many quarrels and hostilities have arisen between Christians and Moslems, this most sacred Synod urges all to forget the past and to strive sincerely for mutual understanding. On behalf of all mankind, let them make common cause of safeguarding and fostering social justice, moral values, peace, and freedom.

4 As this sacred Synod searches into the mystery of the Church, it recalls the spiritual bond linking the people of the New Covenant with Abraham's stock.

For the Church of Christ acknowledges that, according to the mystery of God's saving design, the beginnings of her faith and her election are already found among the patriarchs, Moses, and the prophets. She professes that all who believe in Christ, Abraham's sons according to faith (cf. Gal. 3:7), are included in the same patriarch's call, and likewise that the salvation of the Church was mystically foreshadowed by the chosen people's exodus from the land of bondage.

The Church, therefore, cannot forget that she received the revelation of the Old Testament through the people with whom God in his inexpressible mercy designed to establish the Ancient Covenant. Nor can she forget that she draws sustenance from the root of that good olive tree onto which have been grafted the wild olive branches of the Gentiles (cf. Rom. 11:17–24). Indeed, the Church believes that by His cross Christ, our Peace, reconciled Jew and Gentile, making them both one in Himself (cf. Eph. 2:14–16).

'Declaration on the Relationship of the Church to Non-Christian Religions', *The Documents of Vatican II*, New York, Corpus, 1966, pp. 660–4.

(b) The uniqueness of Christ

[T]he Christian faith is either itself false or 'casts the shadow of false-hood, or at least of imperfect truth, on every other system. This Christian claim' – as Stephen Neill insists – 'is naturally offensive to the adherents of every other religious system. It is almost as offensive to modern man, brought up in the atmosphere of relativism, in which tolerance[1] is regarded almost as the highest of the virtues. But we must not suppose that this claim to universal validity is something that can quietly be removed from the Gospel without changing it into something entirely different from what it is. The mission of Jesus was limited to the Jews and did not look immediately beyond them; but his life, his method and his message do not make sense, unless they are interpreted in the light of his own conviction that he was in fact the final and decisive word of God to men. . . . For the human sickness there is one specific remedy, and this is it. There is no other.'

This seems to me to be the clear import of the teaching of the Bible. . . .

The non-Christian religions seem to me to resemble a patchwork quilt, with brighter and darker components in differing proportions. There are elements of truth which must come from God himself, whether through the memory of an original revelation or through that measure of self-disclosure which, I cannot doubt, God still vouchsafes to those who truly seek him. But there are also elements which are definitely false, and which I, for one, cannot doubt come from the 'father of lies' – whose primary purpose is not so much to entice men into sensual sin as to keep them back, by any means in his power, from the only Saviour. Yet again, there is much that could best be described as human aspirations after the truth, rather than either divine revelation or Satanic deception. . . .

But now, in Christ, the one eternal God has actually become man. He has not merely visited humanity, he has taken our very

---

[1] Tolerance as a social policy is a lesson we have, happily, at least begun to learn. To attempt to *force* on others what we believe to be true is manifestly wrong. But this sort of tolerance should not be confused with 'relativism', or the intellectual flabbiness which sees no essential distinction between truth and error.

nature. Now there is only one teacher, one Lord, one shepherd, one mediator. He has a name which is above every name. 'In no one else can salvation be found. For in all the world no other name has been given to men but this, and it is by this name that we must be saved!' So the attitude of the Christian to men of other religions can only be the attitude of the 'witness who points to the one Lord Jesus Christ as the Lord of all men . . . The Church does not apologise for the fact that it wants all men to know Jesus Christ and to follow him. Its very calling is to proclaim the Gospel to the ends of the earth. It cannot make any restrictions in this respect. Whether people have a high, a low or a primitive religion, whether they have sublime ideals or a defective morality makes no fundamental difference in this respect. All must hear the Gospel.'

J. N. D. Anderson, *Christianity and Comparative Religion*, London, Inter-Varsity Press, 1970, pp. 94, 109, 111.

(c) A pilgrimage to pluralism

[My] own experience, working in philosophical theology, has been one of continually expanding horizons as the investigation of one problem has brought another larger problem into view. . . .

But another major challenge to religious faith was now looming up over the horizon, namely that posed by the diversity of apparent revelations. If what Christianity says is true, must not what all the other world religions say be in varying degrees false? But this would mean that the large majority of mankind, consisting of everyone except the adherents of one particular religion, are walking in darkness. Such a conclusion would be acceptable within a Calvinist theology, according to which much, perhaps most, of the human race is already doomed to eternal damnation (*Westminster Confession*, III.7). But in wrestling with the problem of evil I had concluded that any viable Christian theodicy must affirm the ultimate salvation of all God's creatures. How then to reconcile the notion of there being one, and only one, true religion with a belief in God's universal saving activity?

A move at that time to Birmingham, with its large Muslim, Sikh and Hindu communities, as well as its older Jewish community, made this problem a live and immediate one. For I was drawn into the work which is variously called 'race relations' and 'community relations', and soon had friends and colleagues in all these non-Christian religious communities as well as in the large black community from the Caribbean. And occasionally attending worship in mosque and synagogue, temple and gurdwara, it was evident that essentially the same kind of thing is taking place in them as in a Christian church – namely, human beings opening their minds to a higher divine Reality, known as personal and good and as demanding righteousness and love between man and man. I could see that the Sikh faith, for instance, is to the devout Sikh what the Christian faith is to the sincere Christian; but that each faith is, naturally enough, perceived by its adherents as being unique and absolute. Visits to India and Sri Lanka, amounting together to nearly a year, mainly to study Hinduism and Buddhism, further revealed something of the immense spiritual depth and power of these two oriental religions. Without ever being tempted to become either a Hindu or a Buddhist I could see that within these ancient traditions men and women are savingly related to the Eternal Reality from which we all live.

An important clue to an understanding of the world religious situation came from Wilfred Cantwell Smith's important book, *The Meaning and End of Religion*, first published in 1962 and already now a modern classic of religious studies, with its convincing critique of the concept of 'a religion' and of the notion of religions as contraposed socio-theological communities. We ought instead to think of the religious life of mankind as a continuum within which the faith-life of individuals is conditioned by one or other of the different streams of cumulative tradition. From this point of view it is not appropriate to ask, Which is the true religion? For a true relationship to God may occur in the lives of people in each of the great religious traditions. With the problem in its older and insoluble form having thus been dismantled it was possible to develop, in *God and the Universe of Faiths* (1973), the idea of a 'Copernican revolution' in our theology of religions, consisting in a paradigm shift from a Christianity-centered or Jesus-centered to a God-centered model of the universe of faiths. One then sees the great world religions as different human responses to the one divine Reality, embodying different perceptions which have been formed in different historical and cultural circumstances.

This paradigm shift involves a reopening of the Christological question. For if Jesus was literally God incarnate, the Second Person of the Holy Trinity living a human life, so that the Christian religion was founded by God-on-earth in person, it is then very hard to escape from the traditional view that all mankind must be converted to the Christian faith. However, the alternative possibility suggests itself that the idea of divine incarnation is to be understood meta-phorically rather than literally, as an essentially poetic expression of the Christian's devotion to his lord. As such, it should not be treated as a metaphysical truth from which we can draw further conclusions, such as that God's saving activity is confined to the single thread of human history documented in the Christian Bible. The alternative approach, which sees the incarnational doctrine as a basic metaphor, is supported by a variety of considerations arising in the modern investigation of Christian origins; and others had reached essentially the same conclusion from the point of view of New Testament and patristic studies. Accordingly a group of us met for occasional discussions to write what became *The Myth of God Incarnate*, intending to bring the idea of divine incarnation, which had long been something of a *shibboleth* in British church circles, back into the light of rational discussion.

John Hick, *God Has Many Names*, London, Macmillan, 1980, pp. 4–6.

(d) Race, culture and religion

The Bishop of Truro, I beg to move:

> 'That this Synod recognizes that the emergence of a multi-racial and multi-cultural society lays upon the Church the duty to use the opportunity for the enrichment of our national and personal life.' . . .

The Bishop of Winchester (Rt Rev. J. V. Taylor): I beg to move as an amendment:

> '*Leave out* "a multi-racial and multi-cultural society" and *substitute*: "a society which comprises different racial, cultural and religious groups".'

I support very strongly the contents of the report from the Board for Social Responsibility. It is immensely important that our Church should show that it accepts the pain of the truth as expressed in *The New Black Presence* and that it goes on to commit itself to respond positively to that challenge. It is also immensely important that our Church should stand solidly with the British Council of Churches in that body's witness against racialism, racialism in its more outspoken and in its more covert, unacknowledged forms.

The purpose of my amendment is to bring deliberately into the open the fact that ours is a society in which citizens are adherents of different religions as well as members of different races and cultures. The existence of religious minorities presents us with both problems and opportunities which are distinct from those that arise from the presence of racial and cultural minorities, and should not be lost from sight or evaded.

Therefore, I want to strengthen and enlarge the thrust of the motion by adding the religious factor to the racial and cultural. This could be done simply by inserting 'multi-religious' before or after 'multi-racial' or 'multi-cultural', but I am glad that the Bishop of Truro has already pointed out the greater simplicity of my form of words, in which I also use the word 'groups'. That is an important word, because the two documents before us make it clear that our society does not merely contain individuals who reflect these differences but communities that will go on embodying those differences in their corporate consciousness.

I am aware that the omission of the specific reference to religious differences is probably deliberate in the minds of some. The British Council of Churches from the inception of its Community Race Relations Unit has tended to subsume religion under the general head of culture. The first reason is that it wants these matters to be dealt with as issues of human rights and not of religious differences. The second is that it does not want to arouse the fears and aggressions that always surround the question: 'Is this or is this not a Christian country?'

I can appreciate those arguments, but in fact the religious issue is a distinct element in our situation and continually raises its head and intrudes. For example, some years ago the use of redundant churches as places of worship for other religious communities came up, and there were those in the Unit at that time who at first seemed to imagine that this would be dealt with quite coolly in terms of property on the market and a quite non-discriminatory sale, or even on the basis of a humanitarian concern for the needs of minority groups. But the Unit found itself compelled to research into all sorts of theological questions and take account of religious emotions.

To subsume religious differences under the general head of culture is essentially a sociological way of defining religious affiliation. It is a true way and it is properly humbling for us as Christians to take note of sociological insights, but it is still a very partial way, and if we pursue it we shall be blind to many other aspects of our problems.

So I want to argue on three counts the inclusion of specific reference to religion and religious differences. First, it will help us to recognise that minorities have religious rights and expectations as well as social, political and judicial rights. This will challenge us to care for the moral and spiritual nurture – to refer back to yesterday's debate – of all the children in the realm, whatever their family religious background may be. . . .

I recall the remarks made to me by a convert to Christianity from Islam, a man I met in Pakistan. He said with a deep sadness: 'The problem of all my people is that hardly any of us have ever met Christ. We have only met the Crusaders.' We must realise that the Crusades are an event in history that can cause a different point of view from that of Western Europe. There were those who saw it from the opposite point of view. I am well aware that in addition to a cross-shaped sword there were also sickle-shaped scimitars and that on both sides there was the guilt of reaching for the sword. But if we believe in the Gospel, it is the cross of the humiliated, suffering, self-giving

Christ that constitutes our power – and nothing else. We must think out the theology of those who witnessed to that cross before the members of other faiths, and to another kind of aggression. This will compel us to go on wrestling with the theological questions posed to the Church by the religious experiences and the religious devotion of those amongst us who are of other faiths.

The second reason I want to include the reference to religion is to keep the distinction between cultural assimilation and religious corrosion. 'Culture' is the right word for us to use today. 'Subcultures' will be more accurate in another generation. In our pluralist society there will not only be distinct communities but assimilation into a new pluralist culture. This is inevitable, just as all the different racial groups in the United States, while retaining their separate identities, are nevertheless becoming increasingly American. We shall always have a predominant culture in this nation, and its tap root will be Christian, or the old Christian. It is hard for Muslims to adapt to such a culture and realise that it will not be possible for their community to have the total Islamic law operating within the wider State. But they have done so in India, just as practising Jews have done so in Britain. The Jews demonstrate that assimilation into an overall culture with Christian roots can take place without the loss of their distinctive religious faith. The Sikhs, Muslims and Hindus in our midst need to be reassured that that can happen to them also.

So we must keep religious pluralism as a distinct issue from cultural pluralism in order to ensure that the inevitable assimilation can take place without secularisation.

The third reason I want to keep the distinction in our motion is to keep clear the distinction between religious and cultural identities, for our own sake as a Church. When we talk about our Christian religion here it must not be identified in our minds with the folk religion or the folk residuum of the English culture. Our Christian religion is the religion of millions of Asians, Africans and Latin Americans. They have their cultures – they are theirs, not ours – but their religion is ours. We are impoverished as a Church because we so blandly forget them. I welcome the reference to our enrichment through a greater openness in our discourse with other faiths here in this nation. But we must also remember the need for our openness in discourse with other Christians in other cultures than our own. This is another reason we must not confuse religion with culture. For the sake of our liberation from our proud self-isolation as a Church, we must distinguish between religion and culture.

If we are to deal with the theological problems raised by a pluralist society, why do we not turn to those theologians in Asia in particular who for generations have been living as a Christian minority in a Hindu culture and have insights and answers that we badly lack and could have done with in several recent books? By the same token, we must remember that the religion of the Bradford Pakistani is an international faith also. Indeed, his religious identity is likely to retain that international character far longer than his cultural identity does. Meeting of religions is not the same as the interaction of cultures.

The amendment was put and carried.

General Synod of the Church of England: Report of Proceedings, Vol. 8, No. 2 (1977), pp. 535, 544–7.

(e) *Encounter in practice*

1 November 1983: We have decided as a group to try to make a worthwhile and sustained contact with some local Muslims. I go down to the Islamic centre, which is in the inner-city parish area where I am on the staff, taking with me one of our women students, who is the leading student in our group. It is in a highly concentrated Asian area, and is the centre for cultural, social and religious activity which are all inter-related for a Muslim. We are greeted warmly by a tall, thin, bearded Pakistani. His name is Zaheer. I ask for the co-ordinator of programmes, whom I already know, a retired colonel from the Pakistan army. We are told that he has gone back to Pakistan. I am reminded immediately of the difficulty of keeping up sustained contact. However, we explain who we are and what we want, and, in a short time, we have planned a series of meetings on various subjects, and have been told that they will be 'taken', by a British convert, much learned in Islam, somebody to whom they clearly defer. I make it clear to Zaheer that we do want the participation of born-Muslims too, and he assures me that he will be there, and others from Pakistan. We then go on to ask about his work, and he tells us that he is enjoying it there, co-ordinating programmes and doing social work. But he is on a government employment 'scheme' and so he has only another three months' work more since, after a year, he will be replaced by another person – just when he has gained experience and is really into the work! However, he is resigned to this, and has much to get on with. He is already teaching in a mosque school in the evening, when he finishes at the centre. He will find other voluntary work to do in the community, and will also be freer to pursue his Islamic studies. He came to Britain as a teenager, and worked in engineering for some time, before becoming redundant in the general recession. He went back to his home country, in order to deepen his faith and understanding, which he did quite systematically. He had then come back here, having married, and is now settled and happy. He is quite delighted when we show interest in his school and family, and invites us to visit both.

17 November 1983: We hold the meeting, planned above, on 'prayer'. There is considerable interest in the college, and about 15 of us cram into the small room in the centre, along with the European Muslim speaker, Zaheer, and two others from Pakistan. I have emphasized to the European, whom I have met in preparation, that we are interested in 'dialogue'. But ominously, there is a conspicuous blackboard! It is very hot in the room, with all of us sitting on the floor. After introductions, the speaker takes over, and lectures for over an hour, at the end of which the blackboard is covered in Arabic, which none of us know! It is very informative about Islamic spirituality, but not what could be called 'dialogue'!

Tea was then served by the Pakistanis, which was the only contribution they were able to make to the evening, since they deferred entirely to the speaker's learning. I learnt afterwards from Zaheer that the European was a convert from Catholicism; he had become a Muslim partly at least to shock his parents, as an act of revolt more telling than becoming a Protestant! This came out even more when we had general discussion after tea, which turned into our asking questions, which he answered in a way that showed the superiority of Islam at every point, and also showed he was reacting to a particular form of Christianity, which he assumed was the only form and which appeared to us very much one of his imagination. However, he would not be corrected, nor was he really interested in listening, though he remained both polite and humorous. In the end I called the meeting to an end, and the students left, feeling that there had been no real meeting, and with their prejudices about Islam and its dogmatism confirmed. I felt a little discouraged about where we had started!

1 December 1983: As a follow-up to the previous meeting, we visited the neighbourhood mosque in the largely Asian area of Sparkbrook. Attached to it is a school and a book shop. As always, I wonder at how they can be so welcoming, and so patient with our questions. I ask about this, and they say they feel a clear calling to do something for community in the area and further afield, and opening themselves up to those from the majority community is one way of doing this. Up to 400 children study here two hours an evening, five days a week. We are taken on a tour of their classrooms, and one of our students remarks afterwards that it is like crossing a frontier between continents, walking in from a run-down Birmingham street to find oneself on the North West frontier. We spend time with different classes, and are surprised at the number of girls who are pursuing Urdu, Arabic and Islamic studies. I wonder about the virtue of studying Urdu, since few of them speak it outside the class. And indeed this is a question increasingly occurring to some of those responsible for the teaching; Arabic is crucial because of the Qur'an, and that and teaching about Islam in English may well become the pattern in the future. Many of the students are concerned about the educational method, and wonder how these traditional methods of rote learning contrast with what they are experiencing at day school, by Western methods. All are impressed by the commitment of those involved.

We sit then through the prayers, our women students being allowed to remain at the back, as we witness about a hundred or more men performing their evening prayers. I feel, as always, the beauty and the symmetry of their movements, and the universality of them, as I think of South Indian villages where they follow the same pattern of prayer.

Prayer flowed into relaxed discussion, and we were there for two more hours, and shared tea and biscuits. We talked of education. They were not resentful that little was done in most schools for religious education, but they felt things had improved in some ways. One man said that he had been at school some time ago, and when they asked for a place to pray in, they had been directed to the lavatory. Another, at college, had to pray in his car. But things have greatly improved, and also the Muslims have realized that education is primarily the responsibility of the Muslim community and their families. This is where nurture lies. And Christians should accept the same thing, and nurture children in the Bible and Christian thought and practice, when they are in the community, rather than at school. We feel the strength of their argument, when we think how weak Christian nurture is in so many Christian families and churches! We also wonder whether their own children will always be so co-operative, as they get more and more influenced by their environment here.

2 December 1983: I and my student took up the invitation of Zaheer (see 1 November). We met him waiting for us, outside his house mosque, on a dark winter evening that made the dreary urban surroundings particularly bleak. But large numbers of Muslim children were coming and going, and his welcome and obvious delight that we had come made us feel at home. He exhibited his pupils and their skills to us – they were clearly devoted to him – and then rushed us off to another place where he teaches, less than two miles away, but, in complete contrast, in one of the wealthiest areas of the city. Here, five children gather each evening, members of an extended family, and as bright and shining as the silver and brass ornaments which surround them on all sides. The two fathers have made their money 'in Saudi' and now own a video business. Their wives share the housework, one looking after the children, while the other goes to teach. Zaheer, though from such a different background, is very much accepted and loved by the children, and he clearly loves them. The parents respect him for his wisdom and skills. The four boys put on their caps and recited in turn, their sister sitting amongst them. Meanwhile, the mothers talked with us freely, in a way that could not easily happen in South Asia. They emphasized the importance of understanding, and gave, as an example, the question of a Muslim having four wives, so often raised by Westerners. This they saw as a protection for the woman, who would otherwise be bereft if a husband dies in war or famine. This was seen by them as a means of giving security to women.

Andrew Wingate, *Encounter in the Spirit: Muslim–Christian Dialogue in Practice,* Geneva, World Council of Churches, 2nd edn., 1991, pp. 8–11.

(f) Christian guidelines on dialogue
1 PRINCIPLE I

DIALOGUE BEGINS WHEN PEOPLE MEET EACH OTHER

1.1 People of other faiths do not live in books, but in houses or flats. They wait for buses, look after children, and suffer from backache. They probably know as much or as little about their faith as an average Christian. They may be more aware of being in a minority in Britain, so may have to explain their beliefs from time to time.

1.2 These other people are not simply units of a system. When we speak about other faiths, we need to realise that in the end there is no Hinduism, there are only Hindus. We do not meet Islam or Buddhism, we only meet a Muslim or a Buddhist. It is when people meet, not systems, that dialogue begins.

1.3 This Principle sounds so obvious that some people would leave it out. The trouble is, many people do. They talk and think about members of other faiths, without having truly met a single one. This is especially easy for Christians, or any believers who tend to mix mostly with people of their own belief. . . .

1.4 Once we meet, we realise that Muslims, Hindus, Sikhs or Jews, or whoever we are meeting, are not what we thought. Many of the inherited stereotypes, the images we have subconsciously absorbed, the assumptions we have built up over the years, are simply wrong. What we used to have in mind when we thought of a Muslim, a Hindu or a Sikh does not conform with what we find when we meet Zia or Jyoti or Bhupinder. There are no text-book Buddhists or Jews. There are only people. . . .

2 PRINCIPLE II

DIALOGUE DEPENDS UPON MUTUAL UNDERSTANDING AND MUTUAL TRUST

2.1 Christians must avoid misleading and hurtful terminology. Real meeting takes place only when the participants, as in a marriage, listen carefully to what each has to say to the other. Any attaching of prior labels to other people, such as 'unbeliever', 'heathen' or 'pagan' is not only offensive but also stifles conversation. It devalues other religions and diminishes the Christian claim to be an expression of God's universal love. It makes authentic witness impossible. 'You shall not bear false witness against your neighbour' (Exodus 20:16).

2.2 Christians may not lightly or thoughtlessly dismiss other religions as human attempts to reach God with nothing of God's grace in them. The gifts of the Spirit at Pentecost included not only tongues to speak, but ears to hear, the mighty works of God (Acts 2:11). When a Christian listens to a person of another faith, new discoveries are made. For example, Klaus Klostermaier's Hindu friend, Gopalji, told him, 'It is not we who choose our God, it is God who chooses us' (*Hindu and Christian in Vrindaban*, 1969, p. 84). This recalls St John's Gospel 15:6, 'You did not choose me, but I chose you'.

2.3 Partners in dialogue should be free to define themselves. Dialogue should allow participants to describe and witness to their faith in their own terms. 'Our popular misunderstandings of other people's faiths, and theirs of ours, is one of the most noxious of social and religious poisons. It hurts a Muslim just as much to be told that Islam is a religion of violence as it angers Christians to be told that Christianity is morally permissive. Both ideas are wildly inaccurate, and as long as we live with such caricatures our relationships will suffer' (*With People of Other Faiths in Britain*, United Reformed Church, 1980). Statements about any other religious faith or community should be checked against authentic descriptions or declarations made by members of that community. . . .

3 PRINCIPLE III

DIALOGUE MAKES IT POSSIBLE TO SHARE IN SERVICE TO THE COMMUNITY

3.1 Human community, like orchestral music, depends on the co-operation of all its parts. When the parts consist of people with differing religious faiths, dialogue offers a way towards harmony. . . .

4 PRINCIPLE IV

DIALOGUE BECOMES THE MEDIUM OF AUTHENTIC WITNESS

4.1 Any relationship which passes beyond conventional politeness will involve 'speaking the truth in love' (Ephesians 4:15). The mutual trust which can arise between people of different faiths is likely to lead to questions which begin 'What do you really believe about . . . ?', or confessions of faith which start 'Well, when we reach this point I can only say . . .'. In dialogue we are bound to speak about the bedrock of our faith, and that is not going to be the same as that of the other person. In dialogue there is no way that we can honestly avoid witnessing to our faith. The complaint of some critics that dialogue replaces evangelism is unfounded.

4.2 This form of authentic witness, meeting at depth, depends on each person listening as well as speaking. We are given two ears, but only one mouth, said the Rabbis. Listening always comes first, even when we believe we have the greatest truth in the world to communicate.

4.3 The principle of listening before speaking avoids some in-authentic forms of witness. Many people of other faith communities say they have learnt to dislike or even to fear missionaries and evangelists. All too often in the past 'dialogue' between Christians and other faiths has taken the form of coercion. But God draws free persons, who respond to the divine call. Christians have a centuries-long backlog of barriers to break down. For authentic wit-ness, they need to become ever more closely followers of Jesus Christ, whose life offers an example of dialogue.

Committee for Relations with People of Other Faiths, *In Good Faith: The Four Principles of Interfaith Dialogue: A Brief Guide for the Churches*, London, Council of Churches for Britain and Ireland, 1991, pp. 1, 3, 5, 6.

(g) A statement on inter-religious relations

We, the affiliated organisations of The Inter-Faith Network for the United Kingdom affirm that:

- The United Kingdom is a religiously diverse society: it is only when we recognise and accept this that positive inter-religious relations can be built.
- Differences in terms of ethnicity, class, gender and language also affect our inter-religious relationships, as do the bonds of history, religion and kinship between communities here and overseas.
- We need to find ways of more adequately reflecting both our common citizenship and our religious diversity in the framework of our national life.
- Society is impoverished when religious perspectives on life are excluded or marginalised. A recognition of the extent to which

we share a range of common values and ideals can contribute to a wider sense of community.

- At the centre of all our traditions is a concern for peace but religious people have too often brought suffering, discord and distrust to one another and to the wider community. Constructive inter-religious relations are vitally important to the well-being of our society.

- In overcoming religious prejudice and stereotypes the education system, the media, and our own communities all have important responsibilities. We recognise the need for us to represent accurately the traditions of others within our own religious communities.

- It is only by meeting with those who live another religious tradition and by listening to their beliefs, stories, insights, and experiences that we can learn from others as well as about them, and build relationships of trust through mutual understanding.

- Our sense of community is deepened when we take common action towards agreed social goals, with sensitive consultation at all stages.

- We cannot demand that others engage in inter-religious relations only on our own terms but have to meet with others as they really are.

- We recognise the need to respect the integrity of each other's inherited and chosen religious identities, beliefs and practices. To be able to live by our traditions, share our convictions, and act according to our consciences are freedoms which we all affirm and which we wish the framework of our society to uphold. But these freedoms must never be abused in order to pressurise others into changing their religious identities, beliefs or practices.

- Openness to one another and honest self-criticism are essential to a maturing of inter-religious relations. If we are to transform and enrich our relationships we need to avoid demeaning or disparaging another person's religious tradition. We must always beware of comparing the practice of another tradition with the ideals of our own.

- Sharing our religious traditions in an atmosphere of respect leads to mutual enrichment and transformation. It will lead us to find ways in which we can together build a better society.

Inter-Faith Network, *Statement of Inter-religious Relations in Britain*, London, The Inter-Faith Network for the UK, 1991, Summary.

(h) *Inter-faith worship*

Believing that Jesus Christ the incarnate Son of God, is both God and man, the unique revelation of God, the only Saviour and hope of mankind – we, the undersigned members of the Church of England, are concerned that his Gospel shall be clearly presented in this Decade of Evangelism.

We desire to love and respect people of other faiths. We acknowledge and respect their rights and freedoms. We wholeheartedly support co-operation in appropriate community, social, moral and political issues between Christians and those of other faiths wherever this is possible. Nevertheless, we believe it to be our Lord's command that his Gospel be clearly proclaimed, openly and sensitively, to all people (including those of other faiths) with the intention that they should come to faith in him for salvation.

In this we affirm no more and no less than the Apostolic and Anglican tradition. Article XVIII says: 'Scripture doth set out unto us only the Name of Jesus Christ, whereby men must be saved.'

In consequence we are deeply concerned about gatherings for interfaith worship and prayer involving Christian people. These include the Interfaith Commonwealth Day Observance in Westminster Abbey and other such events in some of the cathedrals and churches of England, whether they refer to Jesus Christ or whether such references are minimal or excluded.

We believe these events, however motivated, conflict with the Christian duty to proclaim the Gospel. They imply that salvation is offered by God not only through Jesus Christ but by other means, and thus deny his uniqueness and finality as the only Saviour.

These events are frequently deeply hurtful to those in this country who have come from other religions into the Christian faith, and also to Christian minorities in other lands, both of whom have frequently experienced persecution from the other faiths, and especially where such faiths are unwilling to tolerate conversions or the existence of minority Christian communities.

We, therefore, appeal to the leadership of the Church of England to oppose and, where possible, prevent such gatherings for interfaith worship and prayer in the Church of England and to seek to discourage them elsewhere. We also call upon Christian people to pray that this will be done.

Our objections to interfaith worship are theological, spiritual and, indeed, constitutional. Recognizing that the Christian faith belongs to all races and nations, we deplore objections to such worship arising from racism or nationalism.

To avoid all misunderstanding, we wish to make it clear that we seek the good of all, of whatever faith, and obedience to our Lord Jesus Christ obliges us to proclaim him as uniquely Lord and Saviour for all.

'Open Letter to the Leadership of the Church of England', *The Church Times*, 6 December 1991, advertisement.

(i) Taking the Gospel to Muslims

Carey College is an inter-denominational initiative which began under the auspices of the Evangelical Missionary Alliance in 1985. The aim of the Carey College programme is to challenge, encourage and offer training to Christians to reach out to their Muslim neighbours in friendship evangelism.

AN OPPORTUNITY FOR CHRISTIANS

. . . A Christian response from the church will bring the Gospel to these previously unreached people who need the salvation which only Christ can give.

Carey college aims:

• to serve church groups, Christian fellowships, missionary

societies and those in training for full-time service, by providing a course of study to help them in their witness to Muslims

- to give understanding about Islam
- to encourage small groups to pray and study together with the help of a leader
- to encourage such groups and individuals to engage in friendship evangelism.

To achieve these aims Carey College has produced study materials for use by church and other groups, and individual correspondence students.

Carey College Prospectus, c. 1992.

(j) A Hindu view of Christianity

The present century has experienced yet another Hindu–Christian encounter, this time in the West between Hindu immigrants and Christians, and interest in Hinduism is increasing in the Western world. Most Hindus in England are from India, particularly from Gujarati business families and the enterprising Punjab. Recently many Hindus have also come from African countries. They remain, on the whole, hardworking and pious people. Their tightly-knit communities, however, are not religion based – as with Jews or Muslims – but cultural-linguistic and based on ethnic background: their Indian or even their state heritage. In towns with large Indian communities Indian associations are seen, but it is not so common to see a Hindu association. While small groups of Jews and Muslims will often establish synagogues and mosques where they settle, religion is mainly a private affair for the Hindu and he feels no urgency about building a temple. Only a few large towns like London and Manchester can boast of a Hindu temple, and often they display pictures of Christ and Mary. There is no special day like the Sabbath for the Hindu and he is not necessarily required or even recommended to visit a temple. A Hindu will often visit a church, and praying in a church is as satisfying to him as praying in a temple, although the solemnity and orderliness of the Sunday Service do

not have the same appeal, accustomed as he is to gaiety and sponta-
neity in congregational worship. Hindu prayer in public takes the
form of music, song, and even dance – all in a spirit of abandoned
joy and devotion. Hindu festivals too are many and joyous, sometimes even boisterous as in *Holi* – the festival of colours. This is
why Christianity sometimes appears cold and gloomy, like a noble-
minded ethical system that takes the fun out of religion. 'And.Jesus
cried' is often the most moving phrase in the Bible for Christians,
but as one agnostic, E. M. Forster, after witnessing a Krishna festival, pointed out: 'One was left . . . aware of a gap in Christianity:
the canonical gospels do not record that Christ laughed or played.
Can a man be perfect if he never laughs or plays? Krishna's jokes
may be vapid, but they bridge a gap.' This gap has perhaps been
recognized by the Church which is to some extent adapting herself
to meet the demand of the times. Such things as the introduction
of pop hymns in some churches here and in America is a welcome
change. One notices too that Christianity is moving away from the
old puritanism and its emphasis on Original Sin. The Christian
insistence on man's sinfulness and the need for repentance are somewhat repellent to the Hindu who aims rather at dispelling ignorance
and thus realizing the Vedantin dictum *Aham Brahmasmi* (I am
God). Perhaps the belief in ignorance rather than in sin, amounts
to the same thing as belief in sin, but the difference is one of
attitude. Hindus generally know far more about Christianity than
Christians do of Hinduism – but then the English of course are
known among foreigners for their insulation (and we have not yet
sent our missionaries to the West!). Often, however, the Hindu
is more knowledgeable about Christianity than English Christians
themselves, and this symptom of the indifference towards religion
of people who are nominally Christian certainly seems strange to
the Hindu and the Indian Christian alike. The Catholic practice
of canonization after a saint is long dead, the officially laid criteria
for determining sainthood and the general disbelief in miracles, are
also noted by the Hindu who often follows a living saint, or saints
– who are so by popular acclaim – and many Hindu saints are
well known for performing miracles, sometimes publicly. But

perhaps the most important difference lies in the pious Christian's insistence on belief in God or Christ as *an act of faith* necessary for meriting grace, and the Hindu's assertion that God or Christ must be and can be tested by personal experience, and that belief will automatically *follow* experience. The former Christian view is no doubt the more humble, but the Hindu would point out that it represents a 'steep and thorny way to heaven'.

Debjani Chatterjee, 'A Hindu looks at Christianity', *Expository Times*, Vol. 88, No. 6 (1977), pp. 179–80.

(k) *Jews and Christian evangelism*

'Bishop Decries the Conversion of Jews' was the headline of an article in *The Times*. Richard Harries, the Bishop of Oxford, has always been very sensitive to Jewish feelings, never more so than on BBC 1's *Heart of the Matter* broadcast on March 31. 'Singling out the Jews for a hard campaign of conversion is a very unfortunate way of understanding the Christian mission to the world'. The Church, he also said, should reflect on its 'terrible history . . . which prepared the way for the Holocaust'.

On the same programme, the diametrically-opposite point of view was argued by the Rev. John Fieldsend of the Church's Ministry Among the Jews: 'I find it offensive that the Church should be told that because of the Holocaust, we should not try to share the Gospel with Jewish people'. He considered it an 'act of anti-Semitism' to withhold the Gospel from the people who gave Jesus to the world.

ULPS Council members at their last meeting, expressed concern about the Decade of Evangelism and its impact upon the Jewish Community, and asked for guidance from the Rabbinic Conference on how to approach this Campaign. The Rabbinic Conference is considering the matter, but has asked me to offer my own views for your consideration. Rabbis, like laymen, will take a deeply personal view on how serious a threat evangelism is to the Jewish Community, and so a consensus will not be possible. A full exploration of the subject can help to clarify our views and feelings on this subject and it is in this spirit that I start the discussion.

The differing views of Bishop Harries and Mr Fieldsend are helpful starters, because both are true. This is not strange as they arise from different perspectives. Bishop Harries has the gift of imagination which allows him to put himself into the position of the Jew. His conclusion is how can Christians who have caused Jews such suffering in the name of Jesus, now offer him as their source of spiritual salvation; how can Jews who are proud of their heritage, be persuaded that the avenue of their redemption can come through an individual under whose symbol of the crucifix so many of their ancestors met persecution and death? Mr Fieldsend, on the other hand, is a Jewish-born Anglican Minister, who sees the faith in Jesus as the key to the spiritual world of fulfilment; how then withhold its message from the Jews?

We, as members of a minority people and faith, struggling for survival, cannot but be more sympathetic to Bishop Harries than to missionaries such as Mr Fieldsend. Accordingly we must do everything possible to assist Jews to find spiritual fulfilment in their own traditions – and not in Christianity or, for that matter, in any other faith.

We should, however, realise that the main thrust of the Decade of Evangelism is not directed towards Jews but to passive and unaffiliated Christians. Of course, there are the fringes of the Evangelical Movement – the 'Mission to the Jews', and the 'Jews for Jesus' who sincerely believe that they are doing God's work by winning converts among Jews. It will break our hearts when we see families divided through their efforts, especially when we feel responsible for this failure to hold on to these lost Jewish souls. But the numbers will be very small and an analysis of those individuals will show that there were extreme personal emotional pressures in their lives which made a religion based on a suffering Christ, so attractive and compelling.

The challenge to Liberal Judaism is to make it more emotionally satisfying as well as intellectually acceptable to individuals in need of spiritual anchors in life. At the end of the day, we are in danger of losing more as a result of the assimilation which arises out of apathy and the seductions of the materialist world, than those declaring the 'truth' of Jesus.

Personally, I believe it is a fruitless and counter-productive exercise for us to condemn evangelists to the Jews, so long as they do not employ bribery or emotional blackmail to further their cause. Far better is it for us to teach with greater emphasis and clarity those Jewish truths and values which have led hundreds of generations of Jews to risk and even suffer death to maintain an identity which has been precious to them and beneficial to humanity. This is the most productive way forward and the one to which we should address our attention.

Sidney Brichto, 'What to do about Evangelism', *Union of Liberal and Progressive Synagogues News*, Vol. 18, No. 9, May 1991, p. 2.

(1) A Muslim perspective

Years ago my community would have regarded interfaith meetings with great suspicion; now they are becoming the accepted thing. Relations between our communities are generally good. We would like the other religions to accept Islam as a legitimate faith community which has a very valuable, sensible system of ethics and belief. We believe in the same One God as you believe in. We have the same commandments as you and the same ethical system. Our community is developing its own western milieu but we are from the same Abrahamite religion. We share so much. The real division is now between secularism and religion. Between people who are committed there is an affinity of faith; they can and do talk to each other.

Generally speaking, Islam has looked on Christianity with greater respect than people realise. The Holy Qur'an says that at the time of the Prophet, the Christians were the people who were the nearest to the Muslims. These good relations have been interrupted by the Crusades and various conflicts; Christians in the West have become very suspicious of Islam. The colonial era produced further attacks on Islam – actually occupying our land and invading our hearts by trying to turn us into Christians. More recently the churches have become committed to freedom of conscience and social justice. Nowadays we can look on Christians with more trust and less suspicion.

But in Britain there is always the worry for the Muslims that our children will become once again objects for conversion. Many are an easy target because their parents are uneducated immigrants; schools do not have a Muslim environment. In some of the church schools we find the head teachers attempting to convert the children quite openly by saying that the children are being handed over by the parents to be taught the doctrine of the school. Happily, this is not very common. But such an attitude does exist and it does frighten parents. Now the Church has changed and is much more accepting of Islam as a legitimate religion which must be respected. Such an understanding is growing and the pronouncements from the Vatican are certainly helpful.

My immediate reaction to the announcement of the decade of evangelism was alarm and fear that the churches with all their financial, political and educational power would be engaging in an unequal battle. We do not have the organisation, the financial backing or the political power. However, I have been reassured by some Christians that the aim of the decade is not conversion. Others may not agree, but they are on the fringes. The decade is about developing the spiritual meaning of Christianity for Christians. This will make the meaning of Christianity much more evident and is not something to fear – for the essential message of Christianity is the same as the essential message of Islam. If this is the idea behind the decade then I should want to be part of it and present God for all to see, to set God against our common enemy, the tide of secularism which is continuing to grow. I hope this spiritual renewal is successful because that would be reassuring to us; we would then expect more sympathy and more understanding.

I am always willing to debate the issue of the Good News and of Christ because I know something of Christianity. In this College, with our courses in comparative religion, we are always attempting to raise awareness of other faiths. We invite our people to study and respect the faiths that exist in this country. What worries me is that the people who evangelise do not understand us; they go to the people who are vulnerable. Of course, there is a duty for the Christian to put the Good News across to others. It is the same for me as a Muslim. I must share my faith with other people. But to persuade a person to leave their community can have tremendous consequences – especially for youngsters who do not understand the implications of what is happening.

Zaki Badawi, 'Presenting God for all to see', *The Month*, September/October 1991, p. 370.

10
CHURCH, STATE AND POLITICS

At the opening of the post-war era the Archbishop of York, Cyril Garbett, envisaged that the Church of England might well find itself obliged within the foreseeable future to accept disestablishment (a). In the event, however, change was slow and piecemeal and the majority of a commission which reported in 1970 proposed modification rather than severing of the ties between Church and State (b). Elsewhere in the United Kingdom the churches also agonised over their place in national life: in the late 1980s the Church of Scotland approved a report from its Church and Nation Committee which recalled and reaffirmed its commitment to devolution (c); while in Wales (as elsewhere) a Christian nationalist vision was qualified by recognition of its exclusive potentialities (d). It was in Northern Ireland that the linkages of religion to political conflict were most apparent: Ian Paisley's brand of Christianity was assimilated in varying ways by his Ulster Protestant followers (e). Christianity also provided a basis for a search for reconciliation in the province, but entrenched positions were not readily shifted, as Cahal Daly, Roman Catholic Bishop of Ardagh and Clonmacnois (later Cardinal Archbishop of Armagh), was all too well aware when he spoke about violence in 1971 (f).

In the mean time the social teaching of the churches had its political impact. William Temple's ideas served as an inspiration for long after his death in 1944 (g). Leading churchmen, notably Michael Ramsey, Archbishop of Canterbury from 1961 to 1974, and Lord MacLeod of Fuinary, a former Moderator of the Church of Scotland, were concerned by the increasingly restrictive policy on immigration apparent in the decision of Harold Wilson's Government in 1968 to legislate to exclude Kenyan Asians (h). By the 1980s social concern was gaining significant ground in the churches, as was evident at the Roman Catholic Pastoral Congress in 1980 (i); in the writings of David Sheppard, Bishop of Liverpool from 1975 (j); in the wider reawakening of evangelical social engagement (k); and in an anxiety to build the 'Kingdom of God' amongst down to earth social realities (l).

Interpretations of the political implications of Christianity diverged sharply, however, as is evident when the address of the Prime Minister, Margaret Thatcher, to the General Assembly of the Church of Scotland in 1988 is read alongside some of the other items printed here (m). A more specific critique of the allegedly 'leftist' leanings of the Church of England was subsequently published by the economist Rachel Tingle (n).

(a) Post-war prospects for establishment

The Church should frankly face the dangers of its position. At the moment Parliament has no desire to exercise active control over the Church or gratuitously to interfere in its concerns. But within a few years a neutral attitude may have changed into hostility, and the Church will find it is then useless to ask for reform or for greater freedom. It should not acquiesce any longer in a relationship with the State which might suddenly prove to be inconsistent in practice as well as in principle with religious freedom. Churchmen are so accustomed to the existing relationship between Church and State that they fail to see how strange and anomalous it appears to other Churches especially those which attach importance to religious freedom. For long Free Churchmen have viewed our position with surprise and dislike. But members of the ancient Orthodox Churches are also perplexed. I can give two examples of this. When in 1943 I visited Moscow I discussed with the Patriarch and other leading ecclesiastics the freedom possessed by our respective Churches. They found it difficult to understand how a Church could be really free when its bishops were appointed by the Crown. I did my best to explain how great was the freedom we actually enjoyed, but I fear that my explanation did not satisfy them, for they kept returning to the point that the Crown in appointing to vacant sees is advised by the leader of a political party who need not be a Christian. A year later I met the Orthodox Synod at Athens; for local reasons its members were then especially interested in the subject of ecclesiastical Courts and asked me about our practice. They did not conceal their surprise and perplexity when I told them that not only did laymen preside over our Courts, but that the final appeal from them on matters of doctrine and worship was to a Court of lay judges appointed by the Crown. Sooner or later by a vote in Parliament, by a decision in the Courts, or by some conflict over a moral problem, it will be brought home to all that the spiritual freedom we now undoubtedly enjoy is on sufferance, and is really inconsistent with the strictly legal relationship between Church and State. The Church is drifting towards disaster if it allows year after year to pass without making a determined and sustained attempt to readjust a position inherited from ages when the Church and the Nation were one, but which now in a time of rapid change has become fraught with danger.

Through its constitutional assemblies the Church should agree on the reforms required to reconcile freedom with establishment. Agreement on a policy is an essential condition of success. Unanimity is impossible to expect, there will always be vociferous minorities who will claim that they speak for the whole Church. It should however be possible after full discussion to secure large majorities in the Convocations, the Church Assembly, and the Diocesan Conferences for four major reforms. First for some machinery by which the Crown could assent to proposed changes in worship without reference to Parliament. Secondly for the establishment of Courts which are really spiritual, and from which an appeal to the Civil Courts for 'redress' would be made only when the ecclesiastical Courts had failed to observe the rules under which they act. Thirdly the Church should be given at some point the right to be consulted in the appointment of its chief officers. Fourthly the Convocations should receive license to frame and enact new Canons. Reform on lines such as these would vindicate the freedom of the Church [which] would still retain its connection with the State.

If however the Church cannot agree to these reforms, or if Parliament after due consideration refuses to accept them, then Disestablishment and Disendowment will be unavoidable.

Cyril Garbett (Archbishop of York), *The Claims of the Church of England*, London, Hodder & Stoughton, 1947, pp. 196–7.

(b) Church and State in 1970

RECOMMENDATIONS

211 1 All matters affecting the worship and doctrine of the Church should become subject to the final authority of the General Synod, with certain safeguards provided.

2 To this end, a Measure should be promoted to ensure that the authority to order forms of worship already granted in part by Parliament should be granted finally to the General Synod, under certain safeguards . . .

3 The same Measure should empower the General Synod to pre-scribe by Canon the forms of subscription to the doctrine of the Church, and to interpret by Canon the formularies of the Church.

4 A Committee or Electoral Board, representing both the diocese concerned and the Church at large, should be formed to present the Church's view when a bishop is to be nominated for election.

   We are not agreed on how such a Committee or Board should take its place in the constitution of the Church.

   (a) Some of us recommend that the Committee should advise the Crown on the names of persons, through the Prime Minister.

   (b) Some of us recommend the part of the Prime Minister should cease, and that the Electoral Board should elect the bishop, and present his name directly to the Sovereign.

5 The choice of suffragan bishops should be brought under the system proposed in either (a) or (b) above, with the proviso that no one should be chosen as suffragan without the consent of the diocesan bishop.

6 Leading members of other Communions, besides the bishops of the Church of England, should be invited to sit in the House of Lords.

7 No one should be excluded, by reason of being a minister of any Church, from his right to stand as a candidate for Parliament and to take his seat in the House of Commons.

8 Even in matters concerning church property the General Synod, in its legislation, should be critical of any proposed Measure which will necessarily lead in time to further Measures. It should be the eventual aim of the Synod to restrict Measures to fundamental changes of constitution or laws of property which affect secular rights, and to avoid all Measures which touch minor matters or matters where the intervention of Parliament is manifestly unnecessary . . .

9 To this end, the General Synod should undertake a programme of legislative consolidation and revision.

CONCLUSION

212 In view of these recommendations, it may be asked, what would be left of 'establishment'? We are not much moved by this question, noticing that when church rates were abolished in 1868, or when the Local Government Act became law in 1894, or when the Enabling Act became law in 1919 (and doubtless on several other occasions), some said that it was equivalent to 'disestablishment'. If we persuade men to get away from loose general terms and consider actual laws, we shall have done a part of what we should like to do.

213 We think that a significant proportion of thinking people in this country would accept the proposition that the Church of England ought to stand further apart from the State than it now does. They would accept this for all sorts of different reasons, and what they mean by it would vary very much. But we have little doubt of that much widespread and basic agreement, though we are the last people to suppose that there would be unanimity on the question.

214 If this is so, there are obviously two possible destinations; (1) a total severing of the historic links, as in Ireland a hundred years ago and Wales fifty years ago; or (2) a form of legal polity resembling that which prevails in Scotland.

215 We have not recommended a total severing of the historic links; first, because we think such a programme to be impracticable in the present state of opinion; and second, because even if such a programme was practicable, most of us would not like it, though we should not shrink from it if the State decided it to be either wise or politically necessary. The people of this country value various features of our polity, and will not favour too much tampering. The people of England still want to feel that religion has a place in the land to which they can turn on the too rare occasions when they think that they need it; and they are not likely to be pleased by legislation which might suggest that the English people as a whole were going unChristian.

216 We have considered a Scottish solution, and reprint in Appendix E a part of what was written for the Howick Commission. What we recommend bears a distant resemblance to the Scottish Establishment. But we have not recommended an imitation of Scotland, because the circumstances which we meet are different from the circumstances of Scotland. The history of Church and State in the two countries has been very unlike since the Reformation if not before. We cannot take a system of law which has arisen in another part of Britain and impose it on England as though it fitted the facts, or the memories, of English life. We have to take English ecclesiastical polity as we find it and then see how it can be adapted.

217 Some people like England to have 'an established Church'. These persons value it for England's sake, less for the Church of England's sake. They think that the Christian tradition and the English inheritance go hand in hand. They do not want changes which end, or which jeopardise, a national recognition of religion, even if such a recognition can often be declared to be symbolic. They do not see how such a national recognition can continue if men make far-reaching proposals for change in the structure of what exists. They have little desire to extend the liberties of the Church, for they believe that the Church has already the liberties which it needs, in teaching, in choice of men, in worship, and in pastoral care.

218 Some people think the words 'established Church' to be an anachronism. Not that it is empty of meaning. But they find it used by different people with different meanings. They see a body of ecclesiastical laws, and ask which laws need altering, and, if they need altering, why? But they do not want to end a national recognition of religion. They want to adapt and amend the laws, so that the recognition may be wider, and less exclusive, and more ecumenical. They are deeply concerned, also, for what they see as the proper liberty of the Church in the things which concern its highest interests in worship or pastoral care or choice of men. One or two features of the law inherited from the past they tend to regard as fetters. They vary between feeling these fetters to chafe intolerably, and finding them comfortable now that we have been used to them for so long.

219 Some people think that 'an established Church' is bad. The State is secular, and the Church will do best not to be linked with it except as all voluntary bodies need its protection. These persons also are concerned for what they regard as the proper liberties of the Church. But even if the Church gained every liberty within a special nexus of law, as in Scotland, they would still think it bad. Only so, they think, will justice to a mixed population be seen to be done. Only so will the layers of the past be stripped away and reality prevail. Thus they have adopted the principles of the Independents in the age of the Reformation, that Church and magistrate must be sundered; forced thereto not by the religious axioms of the Independents, but by the plural nature of modern society.

220 In the light of such differences of approach, we have tried to recommend what the majority of us think to be desirable and practicable in what we judge (so far as we are able) to be the present state of the public mind.

221 The Church should concern itself first, and indeed second, with the poor and needy, whether in spirit or in body. We have been conscious that the first task of a Church is to look outwards, and that you have required us to look inwards, upon the constitution of the Church of England. We have steadily tried to remember that

a constitution is not designed for the sake of a constitution. By lapse of years, or by change of human society, all systems of law must sooner or later be adjusted or become outmoded. We have recommended those adjustments which we think to be good in present circumstances. But we have tried to remember that gospel, sacraments, charity do not become outmoded and that these are the things that matter finally.

Church and State: Report of the Archbishops' Commission, London, Church Information Office, 1970, pp. 64–7.

(c) *The Church of Scotland and devolution*

BACKGROUND

3.1 The 1988 General Assembly instructed the Committee 'to give urgent attention to the question of:

(*a*) the democratic control of Scottish affairs;
(*b*) the creation of a Scottish Assembly;
(*c*) and to the means by which a national referendum on devolution might be effected.'

Events over the past years have given this whole subject added urgency and interest.

3.2 Despite the fall of the Scotland Act, creating a Scottish Assembly, in 1979, the question of the government of Scotland has continued to be raised by political parties and other voices in Scottish society during the 1980s. Ten years after the devolution referendum, in 1989, there is growing support for the Campaign for a Scottish Assembly's proposal, in its document 'A Claim of Right for Scotland', to set up a Constitutional Convention to resolve this question. Once again the Church of Scotland is being asked to consider its own response to these developments. Historical and theological reflection leaves the Committee in no doubt about the nature of the Kirk's response.

3.3 It is time for the Church of Scotland to embody its own theological and constitutional principles in its response to the question of the democratic control of Scottish affairs. This has not always been the case.

3.4 While consistently calling for an effective form of self-government for Scotland within the framework of the United Kingdom since 1948, the Church of Scotland has tended to base its support for this policy upon its own representative role as a national institution responsive to Scottish opinion and responsible for the nation's moral and spiritual well-being. The weakness of such an approach, outlined in the Church of Scotland submission to the Royal Commission on the Constitution 1969–1973, became evident in the 1979 devolution referendum. Without an agreed theological and constitutional basis for its position, the Church of Scotland fell officially silent on its consistent support for self-government, paralysed both by internal disagreement on how that position might legitimately be expressed in the referendum campaign, and by its vulnerability, as a representative national institution, to fluctuations in Scottish opinion on the referendum proposals.

3.5 While the Church's position on the government of Scotland has been a consistent and honourable one for forty years, the lesson is clear. The Church of Scotland can only make a distinctive and effective contribution to the current debate about the government of Scotland if it grounds its position in its own historic theological and constitutional convictions as a national Kirk within the Reformed tradition. Nothing less will do. A growing number of Scots are looking to the Kirk to make such a contribution. In 1988, the Scottish historian Professor Christopher Harvie stated to a Church of Scotland conference on faith and Scottish identity, 'God's will – for Church and Nation – is within our grasp. It is for you to decide whether the Kirk has the heroism to step forward and lead.' The heroism of a Reformed Church derives from its unflinching commitment to fundamental principle. Underlying the proper party political debate and electoral contests on the question of the government of Scotland, there is a fundamental constitutional question which it is proper for the Church to address. . . .

CONCLUSION

3.18 It is the Committee's view that a theologically grounded constitutional principle of limited sovereignty embodied in the proposals arising from a Constitutional Convention and a national referendum offers the best way forward to realise the consistent wish of the General Assembly to see the democratic control of Scottish affairs through a Scottish Assembly established with the support of the Scottish people. It is only by recognising the claim of principle that we can remould our constitution and bring about a change in the foundations of our political institutions that will ensure a stable rational ground for our Scottish democracy, within the framework of the United Kingdom and under the Crown, within Britain and Europe, into the twenty-first century. It is only by grounding its concern for the democratic control of Scottish affairs on the claim of principle that the Church of Scotland can fulfil its calling in national life to speak prophetically to the state and nation on this question. It is time for the Church of Scotland to add its voice in our generation to the historic call of the Reformed faith in Scotland and Europe for constitutionally limited government under the rule of law, and to the Gospel's call for justice among the nations under God the Father Almighty, Maker of heaven and earth.

General Assembly Reports, Part 1, Edinburgh, Church of Scotland, 1989, pp. 144–5, 151.

(d) *Nationhood and religion in Wales*

[In] 1938 [the poet and playwright Saunders Lewis] told a public meeting:

> In his speech in Berlin at the time of the crisis Herr Hitler said that England should, before criticizing him because of his treatment of the Jews and other things in Germany, look after her own problems in Palestine and Wales. The reference by Hitler to Wales was omitted from every report published in the English newspapers!

(Reported in *Y Faner* 25:10:38,
reprinted in *Y Faner* 28:10:88) . . .

[A]ttempts at a definition of Welsh nationality which makes assimilation relatively easy meet resistance from those whom it is desired to assimilate, viz, non-Welsh-speakers. In Germany, Hitler, and many more moderate German nationalists, adopted a different definition of nationality which simply made it impossible for certain groups, such as Jews, successfully to become German, however much they attempted to assimilate. Thus the 'Jewish Question' was in reality a 'German Question' . . . – the question being 'Who is (or can be) German?' In the same way, Saunders Lewis was clearly being tempted to start speculating as to who is (or could be) Welsh.

That such a respected nationalist as Saunders Lewis was tempted by such a form of nationalism, based on the exclusion of certain racial groups from the nation, makes it no surprise that in the 1980s also such a definition found favour with some otherwise reasonable people. Let us turn to the field of the National Eisteddfod in 1987, for the Eisteddfod field is often the best place to feel the pulse of Welsh Wales, and indeed of Welsh Christianity. On that field each year the Evangelical Movement of Wales distributes a pamphlet entitled *Hedyn* (Seed). This publication is usually a vehicle for a proclamation of evangelical Christianity and a call to repentance and conversion. The front page of the 1987 edition shows a map of Wales and a Biblical verse – 'O my God, . . . behold our desolations' (Daniel 9.18). The map points to ten different places in Wales which are evidently particular examples of Wales's desolation. The places are labelled as follows:

- Halal slaughterhouse
- Mormons
- Jehovah's Witnesses
- Orange People (from the illustration, this is evidently an Eastern religion and not Irish Protestantism)
- Sacred superstition in the cult of the Virgin Mary
- Sponsoring Muslim studies (this at St David's University College, Lampeter)

- Hindu Temple
- Witchcraft
- Revival of Popery
- American 'enlightenment' Temple

The references to Roman Catholicism led to the pamphlet's being withdrawn half way through the week, but by then it had already revealed the nature of the nationalism of at least some in the Evangelical Movement – anything which was not pure Welsh Protestantism was 'desolation'.

Like the Archbishop of Wales in his 1988 sermon quoted earlier, they believe that Wales is essentially Christian. But they follow the logic of their belief far further than would the Archbishop. For they conclude that religious faiths other than Protestant Christianity do not enrich the nation, rather, by definition, they despoil it. So it is no surprise that as this essay was being written there were renewed reports of a recruiting drive by the National Front in Wales. *National Front News* called on the young people of Wales to join the 'national revolution', 'a spiritual rebirth which struggles for the benefit of the people'.

Gethin Rhys, 'The Divine Economy and Political Economy: the theology of Welsh nationalism', in Roger Hooker and John Sargant, eds., *Belonging to Britain: Christian Perspectives on Religion and Identity in a Plural Society*, London, Council of Churches for Britain and Ireland, 1991, pp. 68–9.

(e) *Ian Paisley through the eyes of his daughter*

The criticisms were bound to come. Life is like that. It is best to meet them with caution, trying to discern the constructive from the destructive, reacting to each according to their merit. But it is necessary not to let other people's opinions become your guide, otherwise you turn yourself into a pawn. People don't like you to assert yourself.

The fact is that there is a cultural trend in Ulster which I doubt will ever be altered. Here, if you do not agree with someone who has a very rigid and impossibly traditional view, you aren't just wrong, you are a traitor! You aren't just of a different opinion, you are an apostate. Tolerance and forgiveness have been hijacked by insipid clergy and willowy politicians. Tolerance is only tolerance when you can hold an opinion or a belief strongly yet accept the other's right to differ as strongly. It is no test or evidence of tolerance to accept someone's view when you are apathetic or have no strong opinion. Therefore true tolerance has no need to avoid truth. Forgiveness is something which ultimately only God can instigate. We may have the ability – more often due to His grace in us – to have a forgiving spirit towards those who have wronged us, but forgiveness can only be granted when repentance is evidenced. The world has hailed and been inspired by the forgiving attitude of many who have suffered unjustly, not only in Ulster. Those Christians, for example, behind the Iron Curtain, who, after horrific mental and spiritual torture, have survived to relate their experiences, present a rare insight into the power of God in an individual life. . . .

One reason for Dad's falsely belligerent image is that he is not afraid to recognise that contention is the name of the game in both politics and religious matters. We are to contend for our faith. The Christian's lifestyle is not one of inoffensive weakness, it is one of proclamation, and in many ways, it is one of reclaiming what the Church has let slip away. Dad is a defender and a contender for the faith he cherishes. This does not make him a rough man of war, nor an unreasonable man of attack. The greatest contention any Christian knows is not with human beings. It is what Paul describes as a wrestling with principalities and powers, with spiritual wickedness in high places. It is a constant moulding of our natures to do right as opposed to wrong; to be submissive as opposed to wilful, to be Christ-like as opposed to selfish – to be meek. 'Meekness is not weakness.' Dad is a meek man – he is dynamite under control if you like. The control of his life is in God's hands. His goals have fixed his direction and his destiny. Meekness under Christ, I have seen in Dad's life, means strength and ability to be your best. . . .

'Your father's a strong man,' I've often been told. 'He won't let us down.' He is a strong man, I know – but perhaps I choose to view his strength in a different light from many of his admirers who seem to find only its advantages in Protestant rhetoric. When my father dies, someone will no doubt repeat his words and give them a tone of strength appealing to the heart of staunch Ulster loyalism. I will not care to hear those vain repetitions then, any more than I care for them now, but I will always desire to embrace, to hold with all the love I possess for him as my father; the memory of his strength that performed as much and did well that which he put his hand to. It frightens me sometimes that young men who take a pride in their 'contending for the faith' and in calling themselves 'Paisleyites' don't take a pride in developing the meekness which begets true strength. It is not easy to be read a lecture from someone on the intricacies of your father's beliefs and character and informed in the same breath that they 'know' your father. It seems their preconceived ideas make sure they will never 'know' because it is easier to follow blindly than to think! The responsibilities of leadership are vast. My father seeks to make his people think, not just follow. Always there will be some who are content just to follow, but for those who take his leadership and think, the wealth of their future will not lie in rhetoric but in the truths he has sought to uphold.

Rhonda Paisley, *Ian Paisley, My Father*, Basingstoke, Marshall Pickering, 1988, pp. 109, 142–3.

(f) An Irish Catholic perspective

We gather in this holy place at a time when our minds are still numbed by recent shocking explosions and sick and sickening violence in the North of Ireland. We came to pray for peace; and our prayer must now take on a new intensity and urgency, for the danger facing our country at this time is desperate. . . .

It would be foolish in the extreme to think that, if the violence were to continue or intensify, it could be confined indefinitely to the North of our country. What we are witnessing in the North is a possible future for our society in the Republic too. . . .

To speak . . . of the unfinished business of 1916 as though the task were the completion by violence of a national liberation which the struggle of fifty years ago failed to complete, is a crass and perilous misreading of the facts. The 'unfinished business', so far as the North is concerned, is to persuade nearly a million Protestants to enter into democratic union with the rest of the population of this island. It is a noble ideal, which the remaining three and a quarter millions of us, North and South, Catholic and Protestant, as well as the millions of our kin abroad, will never cease to foster and promote by every peaceful and democratic, relevant and rational and Christian means. But who in their sane minds will say that we could bomb a million persons into wanting union with us? Or that we would coerce them into unwilling union, even if we could? When persuasion is of the very essence of our problem, to speak of bombs and bullets is simply irrational. Further violence is monstrously irrelevant to the real national problem in the North. It is, at this time, a betrayal of the national and republican tradition. It is a desertion of our Christianity and a scandal in the eyes of a world that looks to us for Christian example.

The Northern problems are political and social ones, for the solution of which the skill and dedication of political leaders alone are relevant. In one sense it is the truth and indeed the whole truth to say that Christian charity is the only answer. But charity is not alternative to justice. Charity includes justice. Charity needs laws, institutions, structures, embodying justice, penalising injustice. When situations and structures exist which militate against justice and impede human dignity and fulfilment, then charity requires reforms. Reforms in turn demand political action. The Christian call to love our fellow-man includes the command to remove the conditions which make love unlikely and to build the sort of community structures in which love can grow.

Charity therefore must be given political expression and legal formulation and social embodiment. This critical hour in Ireland calls urgently for politicians to deploy their utmost energies and skills in finding solutions to our desperate community problems in Northern Ireland. Their contribution now can be a nobler act of patriotism than any that marks the pages of past history in Ireland. Their positive and peaceful leadership will be a real witness to

Christian faith and indeed a manifestation of secular holiness. Our fervent and continuous prayers will be with the political leaders on all sides, in both parts of Ireland and in Britain, that they may be worthy of the challenge and peril of his hour and that God may make them deserving of His Son's beatitude:

Blessed are the peacemakers;
they shall be called sons of God.

Patrick Marrinan, *Paisley: Man of Wrath*, Tralee, Anvil, 1973, pp. 237–8.

(g) William Temple on the social order

To many it appears evident that we have allowed the making of profits, which is necessary as a means to the continuance of the industry, to get into the first place which properly belongs to the supply of human needs – the true end of industry. We have inverted the 'natural order'. Instead of finance existing to facilitate production and production existing to supply needs, the supply of needs is made the means to profitable production; and production itself is controlled as much as it is facilitated by finance.

If that is true, it is the duty of Christians to become aware of it and to demand a remedy. It cannot be said that it is their duty as Christians to know what the remedy is, for this involves many technical matters. But they are entitled to call upon the Government to set before itself the following objectives and pursue them as steadily and rapidly as opportunity permits:

1 Every child should find itself a member of a family housed with decency and dignity, so that it may grow up as a member of that basic community in a happy fellowship unspoilt by underfeeding or overcrowding, by dirty and drab surroundings or by mechanical monotony of environment.
2 Every child should have the opportunity of an education till years of maturity, so planned as to allow for his peculiar aptitudes and make possible their full development. This education should

throughout be inspired by faith in God and find its focus in worship.

3 Every citizen should be secure in possession of such income as will enable him to maintain a home and bring up children in such conditions as are described in paragraph 1 above.

4 Every citizen should have a voice in the conduct of the business or industry which is carried on by means of his labour, and the satisfaction of knowing that his labour is directed to the well-being of the community.

5 Every citizen should have sufficient daily leisure, with two days of rest in seven, and, if an employee, an annual holiday with pay, to enable him to enjoy a full personal life with such interests and activities as his tasks and talents may direct.

6 Every citizen should have assured liberty in the forms of freedom of worship, of speech, of assembly, and of association for special purposes. . . .

Utopian? Only in the sense that we cannot have it all tomorrow. But we can set ourselves steadily to advance towards that six-fold objective. It can all be summed up in a phrase; *the aim of a Christian social order is the fullest possible development of individual personality in the widest and deepest possible fellowship.*

William Temple, *Christianity and Social Order*, London, Shepheard-Walwyn/SPCK, 1976 (first published Penguin, 1942), pp. 96–7.

(h) Churchmen and immigration

The Lord Archbishop of Canterbury: My Lords, I am going to be brief. I will try not to raise the temperature, and I am going to inject into my remarks some constructive suggestions. I want to dwell first on the subject of race relations within this country and the effect of this Bill upon those relations. My knowledge of the problems is linked with the fact that for the last two and a half years I have worked with the National Committee for Commonwealth Immigrants. . . .

My own share in the work is not a large one. As Chairman, my role has been no more than to help many different people to work together. But I have been able to learn something about the splendid work that is being done for the building up of good community relations in the towns and cities where tensions exist and where tensions are threatened. In particular, through this organisation much has been done in the realm of helping schools to grapple with the problems created by the influx of children from other countries. Much also has been done by voluntary actions in the field of housing – actions to prevent the development of what might be ghettoes in some of the cities. Much has also been done to give a friendly help to immigrants to find their way to places where they will be useful and where relations are likely to be happy. And all the time a good deal has been done through these bodies in the education of public opinion on both sides. This means helping immigrants from other countries to understand the ways and customs in the United Kingdom which are unfamiliar to them, and also helping our own English born citizens to understand the ways, the cultures and the backgrounds of those who come from other parts of the world. . . .

The fact is that the Bill, and the sudden launching of it on the country, has brought a good deal of dismay to many of those who are working in this country for good community relations, and a good deal of distrust not only among the immigrant communities, where a new handle is being given to the somewhat more extremist elements, but also among those who are trying so hard to get on with this devoted work. Why distrust, my Lords? Because the Bill virtually distinguishes United Kingdom citizens on the score of race, and because the Bill virtually involves this country in breaking its word. I use the word 'virtually' because technically arguments can be adduced, and have been adduced this afternoon in the opposite sense.

First, let us take the question of race. Clause 1, on any showing, creates two levels of United Kingdom citizens. Strictly, the level is not that of race; strictly the grandfather clause means not race, but geography. But the actual effect on the bulk of the human situation with which the Bill is dealing is that the one level is the level of the European and the other level is the level of the Asian citizens.

And that is so because the object of the exercise, and the apology for the exercise, is that we must keep an influx of Asian citizens out of the country. It is inevitable, but virtually the clause is thus read in its practical effect and implication and, indeed, underlying purpose. . . .

For that reason, I do not believe it is a misreading of the situation when we say that the Bill virtually implies a race distinction in citizenship in Clause 1; and that it virtually means the breaking of this country's word. In saying that last thing, I am not meaning that particular statesmen made promises and broke them. No. What we are saying is that the country, by its total action, involved itself in a certain obligation, and that this Bill abrogates that obligation. For that reason, however much the Bill may be improved by the efforts of your Lordships' House and the efforts in another place between now and the small hours of the morning, there is at the heart of it something that is really wrong. . . .

But, my Lords, whatever we may do to retrieve the situation, the harm has been done by this Bill. The noble Lord, Lord Brooke, referred to those who opposed this Bill on abstract grounds. I do not know what the word 'abstract' means: I would say ethical grounds; and ethical grounds are never nearly abstract, because ethical grounds always have practical consequences, and it is some of the practical consequences in race relations that are dangerous, on account of what is written into this Bill.

That there is an implicit breaking of something seems to be borne out by the great unease about this Bill. I heard that in another place the Second Reading passed in a kind of sepulchral silence; and I think it will pass, if it does pass, in your Lordships' House in a very sepulchral silence. Why this unease? It really is an unease, and I believe that it is an unease we all share. We all find this vast human problem too much for us, and there can be no sort of 'more righteous than thou' attitude in any single one of us on this matter.

I think the unease is this. From time to time, on occasions when a great event or a great man is being commemorated, Members of your Lordships' House and Members of another place go across the road to Westminster Abbey. I think the last time that happened was when so many of us went to Westminster Abbey for the funeral of Clement Attlee. During that very moving service a psalm was sung, and I think we were all very moved by the way in which the psalm touched us, whatever our religion, or those of no religion. The psalm touched us by its accurate, photographic reference to the character of Clement Attlee. In that psalm, with its description of that man, there was the sentence – and I think it moved us:

He that sweareth unto his neighbour and disappointeth him not: though it were to his own hindrance.

And that, my Lords, is what lies at the bottom of the unease about this Bill. . . .

Lord Macleod of Fuinary: My Lords, it is the known custom of this House that a new Member on speaking for the first time should so declare it, which I now declare. It is the further custom that his words should, as far as possible, be non-controversial, and it is the further custom that he should be short. As regards the last, we have an old riddle in Scotland, 'Why do Presbyterian Ministers speak longer than other men?' The answer is that they do not, but it seems much longer. . . .

I might here declare why it is that in the event I find myself standing here at all. It is because – and I think that this is cogent to the debate – I received more communications from people outside urging me to speak than on any other debate which has taken place since I became a Member of your Lordships' House. Not one such communication has been from a burdened soul, such correspondence as all of us sometimes get, seized of passion or held down by some prejudice. All of those communications have come not simply from individuals but from groups such as the Human Rights Year and other ethical and religious groups. . . .

Without wishing in any way to raise the temperature, is it not worth while to consider the problem of the Irish? I come from Scotland. Why is it that this kind of issue has never been raised although in Glasgow there have been grave problems of an incursion of people who are white? Why never at all has this question been raised? It is important, with all good will and not raising temperatures, to point out that this is a racial issue; and it is a supremely racial issue when we emphasise that it has nothing to do with race! . . .

My last word is on moral grounds, and this to me is the most important. Some weeks ago the noble Lord, Lord Ritchie-Calder, made a notable speech, in which he said that the moment of·truth has arrived. The East–West relations which have been our intense concern for the last 25 years have now been replaced by the problems of North–South relations. These latter are the tragedy of our time, as the noble Lord, Lord Brockway, was so eloquently saying at the end of his speech. We may have it at the top of our minds, but we must realise that a vast change has to take place in the direction in which we must look for the real crisis of our time. We know that Poland and Hungary can talk back to Moscow, and Rumania can talk back to Czechoslovakia. The classical monolith of a vast Marxism is no longer there. . . .

But what is this terrible thing that is coming up between the North and the South? . . .

If this is the world into which we are moving, is it not a terrible thing if we unintentionally lay the seeds of hatred? Can we make it possible to realise the dangers that arise from the 'lesser breeds without the law'? I am sure that every Member of this House and every responsible person regrets anything that gets racial hatred going. Is it not a pity that people are saying that at last the Government are coming level with what they have been saying ought to be done? Do we realise one danger arising? 'The lesser breeds without the law', the prejudiced, the racialists, are beginning to refer to this Bill as proof of what they, in their prejudices, have been saying all along, when it is the last intention of the Government to say any such thing.

Is it for nothing that at the other extreme there is the profoundest danger that race war is going to be started in this country? . . . How far are we quite certain, if this kind of legislation goes through, that it will not start the pulsating beginnings, the germination of race war in this country, and race hatred from all the people in the South of the World. It is no longer East–West. The truth is that it is North–South, and, as has been said, this is the greatest issue of our time.

Parliamentary Debates (Hansard), House of Lords, Vol. 289 (1968), 29 February, cols. 949–54, 976–81 (with cuts).

(i) *Roman Catholics and social justice*

On behalf of the Church in England and Wales, we in the Justice Sector of the National Pastoral Congress feel compelled to begin by placing on record our failure to proclaim the Gospel of Jesus Christ in all its fullness in this land. We regret our failure as a Church to combat the prevailing national mood of insularity, to identify with the poor in our midst and to work vigorously for a more peaceful world. Above all we regret our failure to make our own the declaration of the 1971 Synod on *Justice in the Modern World* which proclaimed that:

> Action on behalf of justice and participation in the transformation of the world fully appear to us as a constitutive dimension of the preaching of the Gospel.

We wish humbly to confess this failure to the poor who live amongst us in England and Wales and to the millions of our sisters and brothers in the Third World whose sufferings and oppression we have in good part caused and are still causing. May God give us the grace to make an entirely new attempt to face up to the demands of the Gospel and to put them into practice in our lives.

Those considering this topic had a mammoth task. But the underlying theme running through the discussions was our responsibility to invite our fellow humans to turn away from false values and look at the world from a new point of view. This means being a sign of contradiction to the world's values. It can be painful. We have to take unpopular stands. But we are also a sign of hope.

Indeed one of the clearest signs of hope was the wide range of issues now seen clearly to be part of our Christian responsibility if we are to be true to the Gospel. These included: housing, unemployment, human rights in the Church, discrimination against women, discrimination against homosexuals, abortion, euthanasia, law and order, Catholic schools and many others. In one sense it was a frustrating task trying to give any measured consideration to a range of topics of such importance but the recurring theme was that as Christians our responsibility was to the poor and powerless. In the words of one group report: 'We do not take the poor seriously. We have sold the Gospel for material values. We idolise the value of becoming conspicuously respectable to the exclusion of the vast growing sector of the poor in our society'.

Liverpool 1980: Official Report of the National Pastoral Congress, Slough, St Paul Publications, 1981, pp. 290, 294.

(j) Episcopal bias to the poor

Bias to the poor sounds like a statement of political preference. My experience has been that some of the most central teachings of orthodox Christianity lead me to this position. I shall argue from Jesus's theme of the Kingdom of God, the calling to the Church to be Catholic, reaching across all human divisions and the doctrine of the Incarnation; they lead me to claim that there is a divine bias to the poor, which should be reflected both in the Church and in the secular world. . . .

Those who belong to more affluent suburbs sometimes resent the claim that there is a divine bias for the poor. They point to particular needs of individuals in their community; are they not also the needy Christ cares for? Yes, He does indeed care for every individual – widow, orphan, handicapped; but it is one of the realities of life, emphasised by urbanisation, that we are all influenced heavily by the group to which we belong. Some whole groups find themselves shut out from the circles in which decisions are taken and where many opportunities exist. Does God not have a word for those who have advantages? He does indeed have a word for all men; it is not always the same word. 'Where a man has been given much, much will be expected of him.' Sometimes His word to the advantaged is that they must surrender their advantage for the sake of the poor. . . .

The call for justice jars on many ears. To those who broadly believed the status quo to be a just one it seems more wounding than the demand for charity or welfare. There is an honest argument here between people who truly care for the poor. To defend the status quo is not necessarily an attitude to be condemned. Those who do so believe that they are realistic about channelling actual resources to the poor; and about the practical difficulties of sustaining any kind of just society in an increasingly violent and libertarian world. They fear that hard-won ground, for example, in respect for authority, in disciplines at work, and in the pursuit of excellence is being put at risk by the call for more equal opportunity for all people to control their own destiny. Such people feel that the call for justice is somehow a personal attack on themselves or on those, whom they admire, who have gone before them. It says that poverty is not inevitable; that those who are better off could actually do something about it if they would try. It feels as though they are being blamed, and they resent that as unfair; they feel they are prisoners of history. . . .

I am aware of four motives which make me continue the argument within Church and society. In a book like this, the first is the compulsion to pass on what I have seen and heard. Society in cities like Liverpool and London is deeply divided. Many are unaware of the experiences of life which others face in the same city. One of the callings of the Christian Church is to be a bridge on which different experiences of life can be given a hearing. I want to show how blocking to God-given talents are some of those experiences of urban life; and to share some of the flickers of hope I see, which help to keep me a believer.

The second motive is to show how false it is to suggest, as is so often done, that two proper Christian callings are posed as opposites – that either you are for changing individuals or you are for changing the structures of society.

When I was first ordained and went to serve in inner city London, I would have said that people are the same wherever they live. I believed that if you could change individuals, that was the only way to change the world. I expected broadly to see the same response to the Gospel, to educational and career opportunities, whatever the context in which people lived. I've learned that there are massive blocks in the way of such responses for inner city people, whether they live in the inner city itself or in vast corporation estates on the perimeter of a city. The Gospel needs to proclaim the need and the possibility for God *both* to change people from inside out *and* to change the course of events to set people free to make such choices.

The third motive is to do with people's response to the Gospel. In my book *Built as a City* I showed that in London visible response to the Churches is dramatically smaller in urban working-class areas than in middle-class or professional areas. The same is true in Liverpool with the exception of the Roman Catholic Church; I will look at some of the reasons for that exception later on. It matters urgently how those who are at a disadvantage see the Church, because their experience of the Church often makes them say that this Christ of the Churches is not for them.

The fourth motive is that the Church is called to reflect God's character in the world. Whether anyone will respond or not, God loves things like mercy, justice and truth, and hates things like greed and oppression. Reflecting this character of God will mean that the Church must risk losing its innocence by becoming involved in the corporate life of cities. It must sometimes take sides, even if that leads to great unpopularity rather than growth in the number of worshippers.

David Sheppard, *Bias to the Poor*, London, Hodder & Stoughton, 1983, pp. 10, 14, 15, 17–18.

(k) A new spirit in evangelicalism

CONVERSION TO WHOLENESS

1984 was a year of intense Christian activity. We met this autumn at the Evangelical Alliance Leadership '84 conference as church leaders, pastors and practitioners of Christian social concern. We have asked how we should assess our faithfulness in obeying the Lord's commission to go and make disciples. 'Should we ask how many people are converted or rather how many people are being made whole?' The gospel of the Kingdom of God is about the love of God in bringing salvation, wholeness and healing to people's creation. In Jesus' ministry, as in the whole of the Bible, such wholeness encompassed both ministries of compassion in ministering to human need and ministries of justice in challenging the evils of society. While evangelical churches in the United Kingdom are involved in a wide range of compassionate ministries, some have more recently been lacking in their engagement with social evils and injustice. If we are to be nation- and world-changing Christians we must be taught, disciplined and enabled to serve from local churches committed to action expressing the Father's love in the surrounding community. . . .

OUR CONTEMPORARY SITUATION

We considered some of the problems and situations of life in Britain today and the forces which shape the outlook of people. For example, we are two nations, comfortable Britain and the other Britain; many are lonely, many lack meaning in life, many are unemployed. Further, we are part of the affluent European community, and we considered how our actions and failures to act cause damage to poorer countries. We need to become more aware of these and other factors in order truly to share Christ with people.

We considered Christian involvement in politics. Politics is first about people and their relationships, and only very secondarily about political parties. God counts the good ordering of relationships in society as so important that those responsible for political affairs are deemed his servants and counted worthy of the respect due to him. We must teach respect for politicians, the responsibility of all to be good citizens, the calling of some in the church to undertake political office and the necessity of the church fellowship to provide them with support and prayer. The church must hold up God's will for society before politicians and protest against bad laws and against bad proposals for legislation in an attitude of love and reconciliation rather than hate and misrepresentation.

Such views may be new for some. We have a history of separation between social concern and the proclamation of Christian truth, and a fear of confronting secular and state authorities, which have contributed to the silence and non-involvement of the church in prophetic social action.

Rene Padilla and Chris Sugden, *How Evangelicals Endorsed Social Responsibility*, Grove, Bramcote, 1985, pp. 20, 21.

(1) The Kingdom of God in north-east England

This book had its beginning in a small group of Christian theologians who met in Durham for several days of discussion scattered between April and October 1985. We were drawn together by a simple, yet challenging question: What meaning has Jesus' talk of the kingdom of God for North-East England today? The basic conviction being, of course, that Jesus' teaching is of primary importance for Christians. It lies at the heart of Christianity, has had an incalculable influence on and through the churches down the centuries, and ought to be allowed to continue exercising that influence today. Meeting as Christians in the heartland of a part of the country notorious for its levels of unemployment and related social ills, we felt no need to apologise for asking the question.

As the question itself indicates, our concern was two-edged. First, to try to hear afresh the teaching of Jesus about the kingdom of God, in the hope that any answers which might emerge to the question should properly represent and re-express the message of Jesus. Second, to keep constantly in view the social reality which is North-East England today, in the hope that any answers which might emerge to the question should have something to say to that social reality.

These twin concerns are not so easily held together as some may think. In the past 'the kingdom of God' has been like a very flexible rubber mould which individuals and groups have been able to pull into a variety of shapes. The resulting impression has often been a jumble of ideas drawn from within the Bible and beyond: the kingdom = the church; the kingdom = the missionary effort round the world; or again, the kingdom = the classless society; or the kingdom = the moral or economic utopia of some political party or sect. The danger of reading our own vision and ideals into 'the kingdom of God' is all too real. We were therefore resolved from the first that our discussion should be controlled by what the New Testament actually says regarding 'Jesus' talk of the kingdom of God'.

At the same time, it was clearly not enough simply to *describe* what the New Testament says about the kingdom. We could not assume that a message delivered to a first-century, largely agrarian, Palestinian society will be immediately and directly applicable to a twentieth-century North-East suffering from the effects of long-term industrial decline. Theological reflection consists of (1) coming to terms with the strangeness and foreignness (to us) of that original message, (2) attempting to hear that message as far as possible in its original terms and with its original impact, and (3) re-expressing that message in equivalent terms and, hopefully, with the equivalent impact. The evidence of the New Testament therefore formed the basis but not the limit of our discussion. And the goal of 'meaning for North-East England' we tried to keep ever before us.

James D. G. Dunn and others, eds., *The Kingdom of God and North-East England*, SCM, 1986, pp. 3–4.

(m) *Prime-ministerial convictions*

I am greatly honoured to have been invited to attend the opening of this 1988 General Assembly of the Church of Scotland; and I am deeply grateful that you have now asked me to address you. I am very much aware of the historical continuity extending over four centuries, during which the position of the Church of Scotland has been recognised in constitutional law and confirmed by successive

Sovereigns. It sprang from the independence of mind and rigour of thought that have always been such powerful characteristics of the Scottish people. It has remained close to its roots and has inspired a commitment to serve from *all* people. I am therefore very sensible of the important influence which the Church of Scotland exercises in the life of the whole nation, both at the spiritual level and through the extensive caring services which are provided by your Church's department of social responsibility.

Perhaps it would be best if I began by speaking personally as a Christian, as well as a politician, about the way I see things. Reading recently I came across the starkly simple phrase: 'Christianity is about spiritual redemption, not social reform.' Sometimes the debate on these matters has become too polarised and given the impression that the two are quite separate. Most Christians would regard it as their personal Christian duty to help their fellow men and women. They would regard the lives of their children as a precious trust. These duties come not from any secular legislation passed by Parliament, but from being a Christian. But there are a number of people who are not Christians who would also accept these responsibilities. What then are the distinctive marks of Christianity?

They stem not from the social but from the spiritual side of our lives. I would identify three beliefs in particular. First, that from the beginning man has been endowed by God with the fundamental right to choose between good and evil. Second, that we are made in God's image and therefore we are expected to use all our *own* power of thought and judgement in exercising that choice; and further, if we open our hearts to God, he has promised to work within us. And third, that our Lord Jesus Christ the Son of God when faced with his terrible choice and lonely vigil *chose* to lay down his life that our sins may be forgiven. I remember very well a sermon on an Armistice Sunday when our preacher said: 'No one took away the life of Jesus: he chose to lay it down.'

I think back to many discussions in my early life when we all agreed that if you try to take the fruits of Christianity without its roots, the fruits will wither. And they will not come again unless you nurture the roots. But we must not profess Christianity and go to church simply because we want social reforms and benefits or a better standard of living – but because we accept the sanctity of life, the responsibility that comes with freedom and the supreme sacrifice of Christ expressed so well in the hymn:

When I survey the wondrous Cross
On which the Prince of glory died,
My richest gain I count but loss,
And pour contempt on all my pride.

May I also say a few words about my personal belief in the relevance of Christianity to public policy – to the things that are Caesar's? The Old Testament lays down in Exodus the Ten Commandments as given to Moses, the injunction in Leviticus to love our neighbour as ourselves and generally the importance of observing a strict code of law. The New Testament is a record of the Incarnation, the teachings of Christ and the establishment of the Kingdom of God. Again we have the emphasis on loving our neighbour as ourselves and to 'Do-as-you-would-be-done-by'. I believe that by taking together these two elements from the Old and New Testaments we gain a view of the universe, a proper attitude to work, and principles to shape economic and social life.

We are told that we must work and use our talents to create wealth. 'If a man will not work, he shall not eat,' wrote St Paul to the Thessalonians. Indeed, abundance rather than poverty has a legitimacy which derives from the very nature of creation. Nevertheless the Tenth Commandment – 'Thou shalt not covet' – recognises that making money and owning things could become selfish activities. But it is not the creation of wealth that is wrong but love of money for its own sake. The spiritual dimension comes in deciding what to do with the wealth. How could we respond to the many calls for help, or invest in the future, or support the wonderful artists and craftsmen whose work also glorifies God, unless we had first worked hard and used our talents to create the necessary wealth? And remember the woman with the alabaster jar of ointment. I confess that I have always had difficulty with interpreting the

243

biblical precept to love our neighbours 'as ourselves' until I read some of the words of C. S. Lewis. He pointed out that we don't exactly love *ourselves* when we fall below the standards and beliefs we have accepted. Indeed we might even *hate* ourselves for some unworthy deed.

None of this, of course, tells us exactly what kind of political and social institutions we should have. On this point, Christians will very often genuinely disagree, though it is a mark of Christian manners that they will do so with courtesy and mutual respect. What is certain, however, is that any set of social and economic arrangements which is not founded on the acceptance of individual responsibility will do nothing but harm. We are all responsible for our own actions. We cannot blame society if we disobey the law. We cannot simply delegate the exercise of mercy and compassion to others. The politicians and other secular powers should strive by their measures to bring out the good in people and to fight down the bad: but they can't create the one or abolish the other. They can only see that the laws encourage the *best* instincts and convictions which I am convinced are far more deeply rooted than is often supposed.

Nowhere is this more evident than the basic ties of the family which are at the heart of our society and are the very nursery of civic virtue. It is on the family that we in government base our policies for welfare, education and care. You recall that Timothy was warned by St Paul that anyone who neglects to provide for his own house (meaning his own family) has disowned the faith and is 'worse than an infidel'.

We must recognise that modern society is infinitely more complex than that of biblical times and of course new occasions teach new duties. In our day the only way that we can ensure that no one is left without sustenance, help or opportunity, is to have laws to provide for health and education, pensions for the elderly, succour for the sick and disabled. But intervention by the state must never become so great that it effectively removes personal responsibility. The same applies to taxation, for while you and I would work extremely hard whatever the circumstances, there are undoubtedly some who would not unless the incentive was there. And we need *their* efforts too.

Moderator, recently there have been great debates about religious education. I believe strongly that politicians must see that religious education has a proper place in the school curriculum. In Scotland as in England there is a historic connection expressed in our laws between Church and State. The two connections are of a somewhat different kind, but the arrangements in both countries are designed to give symbolic expression to the same crucial truth – that the Christian religion, which of course symbolises many of the great spiritual and moral truths of Judaism – is a fundamental part of our national heritage.

I believe it is the wish of the overwhelming majority of people that this heritage should be preserved and fostered. For centuries it has been our very life blood. Indeed we are a nation whose ideals are founded on the Bible. Also it is quite impossible to understand our literature without grasping this fact. *That* is the strong practical case for ensuring that children at school are given adequate instruction in the part which the Judaeo-Christian tradition has played in moulding our laws, manners and institutions. How can you make sense of Shakespeare and Sir Walter Scott, or of the constitutional conflicts of the seventeenth century in both Scotland and England, without such fundamental knowledge? But I would go further than this. The truths of the Judaeo-Christian tradition are infinitely precious, not only, as I believe, because they are true, but also because they provide the moral impulse which alone can lead to that peace, in the true meaning of the word, for which we all long.

To assert absolute moral values is not to claim perfection for ourselves. No true Christian could do that. What is more, one of the great principles of our Judaeo-Christian heritage is tolerance. People of other faiths and cultures have always been welcomed in our land, assured of equality under the law, of proper respect and of open friendship. There is absolutely nothing incompatible with this and our desire to maintain the essence of our own identity. There is no place for racial or religious intolerance in our creed.

When Abraham Lincoln spoke in his famous Gettysburg speech

of 1863 of 'government of the people, by the people, for the people', he gave the world a neat definition of democracy which has since been widely and enthusiastically adopted. But what he enunciated as a form of government was not in itself specifically Christian, for nowhere in the Bible is the word democracy mentioned. Ideally, when Christians meet, as Christians, to take counsel together, their purpose is not (or should not be) to ascertain what is the mind of the majority but what is the mind of the Holy Spirit – something which may be quite different. Nevertheless, I am an enthusiast for democracy. And I take that position, not because I believe majority opinion is inevitably right or true – indeed, no majority can take away God-given rights – but because I believe it effectively safeguards the value of the individual, and, more than any other system, restrains the abuse of power by the few. And that *is* a Christian concept.

But there is little hope for democracy if the hearts of men and women in democratic societies cannot be touched by a call to something greater than themselves. Political structures, state institutions, collective ideals are not enough. *We* Parliamentarians can legislate for the rule of law. *You* the Church can teach the life of faith.

For, when all is said and done, a politician's life is a humble one. I always think that the whole debate about the Church and the State has never yielded anything comparable in insight to that beautiful hymn: 'I vow to thee my country'. It begins with a triumphant assertion of what might be described as secular patriotism, a noble thing indeed in a country like ours:

> I vow to thee, my country, all earthly things above:
> Entire and whole and perfect the service of my love.

It goes on to speak of 'another country I heard of long ago' whose King cannot be seen and whose armies cannot be counted, but 'soul by soul and silently her shining bounds increase'. Not group by group, or party by party, or even church by church – but soul by soul and each one counts.

That, members of the Assembly, is the country which you chiefly serve. You fight your cause under the banner of an historic Church.

CHURCH, STATE AND POLITICS
CHURCH, STATE AND POLITICS

Your success matters greatly – as much to the temporal as to the spiritual welfare of the nation.

Margaret Thatcher, 'A Speech by the Prime Minister, 21 May 1988', in Michael Alison and David L. Edwards, eds., *Christianity and Conservatism*, London, Hodder & Stoughton, 1990, pp. 333–8.

(n) Another Gospel?

1 Synodical Government has provided the mechanisms not only for the Church of England to make more pronouncements on secular political issues, but also for small groups of people to shape what it says. The Church is hence becoming increasingly centralised in spite of the appearance of greater democracy.
2 Reports from Synod on major public issues increasingly reflect a one-sided political stance.
3 The Church of England has been strongly influenced by the ecumenical movement (the World Council of Churches and, in Britain, the British Council of Churches). It has helped to fund the BCC's Community and Race Relations Unit which supports an 'anti-racism' programme virtually indistinguishable from that promoted by many left-wing local authorities.
4 Aspects of the new 'theologies of liberation', which have themselves been criticised for their political bias, have been promoted by some Church of England official reports. Influential Evangelical Christians (the fastest growing group within the Church of England) have also begun to adapt and adopt the concepts of the 'theologies of liberation'.
5 These 'theologies of liberation' are characterised by a transformation of theological into political concepts.
6 There has been a big increase in recent years in the number of Christian political pressure groups in Britain. Many of these are part of an aggressively leftist and anti-Western network. Activists within these groups have held key positions within the Church bureaucracy.
7 The Anglican Communion (the Anglican Churches throughout

the world) is increasingly influenced by the small permanent bureaucracy of the Anglican Consultative Council. This has prepared the agenda and recommended reading for this year's Lambeth Conference.

8 An analysis of the Lambeth preparatory documents show them to be furthering the leftist trend in the Church. They endorse the 'theologies of liberation' and political 'liberation' movements.

9 The implications of these trends are so far-reaching, that there is an urgent need for much more open and informed debate within the Church of England about the theological and political issues involved.

Rachel Tingle, *Another Gospel? An Account of the Growing Involvement of the Anglican Church in Secular Politics*, London, The Christian Studies Centre, 1988, Summary.

11
EDUCATION

F or most of the period the 1944 Education Act (a) was the central statement of the statutory place of religion in schools. It proved a framework sufficiently flexible to permit some adaptation to the needs of a multi-religious society, as was evident in the Birmingham Agreed Syllabus of 1975, drawn up by a working party chaired by John Hick (b). Nevertheless by the 1980s the pressure for modification had become substantial (c). By this date too the newer minority religious communities, above all the Muslims, had found a voice and demand for separate schools and the recognition of distinctive educational needs was growing (d). The 1988 Education Act sought to strike a balance by affirming that 'a broadly Christian character' should be the norm for collective worship in schools, but providing for exceptions to be made and requiring a syllabus that reflected the religious diversity of the country (e, f). Committed Christians however saw the Act as giving them new opportunities for witness, while, conversely, minority religious groups expressed unease (g).

(a) *The 1944 Education Act*

25 *General provisions as to religious education in county and in voluntary schools* –

(1) Subject to the provisions of this section, the school day in every county school and in every voluntary school shall begin with collective worship, on the part of all pupils in attendance at the school, and the arrangements made therefore shall provide for a single act of worship attended by all such pupils unless, in the opinion of the local education authority or, in the case of a voluntary school, of the managers or governors thereof, the school premises are such as to make it impracticable to assemble them for that purpose.

(2) Subject to the provisions of this section, religious instruction shall be given in every county school and in every voluntary school.

(3) It shall not be required, as a condition of any pupil attending any county school or any voluntary school, that he shall attend or abstain from attending any Sunday school or any place of religious worship.

(4) If the parent of any pupil in attendance at the county school or any voluntary school requests that he be wholly or partly excused from attendance at religious worship in the school, or from attendance at religious instruction in the school, or from attendance at both religious worship and religious instruction in the school, then, until the request is withdrawn, the pupil shall be excused from such attendance accordingly. . . .

26 *Special provisions as to religious education in county schools* – Subject as hereinafter provided, the collective worship required by subsection (1) of the last foregoing section shall not, in any county school, be distinctive of any particular religious denomination, and the religious instruction given to any pupils in attendance at a county school in conformity with the requirements of subsection (2) of the said section shall be given in accordance with an agreed syllabus adopted for the school or for those pupils and shall not include any catechism or formulary which is distinctive of any particular religious denomination. . . .

PROCEDURE FOR PREPARING AND BRINGING INTO OPERATION AN AGREED SYLLABUS OF RELIGIOUS INSTRUCTION

1 For the purpose of preparing any syllabus of religious instruction to be adopted by a local education authority, the authority shall cause to be convened a conference constituted in accordance with the provisions of this Schedule.

2 For the purpose of constituting such a conference as aforesaid the local education authority shall appoint constituent bodies

(hereinafter referred to as 'committees') consisting of persons representing respectively –

(a) such religious denominations as, in the opinion of the authority, ought, having regard to the circumstances of the area, to be represented;

(b) except in the case of an area in Wales or Monmouthshire, the Church of England;

(c) such associations representing teachers as, in the opinion of the authority, ought, having regard to the circumstances of the area, to be represented; and

(d) the authority. . . .

'Sections from the Education Act, 1944', in *Agreed Syllabus of Religious Instruction*, Birmingham, City of Birmingham District Council Education Committee, 1975, pp. 17, 18, 22.

(b) The Birmingham Agreed Syllabus

A RESPONSE TO CHANGE

The present 'Agreed Syllabus' replaces one which has been in use within the City of Birmingham for twenty five years. During this period the situation facing those involved in religious education in Birmingham has changed radically. First, there has been a revolution in the understanding of its nature and purpose. Second, profound social changes require that pupils shall be prepared for the realities of life in the twentieth century 'global village'. Third, the City of Birmingham itself now contains sizeable groups of people each loyal to their own particular religious or non-religious commitment and, in addition, many with no deep commitment of any kind. The new Agreed Syllabus is a response to these changes and it may be helpful at the outset to indicate the principles which it embodies.

THE APPROACH TO THIS SYLLABUS

A generation ago the purpose of religious education in county schools was to nurture pupils into Christian faith, and the agreed syllabus of religious instruction was one of the instruments whereby this was to be achieved. In the present circumstances religious education is seen as an educationally valid component of the school curriculum, subject to the same disciplines as other areas of study. It is thus directed towards developing a critical understanding of the religious and moral dimensions of human experience and away from attempting to foster the claims of particular religious standpoints.

The syllabus should thus be used to enlarge and deepen the pupils' understanding of religion by studying world religions, and by exploring all those elements in human experience which raise questions about life's ultimate meaning and value. This involves informing pupils in a descriptive, critical and experiential manner about what religion is, and increasing their sensitivity to the areas of experience from which a religious view of life may arise. It should stimulate within the pupils, and assist them in the search for, a personal sense of meaning in life, whilst enabling them to understand the beliefs and commitments of others.

This view reflects significant changes in the study of religion. First, whereas in the past attention was concentrated on doctrines to the relative exclusion of other aspects, the tendency now is to emphasise that these other aspects – history, mythology, doctrine, ethical outlook, liturgical life, inner experience, artistic and social expression – must also be given their proper weight. Second, the tendency when looking at world religions was towards a comparison of other faiths with one considered as self-evidently superior to the rest; whereas the approach now is to study them objectively and for their own sake. Third, the tradition of studying religion in its relationship to the contemporary world now necessitates reference to stances for living which reject belief in realities transcending the natural order but nevertheless offer an understanding of the universe together with a way of living within it. Such contextual studies contribute towards a critical appreciation of the distinctive features of religious faith.

THE SCOPE OF RELIGIOUS EDUCATION

When applied to the county school, within the context of the profound social changes already mentioned, this approach to religious education requires a much wider range of material than was included in the traditional syllabuses, as well as a fundamentally different treatment. So much material is now relevant that selection is necessary in order to meet the practical limitations of the school curriculum. An attempt has been made to balance the needs arising from the pupils' personal search for meaning, the nature of each pupil's domestic circumstances, the cultural requirements for living in modern Western European society, and the need to understand the outlooks of other people in the world of today.

A generation ago nearly all the children in Birmingham schools came from a Christian background. Today, although the majority of people in our society still have at least a nominal adherence to Christianity, there is far less support for its institutional forms and a high degree of uncertainty is evident on matters of belief and commitment. There are also considerable numbers of pupils whose parents are positive adherents of other world faiths, particularly Hinduism, Islam, Sikhism and of course Judaism, which has been present in Birmingham for more than two centuries. In addition, interest is being shown in many of the ideas basic to what have often been described as 'secular faiths'. The situation is thus a very open one, and its future development is unknown.

Under the basic principle of religious freedom to which this country is committed, and in view of the educational grounds upon which this syllabus stands, there can be no question of making it an aim of religious education in schools to convert pupils to any particular religion or ideology. Everyone should, nevertheless, recognise that education for life in Britain today must include an adequate treatment of Christianity as the faith which has, historically, moulded British life and culture and is still doing so. Further, because of the pluralistic character of this City and of the world, the following world faiths present in Birmingham are also included – Hinduism, Islam, Judaism, Sikhism and, at sixth form level,

Buddhism. Again, on the same grounds, other widely-held stances for living which share many of the dimensions of religion whilst not admitting belief in realities transcending the natural order require serious attention in any realistic programme of education for life today.

Agreed Syllabus of Religious Instruction, Birmingham, City of Birmingham District Council Education Committee, 1975, pp. 4–5.

(c) Educating 'ethnic minorities'

5.1 We believe that religious education can play a central role in preparing all pupils for life in today's multi-racial Britain, and can also lead them to a greater understanding of the diversity of the global community. We feel that religious education of the kind which we have discussed here can also contribute towards challenging and countering the influence of racism in our society. As we have explained, we believe that the phenomenological approach to religious education reflects most closely the aims underlying 'Education for All', in laying the foundations for the kind of genuinely pluralist society which we envisaged at the opening of this report. . . .

5.2 It is important to recognise that the stance which we have adopted in this chapter towards the role of schools in providing religious *education* should in no way be seen as conflicting with the role of individual faith communities to provide religious *instruction* and, as the Durham Report put it:

. . . *to nurture a child into a particular faith.*

Indeed, within a truly pluralist society, in which the maintenance of their religious traditions and beliefs is regarded by some groups within it as of great importance in retaining their group identity and cohesiveness, we would see community-based provisions for religious instruction – whether in the form of a Christian Sunday school, an Islamic Mosque school or organised by the Black

Churches – as complementing rather than in any sense conflicting with the more broadly based religious education which we believe schools should be offering to *all* children.

5.3 More specifically, however, the conclusions which we have reached in this chapter have a direct bearing on the provisions of the 1944 Education Act. As we have already seen, a number of people have suggested that some or all of the sections of the Act relating to religious education should be amended or repealed. During our consideration of religious education we have ourselves found it increasingly difficult to reconcile our own views on religious education with the requirements and the spirit of the Act. Since the Act perceives two distinct elements in religious education, it may be worthwhile considering each of these in turn. With regard to the requirement for a daily act of collective worship in every county and voluntary school, we do not believe that this requirement can continue to be justified with the multiplicity of beliefs and nonbeliefs now present in our society. We would not however wish to restrict the freedom of county schools to make provision for collective worship if it seems appropriate and is acceptable to their pupils and parents. Similarly however we believe the freedom *not* to make such provision should no longer be restricted by law. As we have pointed out, many county schools are in fact already in breach of the provisions of the Act in this respect and this would simply mean therefore regularising their existing practice. Within the existing dual system of education in this country, the trust deeds of some voluntary schools will however still require them to hold an act of collective worship. In relation to school *assemblies*, as opposed to an act of worship, we believe that they can be seen to fulfil a 'social' and an administrative function in schools, especially at primary level, and as such are an important aspect of school life.

5.4 In relation to religious education, or in the terms of the Act – religious 'instruction' – we have already explained that we regard the study of the nature of belief and of a range of belief systems as an essential and integral part of the educational experience of every child. This is not however to say that provision in this area of the curriculum should necessarily be required by law nor that it should be set within the complex framework established by the Act. Whilst we regard religious education *in the sense in which we have discussed it in this chapter* as an essential aspect of the curriculum we would not see it as any more essential than the other aspects of education which we have discussed in this report. If religious education is indeed regarded as such an important aspect of education, it seems difficult to accept the case for legally providing for pupils to be withdrawn from it. This anomalous position in our view raises serious doubts about the justification for the specific provisions of the Act. Clearly if the provision of religious education (instruction) continues to be required by law, and if there is a likelihood that the provision made may adopt a confessional approach, based on a Christian dominated agreed syllabus, then the right of withdrawal must be retained. If, however, as we wish, religious education is broadened to follow a phenomenological approach which seeks to 'inform' rather than to 'convert' pupils, and if the position of religious education within the curriculum is acknowledged and accepted on *educational* rather than religious grounds, then we feel that the legal requirement for provision to be made, the legal provision for withdrawal and the requirement for agreed syllabuses, are no longer justified. . . .

THE 'SEPARATE' SCHOOLS DEBATE

- The right of ethnic minority communities to seek to establish their own voluntary aided schools is firmly enshrined in law;
- We believe that the demand to exercise this right would be much diminished if the policies for 'Education for All' which we have advocated in this report are adopted; . . .
- For some ethnic minority parents the demise of single sex provision may mean that there is no acceptable environment for the education of their daughters. We hope that LEAs with multiracial pupil populations will consider carefully the value of retaining an option of single sex education as part of their secondary school provision and that the Secretary of State will also be

sensitive to the wide ramifications of any decisions he may make on proposals which lead to the loss of single sex provision in multi-racial areas. In cases where an LEA either no longer provides for single sex education at all, or makes only limited provision, we hope that the possibility of establishing or re-establishing single sex schools will be given serious consideration;

- Far more can and should be done by schools to respond to the 'pastoral' needs of Muslim pupils, to ensure that there is a real respect and understanding by both teachers and parents of each other's concerns and that the demands of the school place no child in fundamental conflict with the requirements of his faith;
- As we have observed earlier, the right of communities to seek to establish their own voluntary aided schools is firmly enshrined in the law. At the same time we do not believe that such 'separate' schools would be in the long term interest of the ethnic minority communities.

Education For All: The Report of the Committee of Inquiry into the Education of Children from Ethnic Minority Groups, London, HMSO, 1985, pp. 496–8, 519–20.

(d) A Muslim viewpoint

Islam is a faith that permeates every single fibre of a person's existence and, as such, it moulds and shapes the total personality of an individual or the total culture of a so-called nation or race or nationality.

It is this unique character of Islam and its relationship with Muslims that should be taken into account when anyone formulates an educational policy that would affect them. The Swann Committee has tried to overlook this fact and concentrate, first, on different ethnic groups, and then on the method of integrating all into one broad pluralist culture. Muslims are ready to share those basic values which are common and which are deeply rooted in essential humanity but they will definitely resist and educate their children to resist all those pseudo values which are fleeting fashions or customs or temporary man-made rules such as permissiveness. It is here that the Swann Committee has failed miserably to understand or accept a basic principle and differentiate between the essential foundations of humanity which are divinely sanctioned and the temporary changing rules and regulations constructed by man. Because of their secular outlook they wanted to ignore the religious dicta and went to the extent of regarding religion as a cultural phenomenon and nothing more than that. Their integrational pluralism is based on this secular approach to religion and to all religious communities. Their hope is that in two or three generations the 'education for all' will integrate all these religious communities by brainwashing them and by systematically drawing them away intellectually and emotionally from their different religious backgrounds.

It is here that the Swann Committee has committed a blunder and made a very wrong assessment. It is here that they have been governed by their own irreligious, secularist approach rather than by a detached, objective evaluation, especially of the Muslim community. They should have learnt from history. Islam is such an all-embracing code of life that it is not possible for a person to be partly Muslim and partly non-Muslim. History has shown that wherever they have gone, they have retained their identity. So many different tribes and races entered the Indo-Pakistan-Bangladesh sub-continent and got merged into an amalgam of a multifaceted cultural group but the Muslims did not get amalgamated. They adopted many customs and conventions but they retained their separate Muslim identity. In two or three generations a group of Muslims will emerge who will be British in their use of English, in some of their customs and conventions, even in their love of English literature, but they will be Muslim not only in positive absolute values but in those values that are completely anti-modernist and anti-secularist.

This does not mean that Muslims will be anti-Christian. The Swann Committee should have accepted and spoken of those fundamental absolute values which all religions share, and let each community retain whatever they want to retain, not what they would be permitted to retain. As Muslims do not consider any human law superior to divine law, they will resist anti-Muslim laws and create cores of resistance in the hearts of their children to such laws. At the same time Muslims will readily accept all basic human values which they commonly share with other religions or ethical or humanist groups. Dogmatic secularism is a form of religion and Muslims oppose that 'religion' because they carry on 'jihad' against that force that decides to destroy religion.

That is why Muslims want to set up their own schools and want the government to support the setting up of voluntary-aided Muslim schools. They want their children to grow up as good Muslims and they find the secularist state schools creating non-believers in spite of religious education. All subjects are taught from a secularist point of view. Children are encouraged to be critical of their own traditions and values and even of faith. Doubts are encouraged. Whereas a Muslim teaches a child to pray to God for forgiveness and to strengthen his/her faith, the rationalist teacher teaches the student to explore on his own or with reference to other faiths and ideologies. The Islamic method of removing doubts and the strengthening of faith is completely ignored. It is desirable for a Muslim child to be open-minded and be ready to admit the truth in other religions and ideologies, but it would be wrong to be critical of one's own religion without any norm to judge which is true and which is false. Who will provide the child with that norm? Parents? Teachers? Their own unguided reason?

We want Muslim children to acquire that norm of judgement from Islam. As Islam sums up all the basic values that all the previous religions have taught mankind, that norm will be acceptable, we think, to other religions and the humanist groups as well. As the child grows up he/she learns about other religions and other societies. In Britain it is now a commonplace thing for Muslim children to meet children belonging to other faiths, or children without any faith. Even some of the teachers may be non-believers. That is why it is all the more necessary for the Muslim community leaders to inculcate religious knowledge among its children and help them to grow up as committed Muslims who have learnt the technique of resisting the onslaught of faithlessness. A large number of Muslim families in Great Britain are not educated enough to know even the basic Shari'ah. As a result their children do not grow up with deep faith and knowledge of Islam. They are ready prey of the secular anti-religious environment in which they grow.

Syed Ali Ashraf, Preface to J. M. Halstead, *The Case for Muslim Voluntary-Aided Schools: Some Philosophical Reflections*, Cambridge, The Islamic Academy, 1986, pp. v–vii.

(e) The 1988 Education Act

6 Collective worship
(1) Subject to section 9 of this Act, all pupils in attendance at a maintained school shall on each school day take part in an act of collective worship.

(2) The arrangements for the collective worship in a school required by this section may, in respect of each school day, provide for a single act of worship for all pupils or for separate acts of worship for pupils in different age groups or in different school groups. . . .

7 Special provisions as to collective worship in county schools
(1) Subject to the following provisions of this section, in the case of a county school the collective worship required in the school by section 6 of this Act shall be wholly or mainly of a broadly Christian character.

(2) For the purposes of subsection (1) above, collective worship is of a broadly Christian character if it reflects the broad traditions of Christian belief without being distinctive of any particular Christian denomination.

(3) Every act of collective worship required by section 6 of this Act in the case of a county school need not comply with subsection (1) above provided that, taking any school term as a whole, most such acts which take place in the school do comply with that subsection. . . .

8 Religious education required in the basic curriculum: further provisions . . .

(3) Any agreed syllabus which after this section comes into force . . . shall reflect the fact that the religious traditions in Great Britain are in the main Christian whilst taking account of the teaching and practices of the other principal religions represented in Great Britain.

9 Exceptions, special arrangements and supplementary and consequential provisions . . .

(3) If the parent of any pupil in attendance at any maintained school requests that he may be wholly or partly excused –

- (a) from attendance at religious worship in the school;
- (b) from receiving religious education given in the school in accordance with the school's basic curriculum; or
- (c) both from such attendance and from receiving such education;

the pupil shall be so excused accordingly until the request is withdrawn.

(4) Where in accordance with subsection (3) above any pupil has been wholly or partly excused from attendance at religious worship or from receiving religious education in any school, and the responsible authority are satisfied –

- (a) that the parent of the pupil desires him to receive religious education of a kind which is not provided in the school during the periods of time during which he is so excused;
- (b) that the pupil cannot with reasonable convenience be sent to another maintained school where religious education of the kind desired by the parent is provided; and
- (c) that arrangements have been made for him to receive religious education of that kind during school hours elsewhere;

the pupil may be withdrawn from the school during such periods of time as are reasonably necessary for the purpose of enabling him to receive religious education in accordance with the arrangements. . . .

11 Standing advisory councils on religious education

(1) It shall be the duty of every local education authority to constitute a standing advisory council on religious education –

> (a) to advise the authority upon such matters connected with religious worship in county schools and the religious education to be given in accordance with an agreed syllabus as the authority may refer to the council or as the council may see fit; and
>
> (b) to carry out the functions conferred by section 12 of this Act on councils constituted under this section. . . .

(3) The council shall consist of –

> (a) the representative members required by subsection (4) below; and
>
> (b) where any agreed syllabus for the time being adopted by the authority is in use at one or more grant-maintained schools, a person appointed by the governing body or (as the case may be) by the governing bodies of the school or schools concerned;

and may also include co-opted members.

(4) . . . the representative members required by this subsection are persons appointed by the authority to represent respectively –

> (a) such Christian and other religious denominations as, in the opinion of the authority, will appropriately reflect the principal religious traditions in the area;
>
> (b) except in the case of an area in Wales, the Church of England;
>
> (c) such associations representing teachers as, in the opinion of the authority, ought, having regard to the circumstances of the area, to be represented; and

(d) the authority; . . .

(7) The representative groups on the council, other than that consisting of persons appointed to represent the authority, may at any time require a review of any agreed syllabus for the time being adopted by the authority.

Each representative group concerned shall have a single vote on the question of whether to require such a review.

(8) On receipt by the authority of written notification of any such requirement, it shall be the duty of the authority to cause a conference constituted in accordance with the provisions of Schedule 5 to the 1944 Act to be convened for the purpose of reconsidering any agreed syllabus to which the requirement relates. . . .

12 Determination by advisory councils of the cases in which the requirement for Christian collective worship is not to apply

(1) It shall be the duty of the council, on an application made by the head teacher of any county school after consultation with the governing body, to consider whether it is appropriate for the requirement for Christian collective worship to apply in the case of that school, or in the case of any class or description of pupils at that school. . . .

(2) In determining whether it is appropriate for that requirement to apply in the case of any such school or in the case of any class or description of pupils at such a school, the council shall have regard to any circumstances relating to the family backgrounds of the pupils at the school or of the pupils of the particular class or description in question which are relevant for determining the character of the collective worship appropriate in their case. . . .

(5) Any determination of the council under this section by virtue of which the requirement for Christian collective worship does not for the time being apply in the case of any school or any class or description of pupils at any school shall be reviewed by the council –

(a) at any time on an application made by the head teacher of the school after consultation with the governing body; and

(b) in any event not later than the end of the period of five years beginning with the date on which the determination first took effect or (where it has since been reviewed under this subsection) with the effective date of the decision on the last such review. . . .

(9) The governing body of any county school, on being consulted by the head teacher under this section, may if they think fit take such steps as they consider appropriate for consulting all persons appearing to them to be parents of registered pupils at the school. . . .

Peter Liell, ed., *The Law of Education (Ninth edition): Special Bulletin, Education Reform Act 1988*, Butterworths, 1988, pp. 69–76 (extracts).

(f) *The future of Religious Education*
THE CONTENT OF RELIGIOUS EDUCATION AND THE 1988 EDUCATION REFORM ACT

One of the most significant features of the new Education Act is that religious instruction has been abolished. In Section 1 of Chapter 1 ('The Curriculum') we are told that the authorities responsible for the schools shall 'exercise their functions (including in particular the functions conferred on them by this chapter with respect to religious education, religious worship and the National Curriculum) . . .'.

This is the first time in law that religion taught in the classrooms in England and Wales has been called 'religious education'. The expression used in acts of Parliament from 1870 to 1944 was 'religious instruction'. The expression 'religious education' had been increasing in popularity steadily during the previous fifty or sixty years. It was widely felt that the word instruction suggested something too narrow, too authoritarian, and too suggestive of the transmission of a set body of knowledge or doctrine. . . .

CONTINUITY RATHER THAN CHANGE

Many people have emphasized the changes which the Act requires, but it would be easy to exaggerate these. Most educational legislation gives legal sanction and official support for what schools have long been doing. That was the case in 1944. Agreed Syllabuses, for example, were not created by the 1944 Act. They had been in great popularity during the 1920s and 1930s, and the Act merely ratified and clarified their use, making mandatory what previously had been done for purely professional reasons.

The 1988 Act is no exception. There are certainly changes, and some of them are important, but the major emphasis is upon continuity. This is apparent in section 8 where the special provisions for religious education are set out. The first thing that is said about religious education here is that it shall be 'of the kind required by such of the provisions of sections 26 to 28 of the 1944 Act . . . as apply in the case of that school'. This means that religious education shall be given to all pupils in attendance at the school, and shall be given in accordance with an Agreed Syllabus. . . .

Christianity is regarded as one of a class. The class is 'the religious traditions of Great Britain' and of these Christianity is regarded as the principal group. The plurality of Christianity is acknowledged, since the wording does not speak of the Christian religious tradition but of the religious traditions which are Christian. It is thus clear that the old fashioned practice of presenting Christianity as a unified entity must disappear. Full weight must be given to the range and variety of Christian religious traditions.

In the case of the other principal religious traditions of Great Britain, the new syllabuses must take account of both their teaching and their practices. We see thus that the doctrine (i.e. the teaching) of several religions becomes an integral part of religious education. Once again, the Act is supporting what has become the practice in the Agreed Syllabuses of the past fifteen years or so.

The significance of this emphasis upon plurality must be emphasized. A traditional feature of many Agreed Syllabuses has been the local history of Christianity. It has sometimes been argued that in counties where Christianity is virtually the only religious tradition there was no point in including the teaching and practices of Islam and Hinduism. Such a position will no longer be valid, since the new Act requires each local Agreed Syllabus to take account not so much of the religious traditions present in the locality but those represented in Great Britain. On any reckoning, Judaism, Islam, Hinduism, the Sikh faith and Buddhism are major religious traditions which are represented in Great Britain. Whether or not they are religious traditions *of* Great Britain is not the point. They do not have to be. They are certainly principal religions *represented* in Great Britain, and no Agreed Syllabus will meet the requirements of this section of the Act unless it takes account of their teaching and practices.

THE TRUTH AND THE RHETORIC

Many people have got the impression that the new Act announces a period of Christian aggression in education. Alarm has been expressed by thoughtful Muslims, Jews and others about the effects of this upon religious harmony in this country. The fact is that the Act gives no support whatever to Christian supremacy in the classroom. It is true that Christianity is mentioned on the face of the Bill but so are the other principal religions. Placed in the context of the educational emphasis which religious teaching is to have, this represents no more than an official support for the curriculum development which has been going on in religious education in recent years. Misguided Christians who are inspired more by tribalistic enthusiasm than by a responsible Christian concern for the Kingdom of God in Britain today must be gently but persistently reminded of the actual wording of the new Act.

Editorial, *British Journal of Religious Education*, 11 (1989), pp. 59–61 (with cuts).

(g) *Christian and Muslim perspectives on the 1988 Act*

Built largely on Christian foundations, the British national educational system has in the last twenty years become increasingly secular. This has given rise to a concern among Christians about various areas of education such as children's literature, the occult, sex education, and multi-faith RE, which all reflect this overall secularisation of our schools. However, recent changes in government legislation have opened new opportunities for a Christian presence in schools, and the growing disquiet among Christians is being translated into positive prayer and action.

Christians in Education is a charitable trust established to address this situation, aiming to encourage a biblical perspective on education and serve the Christian community in its involvement in schools.

One aspect of school life about which we are continually being asked is school assemblies. Under the 1944 Education Act, a daily act of collective worship was required for all pupils. At the time of the Act it was presumed to be Christian but was never actually stated to be so. Increasingly in the seventies and eighties that piece of legislation was seriously neglected, and school assemblies in many places, especially at secondary level, became both secular and multi-faith.

A concern about this situation gave rise to a series of amendments to the 1988 Education Reform Act being tabled in the House of Lords. These strengthened the requirements for a daily act of worship and prescribed that they should be 'wholly or mainly of a broadly Christian character'. The reaction to these requirements is mixed, and they will clearly present many schools with problems.

Whatever is prescribed by law, however, what matters most is what actually happens in the schools. The intention of the 1988 Education Reform Act is to see Christian worship in schools. Whether that becomes the experience of young people around the country depends not only upon the teachers but upon the prayer and participation of the Christian community.

It is not only difficult but inappropriate for unbelieving teachers to conduct Christian acts of worship. The Department of Education and Science (DES) in its guidance to local education authorities (Circular No 3/89) has therefore stated that:

Where there are insufficient teachers in a county school who are prepared to lead an act of collective worship in accordance with the requirements of Section 7, it is for the head teacher to take all reasonable steps to find persons not employed at the school who would be willing and able to conduct such acts (section 48).

Although this does not give members of the Christian community any legal right to go into schools, here is a door of opportunity for Christians to convert their concern into constructive Christian service. In many places schools are positively open to receiving sensitive offers of help in this sphere in a way which would have been most unlikely only a short time ago.

Christians in Education has written this book in the hope that it will encourage Christians to be 'willing' to take Christian acts of worship and 'able' to do so in a way which is well prepared, interesting, and appropriate to the individual school.

Lynn Murdoch, Preface to Janet King with Christians in Education, *Leading Worship in Schools: An Open Door for Christians?*, Monarch, Christians in Education, Eastbourne, 1990, pp. 7–9.

Rt. Hon. Kenneth Baker MP,
Secretary of State for Education,
Elizabeth House,
York Road,
London, SE1 7PB   29th June 1988

Dear Mr Baker,

Re: AMENDMENTS ON RELIGIOUS EDUCATION INTRO-
    DUCED BY THE BISHOP OF LONDON . . .

While we are in favour of the natural primacy of Christianity in the collective worship and in the religious education for Christians, at the same time, we would ask for explicit provision in the

Education Reform Bill for the minority faiths to pursue their own forms of worship and religious education.

We firmly believe that you have no intention to impose Christianity on non-Christians and deprive the minority faiths of their legitimate rights. We rather hope that you will do everything possible to allay any fears of the minority faiths resulting from the amendments.

In the context, I would like to reiterate some of the basic educational concerns of the Muslim community:

1 The right to withdraw Muslim children from the collective worship and religious education must be preserved in the Education Reform Bill.

2 Muslim children must be provided with the necessary facilities within the school premises to hold their Islamic assemblies and receive Islamic education.

3 Section 26(b) of the Education Act, 1944 should be amended to allow the Local Education Authorities to facilitate and meet the cost of religious worship and religious education of the minority faiths.

4 Suitable facilities should be provided by the LEAs to Muslim children to offer their prayer in schools with 10 Muslim pupils on its roll.

5 Muslim girls of secondary school age should be allowed to observe their religious rules to wear modest dress and headscarf conforming to the colour of the school uniform in order to enable them to do their Islamic worship and attend Islamic religious education. . . .

Yours sincerely,

Ghulam Sarwar
Director

Ghulam Sarwar, *Education Reform Act: Compulsory Christian Collective Worship and Christian Religious Instruction (RE) in Schools: What can Muslims Do?*, London, The Muslim Educational Trust, 1989, pp. 8–9.

12
WOMEN

<u></u>

*T*his *section is designed to illustrate, through a range of short extracts,*
something of the diversity of women's religious experience and concerns.
Material is concentrated on the later years of the period when the growth of
feminist and female consciousness resulted in an increasingly serious
challenge to traditionally patriarchal structures. Women wrestled with the
constraints of language and image (a), but were increasingly articulate
about their own spiritual resources (b). For Christians the issues were focused
particularly by the debate over the ordination of women to the priesthood of
the Church of England, but much wider matters were seen to be at stake (c).
Liberal Judaism affirmed the equality of the sexes, while Jewish women explored
the nature and historical roots of their identity (d). For Muslims the hijab
(veil) was a central issue (e), while there were some radical voices
challenging the whole perceived framework of male domination in the Asian
religions (f). Even Sikh women, who were able to assume roles of considerable
responsibility in community organizations, were not necessarily satisfied with
their situation (g). For others (in this case Buddhists) an alternative radical
option was celibate communal life (h). Meanwhile the growth of New Age
spiritualities offered further potentialities (i). (Note also the article on Hindu
women in section 4(c) and an Afro-Caribbean female perspective in section
6(c).)

(a) Language and tradition

Language: At this conference we had been speaking to each other
in English which created a number of barriers for a range of women
who brought with them different understandings of the same words
(such as 'fundamental'). We must not develop a false sense of security, believing we have everything in common: one of the difficulties
of talking in an adopted language was that many difficulties were
not vocalised, because women could not begin to articulate what

they really wanted to say. It was also recognised that by speaking in English we were using a western-defined and largely male-dominated language. Words were not always adequate, in whatever language we spoke, to capture the way we wanted to talk about the spiritual, and one participant thought that we would do well to use other channels, such as nature, to image the religious dimension in our lives. It was also suggested that our gestures and actions should be filled with spiritual sincerity, as actions indeed speak louder than words.

Cultural and religious traditions: It was noted that many of the difficulties women encountered within their faith communities were more influenced by cultural traditions rather than religious laws. In many cases it was difficult to distinguish between cultural and religious practices, as for most women present, both fused into a single way of life. It was also important to acknowledge that it was both western and eastern cultures that could oppress women. It was often assumed that only eastern cultural practices restricted women.

Religion affirming or oppressing women: A number of women present told stories about their own religions and how they affirmed their roles as women. For example, some faiths encouraged women to become spiritual teachers; religious teachings accorded dignity and respect to women's gifts; some faith communities consulted both women and men before policy decisions were made or allowed women and men to take up the same roles in their place of worship. But it was acknowledged that while all our faiths could proclaim ideals wherein women were treated with dignity and respect, the good news our faith offered had often been distorted and suppressed in the course of time. It was also noted that women's traditional role as mother was to be affirmed and celebrated, and that faith traditions were rich in this respect. However, motherhood was not the only model for women and it was necessary to hold its affirmation in balance with similar respect for women who chose other roles.

Women's needs and expectations: It was easy to assume that all women were seeking the same things and it was important to remember

that women had different needs and expectations. It was acknowledged that 'feminist' language could be as threatening to some
women as 'male' language. It was necessary to be clear about what we
were saying in order to avoid isolating and confusing some women. It
was not appropriate to build a false dichotomy between liberal and
conservative women. One participant shared her experience of
meeting two conservative women, one a Christian and the other a
Muslim, who had encouraged her to pursue inter-faith dialogue. It
was not always necessary to agree with one another in order to
achieve good inter-faith dialogue. Dialogue must not be restricted
to a particular group of liberal women. It was also important to
recognise that the needs and expectations of our different faith
communities were constantly shifting and difficult areas such as
morality were not as clear cut as were sometimes assumed.

Images of women: There was some debate as to how we defined what
were positive and negative images of women. Some women felt that
they had been stereotyped by others because of the clothes that they
chose to wear. It was assumed that women wearing saris and veils
were oppressed and this made those women angry. One professional
woman said that she purposely wore Indian dress at work to actively
break down the negative stereotype that all Indian women were ill
educated and poverty stricken. What did it mean for women
from other cultures to integrate with British society? If black women
wore white women's clothes, it would not make them white.
Wrongly or rightly, the way we dressed did influence the way we
were treated. We needed to dress to please ourselves, but we also
needed to be aware of the sensitivities of our cultural and religious
communities.

'What women of faith are saying', Report of a day conference run by the Inter-Faith
Network, 1992, pp. 12–14.

(b) *Women's spiritual resources*

In answering our question we must emphasise first of all the rich
resources which women possess within themselves and which they

have manifested frequently enough throughout history. These are resources primarily linked to women's biological, emotional and psychic attributes and abilities. There is perhaps first and foremost the immense resource of suffering as a source of strength to overcome adversity and affliction. There are the pain, the tears, the agony, the immense labour in bringing new life into the world and attending with equally immense patience to its slow and imperceptible growth. These are the roots for women's resources of compassion, of insight, and ultimately of wisdom.

There is also women's attention to detail, to the *minutiae* of life, the faithfulness to the daily round of duties which ensure personal and social wellbeing and make the smooth running of ever so many activities in the world possible and bearable. Then there is women's power of listening, of pacifying, of soothing and healing many a wound and settling many a quarrel and dispute. There is the strength of an encouraging smile and the gentle touch of love, the experience of generous selfless giving, of comfort, warmth, patient encouragement and recognition, the adaptability to people and their personal needs, the caring concern and understanding of others.

Peace, love, joy and harmony are all fruits of the spirit found in people of spiritual power and presence. They are not qualities unique to women but women, by the very nature of their traditional tasks and experience and by the social pressures and constraints put upon them, have often developed and embodied these qualities to an unusual degree. . . .

To put into practice the spirit of peace, of friendship and love, humankind must become fully aware of all the potentials of our global spiritual and moral resources, an essential part of which is represented by the spiritual heritage and resources of women. More than anything else this heritage of women consists in the celebration and affirmation of all life – the life that flows in our veins, the force that lives in nature all around us, the life that animates us within, and the life of the spirit which continually renews us. This is a most precious heritage for the renewal of our world and the life of all people, but women in particular can draw great strength not only from the spiritual resources within themselves and their sisters, but also from a rich and diverse heritage of symbols, beliefs and exemplary lives in the cultures and religions of the past.

U. King, *Women and Spirituality*, London, Macmillan, 1989, pp. 92–4 (with cuts).

(c) Challenges for the churches

I remain of the conviction that the ordination of women to the priesthood ought to be construed as an enlargement and extension of the historic Christian ministry. For a number of years I have done my best to present the ordination of women in the Anglican Communion to Orthodoxy and to Rome in terms of development rather than revolution.

Theological arguments can justify and indeed increasingly require the ordination of women to the priesthood. It cannot be irrelevant to evangelism that so many unbelievers think the place we give to women is frankly absurd.

Robert Runcie,
Archbishop of Canterbury,
General Synod,
November 1989

Robert Runcie, quoted in *Women Priests: Which Way Will You Vote?*, London, SPCK, 1990, p. 6.

What is most noticeable to onlookers is that women are trying very hard to say something of great importance to the Church, and *they are not being listened to*, much as Florence Nightingale was not listened to, to the disgrace and folly of the institution she sought to love and serve. Women are trying to say 'You have denied our very personhood, you have cut us out of your pictures of God, you have told us to be quiet, you have not consulted us. Now that we can speak for ourselves, we intend to do so. It is *our* church every bit as much as it is yours, and we don't like it the way it is. We don't want to be patronized or condescended to, we expect to share jobs and rites and language, theological ideas and ecclesiastical decisions, on equal terms. We dislike the "old boy network" and "jobs for the boys", and don't believe they are relevant to Christian belief. We don't want our daughters brought up on patriarchal lines or damaging theological ideas, we don't want to be flattered, or idealized, or told we are "an influence" behind the scenes. We don't want to spend all our time as secretaries, typists, flower arrangers, floor scrubbers, surplice washers, sandwich cutters, bazaar organizers, though we may choose to do our share of such things. We have strength, power, wisdom, commonsense, just as men have, and we would like to use it justly, straightforwardly and efficiently, not covertly in order to simulate weakness and helplessness.'

M. Furlong, *A Dangerous Delight*, London, SPCK, 1992, p. 148.

Until women are ordained as priests it is difficult to see how a balance can be given to the leadership of the Church. But the ordination of women does not stand or fall on that, rather it is related back to our understanding of God and of men and women created and redeemed in that image. Bishop Oliver Tompkins has written:

Christian priesthood is called to be fully human if God is to be known as fully God.

Here is the central issue in the debate over the ordination of women.

It is not primarily about rights for women. It is not a political issue about women sharing a function hitherto assigned to men.

It involves at one and the same time our understanding of the nature of God, of the nature of humanity, and of the real depths of the life and unity of the universal Church.

It is a search for wholeness in life which expresses, reflects and is grounded in the wholeness of the Triune God and a transformation of our Christian system.

The key question is: Can the churches open themselves to receive that vision? Can they open themselves to this source of energy, this fresh spring of water, this new wine, this 'women spirit rising', and change and be changed in the process?

Mary Tanner, 'A Wider Vision', in *Women Priests: Which Way Will you Vote?*, London, SPCK, 1990, p. 24.

It is one thing, however, to analyse our uneasiness with unduly masculine language and quite another to provide usable and wor-shipful alternatives. Along with others, I have been engaged in both activities in recent years, and I have found that the second process, of trying to find 'a language which positively celebrates the "feminine" we presently fear', has involved me in a deep and search-ing exploration of what liturgical prayer is *for*, in a way that has been much more demanding than I had anticipated. . . .

A . . . creative danger associated with women's liturgies is their potential to reveal some political realities that underpin our worship practice, in ways that sharpen the theological words and images we are so accustomed to. The St Hilda Community in east London is a mixed group of Anglicans committed to the active ministry of women, including presidency of the Eucharist. Last Easter, it was planned that a woman priest should preside in the chapel normally used by the Community. But it was made clear by the diocesan authorities that, if this went ahead, the incumbent's job might be at risk, and so the decision was taken to hold the celebration in an adjoining common room instead. The altar table was placed across the entrance to the empty chapel, and the service took place outside the officially hallowed space. Immediately, the hollow, dark church became a graphic image of the empty tomb, visited first by women, as the preacher stood in the doorway and repeated: 'He is not here. He is risen. He is gone before you.' Rather frightening implications for the Church did not need spelling out; but they arose, not because of someone's imaginative aesthetic liturgical ideas about space and movement, but because we were *really* not allowed to be in the church. The current political realities about who may take liturgical authority, and where, themselves commented on our theology.

Other groups have discovered that to take seriously the agenda set by women in this time, and to bring Christian tradition into contact and dialogue with that, has liberated liturgical action from its necessary connection with church buildings at all, and set free its capacity to subvert some cherished political assumptions. Inspired by the witness of those women at Greenham who have for years put their bodies outside the camp to protest at preparations for nuclear war, and believing also that the Christian witness 'outside the gate' is relevant here, a group of Christian women come monthly to the Blue Gate at Greenham. Here they keep vigil overnight, using a liturgy based on the passion narrative in Mark's gospel, interspersed with psalms and other biblical readings. To commemorate the passion, squatting in the mud by a campfire, in the dark and wet, and facing a sentry box and razor-wire, is a quite different experience from doing so in church. Reminders of the women who 'watched from afar' take on a peculiar concreteness; but once again, this is not someone's bright idea for re-living the gospel story with convincing special effects. It is to partake in an actual vigil that is kept, while a potentially cosmic passion is prepared – and it is in any case only what the Greenham women do nightly. The danger is not faked; and it is appropriate to bring the risky activity of communal prayer into the place where that appalling danger can be visibly confronted. Strangely (or perhaps not so strangely), most of those who participate in the Greenham vigil find themselves not only cold and tired, but also moved and actually hopeful. For to engage in such an activity in such a place is not only to emerge from the safety of the church building; it is to call in question the kind of 'security' that can be derived from the possession and deployment of weapons of mass destruction by opposing this with the radical insecurity we are called on to embrace as Christians. To give up the idea that liturgical practice should be free from danger can offer us a position from which to confront our fears for the world. It is in this kind of context also that it becomes clear that liturgical language is a form of *action*, taking a particular stance in the interactions of the world, rather than a retreat into an apparently abstract and apolitical space. The inextricable connection between liturgy and human polemic is once more made visible.

And so, devising new liturgies as women is dangerous because it risks exposing conflict. . . .

But perhaps the greatest danger we should avoid is the feminist version of the one I began with: namely the illusion that there exists, at least potentially, a 'pure', adequate, right, *safe* language about God that we have merely to discover and then implement – a solution to our present uneasiness about male-centred terminology.

J. Morley in M. Furlong, ed., *Mirror to the Church: Reflections on Sexism*, London, SPCK, 1988, pp. 24, 33–5, 35 (with cuts).

(d) The place of women in Jewish life

We affirm the *equal status of men and women in synagogue life*. The Liberal Jewish movement has been the pioneer in that respect in Britain. There is no sex segregation in our synagogues. Women may lead services, become rabbis, and hold any synagogue office.

We affirm the *equal status of boys and girls in religious education*. Accordingly, we have introduced the ceremony of *Bat-Mitzvah*, 'Daughter of Duty' to complement the traditional *Bar-Mitzvah*, 'Son of Duty' at the age of thirteen, and we attach great importance to the further ceremony, created by Liberal Judaism, of *Kabbalat Torah*, 'Acceptance of Torah' or 'Confirmation' at fifteen or sixteen.

We affirm the *equal status of men and women in marriage law and ritual*. With us, therefore, bride and bridegroom alike play an active role in the marriage service. Similarly, we object to the traditional *Get*, Bill of Divorce, by which the husband unilaterally 'sends away' his wife.

'On the status of women', *Affirmations of Liberal Judaism*, Nos. 32–4, London, Union of Liberal and Progressive Synagogues, n.d.

There was no link between history as we knew it from home and our place in modern Britain, between childhood stories and our adult experience. Our parents' stories belonged to a different history; they lived on the margins of the textbooks we met at school.

For those of us who grew up in Britain, the school history we learned was the one in which English kings and one or two queens led a triumphant march from the Stone Age to the present day. It was followed by a history of the Greeks and Romans which didn't mention their occupation of the Jews' land and the consequent oppression of the Jews, or the contribution the Jews made to resistance against their empires. The rest of school history was a cosy anglocentric celebration of a past in which the other peoples of the world were by and large either subject peoples or enemies. . . . Usually, that history stopped at the First World War. And the ordinary people of Britain were presented as a monolithically white, English-speaking mass who either lined the streets to cheer the great or erupted dangerously as mobs.

Some of us encountered Jewish history at school in the shape of scripture lessons; some of us went to *cheder* as well, where we also learned to read Hebrew. This history was largely based on Bible stories of the tribes of Ancient Israel. Where women played any part at all, they were just as likely to have been temptresses and schemers, like Jezebel and Delilah, as heroines, like Esther and Deborah.

Our mothers' stories were very different. For most of us, 'our' history was one which included flight from persecution and sometimes the threat of death, and subsequent migration from country to country. There are few of us who have grown up in the same countries as our mothers, and some of them in turn had come to live in different countries from their mothers or their grandmothers. The stories they had to tell us were often of the ways of their own families as part of the Jewish communities of Middle and Eastern Europe. . . .

Through these stories many of us learned that it was the women in our families who had so often been the ones responsible for taking on those movements across continents to safe homes. It was the women who kept the memory of who and what had been in the past. For those of us who came from religious backgrounds, it was often the women who found ways to give us a consciousness of Jewishness as more than a religion, a nationality, a personal identity.

For them, it meant a way of life which shaped every aspect of their existence.

We wanted to know what Jewish women's lives were like. But women are scarcely mentioned in conventional Jewish histories. It is an irony that histories of Jews by Jews, which are scarcely acknowledged in mainstream historical accounts of countries where Jews lived for centuries, echo the marginalisation of women in orthodox academic history. Jewish women's experiences and perceptions have either been obscured or absorbed into descriptions of men's lives. Yet we know that Jewish women's contributions to the family economy in Eastern Europe prior to their arrival in England were vital, often the only ones when men were absent in the army or peddling or studying, or had gone abroad in advance of the rest of the family.

Like other historians of lives which have not to date been considered worthy of documentation, we turned to oral history. We wanted to talk to Jewish women about their personal experiences of living through the great upheavals of Jewish life in this century. . . .

The task was far greater than we had ever imagined in 1984, when we first formed as a group, for there is no single Jewish women's history. Instead, there are a number of Jewish women's histories, for Jewish women have lived in countries as diverse as the Yemen, Lithuania, Germany and India and their lives are shaped by the histories of those countries as well as having an internal dynamic of their own. We wanted to represent the range and diversity of Jewish women's experience and set out to explore the ways in which Jewish women's identities are constructed and developed, within and against historical and life events.

Jewish Women in London Group, *Generations of Memories: Voices of Jewish Women*, London, The Women's Press, 1989, pp. 6–7.

But the way I read Judaism is almost like standing on its head all the conventions about Judaism, especially those which have been talked about by gentile feminists. I see Judaism as first of all a religion and a tradition which have always taken a very strong lead from 'the people'. There's great attention paid to the wishes of the people, with the rabbis following the congregations, not leading them, in the sense of altering the rules or reinterpreting the rules to respond to the needs and desires of the people. Take the tradition, for example, of separating women and men in the synagogue, which comes from the demands of women in the time of the Temple that they have a women's space. That women's space in the Temple was called *ezras nashim*, which means 'help for women' – it literally means women's aid. I love that tradition in Judaism which separates men and women, because I am a radical feminist and a separatist and so therefore Jewish practice which separates women and men, I think absolutely wonderful! There are feminists who read that as saying, that's an oppression of women. There is so much evidence in the history of *halachic* practice that women have succeeded in changing the law by pressure that I just don't believe that it's a correct interpretation of either women or Judaism to say these things happen because women were oppressed. I'm not trying to deny that they were oppressed but I don't think that the *halachah* is there as a simple projection of the particular forms of oppression which Jewish women experience. But I rather think that Judaism is full of recognition of the need for women's separate space, recognition of the innate violence of men, and therefore there are a whole load of obligations on men that they should constantly be praying, that they should cover themselves with symbols which tell them not to sin, like the *tallis* and the *tsitsis* and so on. It's almost as if Judaism is saying, yes, men are violent, they need restraining, and they have to fill up their lives with *mitzvahs*. Jewish tradition is absolutely against anything like pornography and out-of-control sexuality. And I more than appreciate it, I feel utterly at home with that.

Jewish Women in London Group, *Generations of Memories: Voices of Jewish Women*, London, The Women's Press, 1989, p. 238 (Miriam Metz).

(e) *Muslims and the veil*

Wearing the *hijab* can be a liberation, freeing women from being sexual objects, releasing them from the trap of Western dress and the dictates of Western fashion. Just as feminists in the West have reflected on the connection between 'feminine' clothes and female oppression, so Muslim feminists reject the outward symbols of sexual allure. In favour of the *hijab* it can be said that by distancing its wearer from the world, it enriches spiritual life, grants freedom from material preoccupations, and erases class differences by expressing solidarity with others in the same uniform. Since all women look the same in it, it is a most effective equaliser, and since it camouflages rich clothing, it is in keeping with the Islamic injunction against ostentation. The long dull coat usually worn with the *hijab* is of similar significance and may be compared with the dun-coloured cloak favoured in Renaissance Florence after the passing of the anti-luxury laws.

R. Kabbani, *Letter to Christendom*, London, Virago, 1989, pp. 26–7.

Rana Kabbani also argues that the *hijab* has become a symbol of resistance from the imperialist, racist, and Christian forces of the West, which demand assimilation, and overpower and destroy Eastern cultures. I accept that this perspective exists, even in Britain, where, after the Rushdie affair, some women are reasserting their Muslim identity by taking up the *hijab*, but I believe that such a perspective mitigates against the long-term interests of women. It poses dangers for those of us who have been working to liberate ourselves from these restrictions. These developments have to be seen in the context of wider pressures to control women. For example, the demand for separate religious schools, especially for girls, is a serious setback, because it will lead to indoctrination and pressure to return to the traditional role for a Muslim woman, that of mother and wife.

H. Siddiqui, Review of *Letter to Christendom*, *Feminist Review*, **37** (1991), p. 81.

(f) Dignity in dissent

On 27 May 1989 when the Muslim fundamentalists marched

through Central London against Rushdie, I was there not as a part of their demonstration, but as a part of the women's counter picket organised by Women Against Fundamentalism.

The full realisation of why I was there did not dawn on me until the Muslim demonstrators marched past us at Parliament Square. When I saw thousands of angry Asian male faces, it reminded me of the faces of my father, my brothers, my uncles. Of my whole family and community. Of a culture and religion which intertwine to sanction and reinforce male power and domination. It looked and felt so familiar.

The fundamentalist cries of whores and prostitutes reminded me of the insults I had to bear when I went out with my friends and exposed my legs. When I refused to marry and had boyfriends. When I wore make up and cut my hair. Once I said I wanted to be an actress, my father slapped me. This slap of authority sought to punish, silence, and control me. This slap came from my father, my family, my community.

Separate Muslim schools for girls is yet another slap. My father always worried about my co-education in Britain – the corrupting influence of the West, of disbelievers, of Christians, of boys who would soil my virginity with a look, of girls who would lead me astray. Separate schools seek to segregate and control my sexuality, limit my world vision, and curb my aspirations, to destroy my chances of higher education or of a chosen career. Indoctrination which prepares me for my role as a good Muslim wife and a mother. A school which keeps me in ignorance of the alternatives.

The fundamentalists are supported by the state, the multiculturalist, and the liberal anti-racist lobby. The multi-culturalists see the community as a unified whole. The only demands they listen to are those defined by conservative, religious, male leaders. They refuse to recognise the demands of women within our communities. At SBS, Asian women come in on a daily basis experiencing violence, rape and sexual abuse. Women are being forced into arranged marriages, homelessness, and denial of education. The multi-culturalists fail to intervene and support these women. For them, it is all part of a culture and religion which must be tolerated. And the anti-racists allow this to continue because they see the fight against racism as the central struggle.

At the picket, my past of daily battles had now been transformed onto the streets in new and dangerous ways. My heart pounded with fear and excitement as it did when I questioned and challenged my father. However, as then, I did not put down my banner and walk away. Even when the fundamentalists attempted to physically assault me, I did not walk away.

I shared this battleground with other women from diverse religious backgrounds. But we were all doubters and dissenters. We oppose the supreme court ruling on abortion in America as we oppose the Muslim fundamentalists. In both cases, fundamentalists are attempting to control women.

I do not want men and mullahs to build my future. I want to create my own future in a world where women can choose to live as they please. I want a secular state without blasphemy laws which impose religious censorship. I support Salman Rushdie's right to write *The Satanic Verses* because his right to doubt and dissent is also my right to doubt and dissent. For me, it represents a lifetime of struggle and a refusal to submit to the slap of authority.

Hannana Siddiqui, 'A Woman's Banner for Doubt and Dissent', in Southall Black Sisters, *Against the Grain: A Celebration of Survival and Struggle*, London, Southall Black Sisters, 1989, p. 2.

(g) The contribution of women to Sikhism

Sikh women have come in the forefront and have shown their ability and stamina to work outside Punjab. In 1966 in Smethwick (Midlands) a serious dispute arose between the two parties of the Gurdwara Management Committee. The women took charge of the Gurdwara affairs and for a whole year very successfully conducted the affairs till the men cooled down and got ready to work together.

Bibi Balwant Kaur in Birmingham has contributed greatly to the social and religious welfare of Sikh women by establishing Bebe

Nanaki Gurdwara in Birmingham, where mostly women manage all the affairs of the Gurdwara. In Kenya, she helped widows to become self-supporting by giving them tailoring techniques and providing sewing machines. For the recent famine in Ethiopia, she collected funds and personally visited the famine-stricken areas.

Many women have and are currently occupying positions of Presidents, secretaries of Gurdwaras and other similar Sikh organisations. In almost every Gurdwara, women are seen organising functions to collect money for charities. In spite of her active participation in all religious, political, social and cultural affairs, the position of Sikh woman is far from satisfactory. Her status in life is still lower than man. The birth of a female is still less welcome than the birth of a male child. There still exists the dreaded dowry system that puts the woman a few pegs lower than the man. The Sikh man will quite happily cook, clean and serve food in the Langar in the Gurdwara but would still think those very jobs belonging to woman as in his mind it is engraved that household chores are low and need less intelligence.

Despite the Gurus' teachings of full equality, the Sikh woman still suffers from submerged prejudices and stereotyping. The male dominance has led to the exclusion of women from being one of the Panj Piaras (five beloved ones) to administer Amrit. No woman has even been elected as the president of S.G.P.C. (the Central Management Committee to manage the affairs of the Gurdwaras in Punjab); no woman has been appointed Jathedar (head) of any of the five Takhats (the thrones of authority); and the number of women, who have been the members, secretaries or presidents of Gurdwara management committees is very small.

Sikh history has been written by men only, who either chose to disregard women's contributions or did not think their contributions worthy of note. Whatever the reason, women's contributions have been kept off the record and as a result Sikh women could not transmit their achievements to the next generation so that the next generation could have positive images to look upon and emulate. Even today there is not a single research book – or any other book – written on the contribution of Sikh women.

I think to some extent the fault also lies with Sikh women themselves. They have collaborated with men in stereotyping the role of women. Sikh women should teach equality of the sexes within the family unit by welcoming the birth of a daughter and celebrating this on the same scale as those of sons and providing equal opportunities for their higher education and challenging careers.

Kanwaljit Kaw Singh, 'Sikh Women', *The Sikh Messenger*, Spring/Summer 1990, pp. 24–5.

(h) *The making of Buddhist nuns*

In Britain over the past 8 years, first at Chithurst Forest Monastery and since 1984 at Amaravati Buddhist Centre an order of nuns has gradually come into being. Like a tiny shoot grafted on to a strong and healthy plant it has begun to take shape. I was among the first 4 women to arrive – inspired by the teaching and example of Ajahn Sumedho and the other western born bhikkhus who had been trained at Ajahn Chah's monasteries in North East Thailand. We lived in much the same way as the postulant monks, following a discipline comprising the Eight Precepts combined with a fairly rigorous monastic routine. Our work in the community was for the most part menial – cooking, gardening, cleaning, running errands and arranging flowers for the shrine. We were very different in background and temperament but, with the constant support and encouragement of the monks who were our teachers, our practice began to take root and gradually we discovered how to live together harmoniously. We learned to forgive ourselves and each other for our inevitable short-comings, to begin again: 'not making problems about the world', as Ajahn Sumedho would say. So the foundation for an order of nuns was laid.

Over the years which followed we were joined by others and in 1983 Ajahn Sumedho, having hesitated out of sensitivity to the somewhat conservative sangha in Thailand, took the step of allowing the first four of us to 'Go Forth'. We avowed the Ten Precepts and, relinquishing personal wealth, we became totally dependent on the generosity of others. The white robes and tin bowls of anagarikas were replaced by dark brown robes and ceramic alms bowls of 'Siladhara'.

Ayya Candasiri, 'Going Forth', *Shap Mailing 1988: Women and Religion*, p. 23.

(i) New Age and matriarchy

We are women who have been meeting to celebrate and exchange knowledge at the full and dark moons and at the eight festivals of the old religion. We have shared our feelings, discussed our ideas. We are women who want to discover or rediscover our spirituality and to affirm and work with energies which are specifically female.

'Who We Are', *Arachne: A Magazine of Wimmin's (sic) Spirituality*, 1, May 1983.

Matriarchy does not mean power of the mothers or rule of the mothers. But what matriarchy actually means is: In the beginning was the Mother. The Mother created All . . . Motherhood is creativity, invention, renewal of life in every aspect. To be a matriarchalist is to state that Our values are different from Theirs, and to state without fear, but loudly, that Matriarchy, a Different kind of society Did Exist and Will exist.

Matriarchy Research and Reclaim Network Newsletter, 19, n.d.

13
CHRISTIANS AND SEXUAL MORALITY

*T*he 'permissive' trends of the 1960s were met with a variety of reactions
from the churches, including cautious adjustment (a), conservative
restatement (b), and radical reassessment (c). Meanwhile evangelicals in the
Festival of Light movement developed a vigorous critique of 'permissive' trends
in the media (d). For Monica Furlong, on the other hand, the issues were by
no means so clear cut (e). The 1980s saw the continuance of longstanding
debates, notably on abortion (f), and also some creative reinterpretation of
traditional teaching (g). Meanwhile arguments raged over the morality of
homosexual relationships (h). In the latter part of the decade the challenge of
the AIDS virus dramatically raised the emotional and theological stakes (i).

(a) The role of sex in marriage

During the past thirty years theological thought about marriage has
developed considerably.

1 Full weight has been given to New Testament teaching about the
union of man and woman in 'one flesh' and the analogy it bears to the
union of Christ and his Church. It is now fairly generally recognized
that the union of man and wife ought not to be regarded mainly as a
means to bringing children into existence, but as a 'two-in-oneship'
which has value in itself and glorifies God. It has become common to
think of children as the 'fruit', rather than as the 'end' of the marriage
union; and monogamy is more often defended by reference to the
demands of love and of the gift of self which is made in marriage than
by reference to the needs of offspring.

2 In keeping with this development a new value is ascribed to
coitus, which, as the specific and consummating act of marriage, is

seen to be no mere means to generation, but an act of positive importance for the marriage union and for the perfecting of husband and wife. This intrinsic value is affirmed as against the old opinion that *coitus* always needed the 'good' of generation to justify it. Since the unitive virtue of the act depends partly on the manner in which it is performed, value is attributed to love-making also.

3 Lest the new orientation of thought about marriage should cause procreation to be regarded as merely subsidiary to the personal relationship of husband and wife, there is renewed insistence in some quarters on the dignity of parenthood as participation in the creativity of God and on the fact that the procreative purpose is part and parcel of marriage, not an optional *addendum* to it.

4 Increased understanding of the cycle of fertility in woman has made deliberately non-generative *coitus* a practical possibility even for those who reject contraception. In consequence new moral questions are posed. On the one hand, to what extent may man and wife rightly use *coitus* with sole reference to their own relationship? On the other hand, how are man and wife to determine the extent of their procreative responsibility? Is there a discoverable 'duty' to have children, or should procreation be regarded as a matter of vocation rather than of duty? In addition there is still the vexed question whether contraception is admissible or, if it is admissible, in what circumstances it may rightly be used. On these matters which are relevant to population problems, debate continues.

'The Family in Contemporary Society', in I. T. Ramsey, ed., *Christian Ethics and Contemporary Philosophy*, London, SCM, 1966, pp. 341–2.

(b) An evangelical perspective

LEGISLATION

The Church must be loyal to God's absolute standards and practical in its application of them to legislation. We maintain that the law of our land still primarily reflects Christian morality, but we recognize that the full Christian ethic cannot be enforced by law.

DIVORCE AND ABORTION

The law of divorce provides a case in point. Christ unequivocally stated that God's purpose for man was lifelong fidelity in marriage, but He in no way suggested that the Mosaic concession to the 'hardness of men's hearts' was not made by divine permission. This does not mean that we believe in two standards, one for Christians and the other for non-Christians. We accept one fundamental standard, but we believe that we may rightly take our part in framing a civil law of divorce which will best combine such concessions to human frailty and sin as the circumstances of society may require, with maintenance of the greatest possible stability in marriage.

Similarly, in regard to abortion, we judge that the life of the mother and her physical and mental health, must have priority over the potential personality of the foetus. We therefore urge that questions such as alleged rape, the possibility that the embryo might be malformed, and social considerations, should not be regarded as grounds for abortion unless the mother's health is in danger.

The problem of abortion troubles so many minds and consciences that it merits investigation by a Royal Commission.

SEXUAL MORALITY

Whilst sympathizing with young people concerning certain social customs and the resulting temptations which press upon them today, we assert that marriage is the divinely ordained state in which complete sexual fulfilment is to be sought. Pre-marital and extra-marital intercourse are therefore contrary to this principle and are responsible for much unhappiness.

We urge local churches to provide adequate instruction about sex and sexual morality, both for young people in general and for engaged couples in particular, and we believe that self-control should be encouraged as the basis of future family happiness and stability.

Philip Crowe, ed., *Keele '67: The National Evangelical Anglican Congress Statement*, London, Falcon, 1967, pp. 27, 30.

(c) A new Christian morality?

I chose the title *Christian Freedom in a Permissive Society* because, from the time that it served as a chapter heading in *Honest to God*, 'the new morality' has been, as a household phrase, equated with 'the permissive society' and all that it stands for. But my plea was in fact for a criterion of response and responsibility more rather than less searching than that of the old code morality. . . .

Permissiveness – what does it suggest both to those who like and to those who dislike it? Freedom from interference or control, doing your own thing, love, laxity, licence, promiscuity – and in terms of verbs, swinging, sliding, eroding, condoning.

Christian freedom, on the other hand, has its ambience, both in the New Testament and outside it, in a very different language world – that of freedom *for* self and others and God. Its concomitants are truth, grace, love, service, responsibility, wholeness, authenticity, authority (the freedom which Jesus had that comes from going direct to source), maturity, sonship, coming of age, self-possession. . . .

In what sense are Christian morals today different from Christian morals yesterday? Is there not an abiding Christian ethic? Indeed, can you have a new morality any more than a new gospel? The tension here is between the constant and the variable, the absolute and the relative, the eternal and the changing.

Now, neither side in the present controversy, I would submit, has any interest in denying either of these complementary elements. But to the 'old morality' it *looks* as if the advocates of the 'new' are betraying the absolutes of right and wrong and selling out to relativism. What I would seek to urge is that they have equally vital concern for the element of the unconditional but are placing it elsewhere.

The 'old morality', if we may continue to use these terms as counters, locates the unchanging element in Christian ethics in the *content* of the commands. There are certain things which are always right, and others which are always wrong. These absolute Christian standards are eternally valid, and remain unchanging in the midst of relativity and flux. And it is this body of moral teaching, grounded firmly on the laws of God and the commands of Christ, which the church exists to proclaim to every succeeding generation of men and women, whether they hear or whether they forbear.

Christian ethics, according to this view, is concerned with *applying* these standards to the changing situation. It starts from the fact that the Bible supplies a God-given 'net' or framework of conduct for human affairs. The task of moral theologians is to keep the net in repair for each generation, and to define its mesh more closely as new occasions teach new duties. There is nothing static about this conception of Christian ethics as long as it does not become ossified, and casuistry at its best has conserved fluidity with fixity in a way that compels the reluctant admiration even of those who most distrust it. But I will not expound this view further. It is the one in which most churchmen have been nurtured, whether catholic or protestant (the difference of emphasis being that the catholic tends to maintain the net by narrowing its mesh, the protestant by strengthening its cords). Rather, I should like to move on to try to interpret the opposite approach, which is in greater need of exposition.

This view starts from the other end. It does not in the least deny the need for a 'net'. No person, no society, can continue or cohere for any length of time without an accepted ethic, just as ordered life becomes impossible without a recognized legal system or a stable economy. And the Christian least of all can be disinterested in these fields. The more he loves his neighbour, the more he will be concerned that the whole *ethos* of his society – cultural, moral, legal, political and economic – is a good one, preserving personality rather than destroying it.

But he will also be the first to confess that Christ does not supply him with an ethical code, any more than he supplies him with a legal system, or a polity, or an economy. For it was not Jesus's purpose to provide any of these. Jesus's purpose was to call men to the Kingdom of God, to subject everything in their lives to the overriding, unconditional claim of God's utterly gracious yet utterly demanding rule of righteous love. And men could not acknowledge this claim without accepting the constraint of the same sacrificial, unselfregarding *agape* over all their relations with each other. It is this undeviating claim, this inescapable constraint, which provides the profoundly constant element in the distinctively Christian response in every age or clime. For it produces in Christians, however different or diversely placed, a direction, a cast, a style of life, which is recognizably and gloriously the same. Yet *what* precisely they must do to embody this claim will differ with every century, group and individual.

The elements of fixity and freedom are still there, but the mixture is different; and it allows those who start from the second end to treat freely what, for those starting from the other end, seems most fixed. And this not unnaturally is disconcerting. To those for whom the element of constancy in Christian ethics is content-centred, changes in what the Church teaches in different generations or cultures must inevitably appear as a threat – or as a mark of imperfection. Ideally it always ought to be the same for all men everywhere. If this is not, it is a sign of unhappy division or of moral decline. And the answer in either case is a reiterated affirmation of the abiding, unchanging values.

But realism, if nothing else, requires us to admit that the situation is not so simple. The *content* of Christian morals has over the centuries changed considerably. And I believe that Christians should not have too troubled a conscience about the fact that *what* their brethren have believed to be right and wrong in different situations has differed, and still differs, widely.

John A. T. Robinson, *Christian Freedom in a Permissive Society*, London, SCM, 1970, pp. ix, x, 11–13.

(d) Moral resistance in the 1970s

Literature, the cinema and the theatre are all indulged in as a matter of positive choice. The broadcasting media are in a different category, being virtually on tap directly within the home. In so far as television and radio have mirrored developments in the arts and literature they have of necessity included increasingly in their programmes material which emphasizes sexual infidelity and lust together with the gratuitous use of violence. It is in the field of television drama where the all-pervading permissiveness is mostly evident, with plays emphasizing infidelity in marriage, promiscuity and sexual deviancy outside it, and virtually writing off traditional standards of sexual morality. . . .

A wave of cynicism and irreverent satire begun with *That Was The Week That Was* in 1963 and continued in similar programmes, was the prelude to a period when under a very liberal-minded director-general 'a fall occurred in BBC standards which unfortunately is still continuing', to quote John Stokes MP writing to *The Times*. There was some correspondence in the *Daily Telegraph* in the Autumn of 1971 concerning the charge that there was a general bias in television, during the course of which both David Holbrook, the writer, and Malcom Muggeridge, accused the broadcasting media of 'unfairness, impertinence and bias' concerning those 'opposed to the prevalent dogmas of permissiveness'. There has been much public agitation in this field over the past eight years as a result of the work of Mrs Mary Whitehouse, whose Clean-up TV Campaign and subsequent National Viewers and Listeners Association has attracted much support from the British public, and it must be added, a measure of scorn.

Sex education for children has mushroomed during the past twenty years. Whilst most rational people welcome the open and frank discussion of sexual matters which has been a feature of recent years more recently there have been some disquieting developments. The schools radio programme *Leaving about Life* intended for the fourteen to sixteen age group, has, amongst other things, advocated the practice of masturbation as a preparation or rehearsal for sexual intercourse, taken a virtually amoral attitude to homosexuality and sexual intercourse outside marriage, and implied that responsibility in sexual relations between the partners was simply a matter of considering each other's sexual needs and choosing an effective contraceptive.

During 1971 a sex education film entitled *Growing Up* was shown by Dr Martin Cole of Birmingham, which contained film of masturbation and also full sexual intercourse, together with a commentary which completely divorced the subject from any moral considerations. . . .

The extent to which what has been mentioned in this chapter is obscene in the terms of the 1959 Obscene Publications Act is a matter for some speculation. Whether it is or is not, most of it is pornographic in the sense that it exploits depersonalized sex for commercial or ideological gain and is also likely to lead to a coarse animalistic attitude to sexual relationships. The stakes in the pornography business are high. There are many fortunes to be made and as each barrier is overrun, as each convention is discarded, so inevitably pornographic material will move away from 'straight' sex to deviations, perversions, sadism, violence and cruelty, with incalculable results.

This is not just scaremongering talk. It is already happening in some of the highly competitive areas that have been discussed. And while the chief cause for concern may well be the mass media of press, radio and television, what happens in the theatre, the cinema and literature inevitably has an increasingly significant effect upon the more popular mass media. Children growing up today may well have a much more open and uninhibited attitude to sexuality, which will be all to the good, but they are nevertheless being exposed to material freely available as it is through many outlets, which no one has yet clearly shown could not cause grave damage to their developing attitudes towards sex.

John Capon, *. . . and there was light: The Story of the Nationwide Festival of Light*, London, Lutterworth, 1972, pp. 99–102 (with cuts).

(e) *Christian uncertainties*

Trying to tell the Editor what I had in mind for this series, I used the shorthand, 'hot potatoes': that is to say, the sort of subjects that *Church Times* readers get most worked up about in the correspondence columns. Abortion and women priests were the first two that came to mind, with divorce, homosexuality and extramarital sex following hard on their heels.

I think that what drove me on to write the series, as well as to give it its rather tentative title, was the feeling that I have not got these questions worked out to anything like my own satisfaction, and that I need to think about them a lot more.

Of course I know that even to wonder and puzzle about them causes offence in certain quarters – the quarters where there is a 'Christian answer' to every question. But what worries me about 'Christian answers' of that kind is that they nearly always seem to be 'tough' (not to say brutal) answers, giving blanket commands to people to do what often turns out to be the impossible; and my experience of life does not lead me to think that this is the way of love.

Blanket answers seem, superficially, to be based on appeals either to the Bible or to 'authority'; but underneath I sometimes think I discern an overwhelming attraction to 'simplicity' of thought. It really is so much simpler, neater, if you condemn, for example, all abortion whatever the reason, and give it a title like 'murder'. You then do not have to bear the agonising uncertainties and doubts, possibly the guilts. It asks of you no inner struggle, no admission of conflicting or upsetting evidence; you simply do either what your own emotions, or some external 'authority', tells you is the 'right' thing to do.

I am no moral theologian, but I have slowly and painfully come to the conviction that there are no simplicities, and no blanket answers; and, if we want to love others and not rush them into quick, and bad, solutions, then we have to remain open to all kinds of answers – some of them personally upsetting and offensive, no doubt.

What is so hard for every one of us to believe is that others are not made like us (quite apart from the fact that they exist in entirely different situations), and that life is not neat but messy, as well as being paradoxical, contradictory and full of surprise. This is why we need an extraordinary mental flexibility in looking at everything from moral questions to the economic situation, trying to perceive in the tangle of threads the one that will lead us home. . . .

Let me come clean about my attitudes to the subjects mentioned above, so that you can see where my bias lies.

I do not feel able to utter a blanket condemnation of all abortions, all divorce, all homosexuality or all extramarital sex, though I can think of many situations where I would deplore one or more of them in practice. Because orthodox opinion has been so strongly against them, and because I have an immense respect both for Biblical insights and for Church teaching, I feel obliged to question myself continually and not to adopt any sort of complacent attitude. But, the more I question and the more I look at actual situations, the more I continue to feel that sometimes the 'hard' and sometimes the 'soft' solution is the right one. . . .

Since I have already stuck my neck out, let me stick it out a few inches farther and say that I do not believe there is a 'Christian answer' to anything at all; and I deplore the tendency to 'make man for the Sabbath' that suggests that there is. All that is available to us is a 'human answer', one that exists in the same way for those who are not practising Christians as for those who are; and it is an answer (if I have understood Christ at all) which tries to set pre-judgements on one side and see what is the most loving solution for the greatest number of people.

Sometimes a loving solution can cause agonising and guilt-producing feelings (as in the decision to end a marriage which is no more than a sham) yet which are unavoidable. Sometimes it can produce the sort of self-sacrifice with which Christians have tended to feel more at home. I don't believe that there's a hard-and-fast rule, only the rule of people's human and spiritual growth. And a painful business *that* is.

Monica Furlong, *Christian Uncertainties*, London, Hodder & Stoughton, 1975, pp. 105–7 (with cuts).

(f) The abortion 'crisis'

Easy abortion is something with which we have become very familiar. In almost every country in the world it is legal in some circumstances, and in many – including our own – it is very common. Abortion is the subject of heated emotions on the part of those who favour it and those who do not. Where does the balance of the argument lie?

The strongest supporters of abortion are those who see it as an essential element in 'women's rights'. Every woman, they claim, has an absolute right to control the functions of her own body. She has a right to stop herself becoming pregnant, and if that fails she has an equal right to stop herself giving birth – so that both contraception and abortion are methods of 'birth control'. The fetus, it is alleged, is merely part of the woman's body. No-one else can challenge her right to dispose of it should she so choose.

The most public opponents of abortion have been seen as the Roman Catholic Church, and in consequence the debate about abortion has been regarded by many as a debate between a particular religious standpoint and everyone else. But this view is seriously mistaken. Opposition to abortion has come not merely from Roman Catholics but from Protestants too, and one of the most significant features of the recent development of the debate has been the public commitment of leading Evangelicals to the anti-abortion cause. . . .

More recently, of course, many of the Protestant churches have taken up very different positions, which while continuing to stress the significance of the life of the fetus have often come to terms with abortion for reasons which would earlier have been considered unthinkable. It is difficult not to see this change of climate as the result of liberalizing tendencies in the theology of the churches, which have in many areas produced less clear-cut notions of right and wrong. The contradictory nature of the position which results is evident in many church pronouncements, which have plainly been devised to use the old words while making room for the new ideas. For example, in the fateful year of 1967 the Archbishop of Canterbury, when addressing Convocation, could speak of the 'general inviolability of the fetus' as 'normative', while going on to list the categories of possible exceptions: 'the risk of birth of a deformed or defective child; conception after rape; circumstances when the bearing and rearing of the child would prove beyond the total capacity of the mother'. Again, the Church of Scotland stated in 1966 that 'we cannot assert too strongly that the inviolability of the fetus is one of the fundamentals and its right to life must be strongly safeguarded', but then went on to add, in an almost sinister fashion, that 'we recognise that this general right is, in certain circumstances, in conflict with other rights', thus effectively torpedoing the significance of the statement of principle which had just been made. The national churches therefore offered little real opposition to the passage of the 1967 Act.

IS THERE A CHRISTIAN VIEW?

So what, we may ask, is *the Christian view* of abortion? Until recent years it would not, as we have seen, have been difficult to answer that question. What began as a distinctive position over against that of Greek and Roman paganism, inherited by the first Christians from the people of God in the Old Testament, developed into the universal teaching of the church. The present acceptance of abortion, in liberal Protestantism and, indeed, in some evangelical circles, is a mark of the degree to which Christian thinking can be influenced by the pragmatism of those who have little respect for human life. Of course, present-day defenders of abortion within the Christian church vary from those who are entirely happy with the practice to others (evangelicals in particular) whose deep unease can nevertheless come to terms with what they see as sometimes a sad necessity. Yet even this position is poles apart from that of the first Christians which became the conviction of the whole church of Jesus Christ. In claiming that the church's ancient repudiation of abortion is alone biblical and fully Christian we do no more than call those modern Christians who have taken another stance back to the historic moral teaching of the church, whose origins lie in the distinctive character of the people of God in Old Testament times.

Nigel M. de S. Cameron and Pamela F. Sims, *Abortion: The Crisis in Morals and Medicine*, Leicester, Inter-Varsity Press, 1986, pp. 7, 31–2.

(g) Marriage without marriage?

To this very day so many theorists assert that there is no link between sexual pleasure and love that it is important to have a full understanding of human nature in which the two are essentially linked. This link is the answer to pursuing sexual pleasure separately from a personal interaction of love. But if the hedonist needs correction, so does the Christian fundamentalist who sees the essential link to be between sex and procreation, as the Catholic Church still teaches us in the encyclical *Humanae Vitae*. This tradition has yet to learn that before sex was linked with procreation, it was connected with personal love in the depths of interpersonal communication.

In referring to *Humanae Vitae* it is vital to remind ourselves that this remains the official teaching of the Roman Catholic Church. The fact is that the overwhelming majority of Roman Catholic moral theologians and the faithful have rejected this teaching and there is a continuous tension between the teaching authority and the rest of the Roman Catholic community. The essence of the teaching depends on the view that there is an essential link between sexual intercourse and procreation which must not be denied. At the heart of this view is an instinctual, biological view of sexual intercourse which in the light of all I have said is inconsistent with reality. At the centre of sexual intercourse is a duality of biology and personal love, and of the two the latter has always the overwhelming priority. This does not mean that contraception cannot be misused. It can and frequently is, in the sense that it is used to offer a safeguard against fertilization in the absence of a loving encounter. But the fact that contraception can be misused does not render it invalid in the proper circumstances when it is used to facilitate love. . . .

COHABITATION

The final issue which must be tackled is cohabitation. This is a state in which a couple are living together as husband and wife. Cohabitation may be followed by formal marriage, but increasingly couples are deciding to cohabit, have children and not marry. What is the moral status of cohabitation?

In so far as such a couple have not undertaken a formal ceremony of marriage, they are in fact formally fornicating. However, they would not see themselves in that light at all. By the criteria I have set out, they are in fact in a state of committed love which is marriage. The concept that they are married without going through a formal ceremony is not a leap of the imagination or an externalizing liberal handout. There is a deep-seated theological tradition that the essence of marriage is to be found in the commitment and donation of a man and a woman of their person to each other in a committed relationship which is consummated by intercourse. It is not the priest who confers marriage. He is a witness to the marriage event which the couple enact for each other. The public dimension of the wedding ceremony was introduced as a compulsory element to safeguard that commitment. I believe that the need for a public dimension of marriage is as relevant today as when it was introduced three hundred years ago. Nevertheless, the status of cohabitation is far from clear in the moral sense. Whilst such patterns of behaviour are clearly breaking ecclesiastical and legal laws, are they repudiating the essence of marriage?

SUMMARY

Let me summarize what I have said in this chapter. For thousands of years the key to sexuality was to be found in procreation with the accompanying pleasure, a reward for this deed. The teaching on contraception in the Roman Catholic Church which insists that every act of intercourse should be open to life is the last remnant of this tradition. No one can dismiss the biological link between intercourse and new life, but the connection has become markedly reduced, and in my view a deeper understanding of the human personality shows that it is the link between sex and love that has the supreme value and that all intercourse has ultimately to be assessed by the presence or absence of love. . . .

In the last twenty-five years, the permissive society has attempted to liberate sex from the confines of the furtive, the secretive, from shame and guilt. At the same time it has, at its worst, trivialized, cheapened and dehumanized it. Christianity has been shocked and its ethical foundations challenged. Crisis is a time of opportunity. Whilst we can thank the world as Christians for demystifying sex, we have an opportunity to offer back to the world a value of sexuality steeped in love which accords with the findings of psychology, the insights of the Bible and tradition, for sex has always been held in high regard. Today we can see it as a precious gift from God which demands a morality to protect not something we should feel embarrassed about but an experience that reflects the divine in each one of us.

Jack Dominian, 'Masturbation and Premarital Sexual Intercourse', in Jack Dominian and Hugh Montefiore, *God, Sex and Love: An Exercise in Ecumenical Ethics*, London, SCM, 1989, pp. 25, 34–6.

(h) *Christianity and homosexuality*

In 1977 SCM Press published 'Towards a Theology of Gay Liberation', a symposium of papers and articles on various aspects of gay life and sexuality. Malcolm Macourt concluded his essays called 'A Framework for the Debate' by saying, 'It will only be when theologians face fairly and squarely the question about "Chris and Pat" (the gay couple) knowing that Chris and Pat exist in large numbers, that there will be any real dialogue between the church and gay liberation – and only then will we be able to progress towards a theology of gay relationships and a theology of human sexuality appropriate to our times.'

Since then there has been little sign of such a process taking place, indeed largely because of AIDS and the hostility of the tabloid media, homophobia (albeit with a kind of pastoral face) has taken on a new vibrancy culminating in Tony Higton's infamous motion to the General Synod, and much Christian support for Clause 28. As a result, those of us who are gay men, lesbians or bisexual have been forced to continue the same old battles over exegesis of a limited number of texts, the validity of our lifestyles and even our right to be called 'Christian'. . . .

CONCLUSION

The context and criteria for gay interpretations of the Bible and for doing gay theology, is the community of gay people in the church. We are the only people who can take responsibility for our own liberation. There lies the future. To voluntarily leave the church is to accept voluntary marginalisation and to ensure that the church – which is our church too – is never confronted or challenged.

We must guard against the desire for validation and acceptance within the patriarchal church on its terms. Otherwise, we will never be able to determine the agenda or parameters of discussion but will be trapped within the church's priorities. Then the church will never be confronted with its guilt in our persecution or moved to repent. The process I have outlined will enable us to begin the reclamation of our history and in so doing acquire perspective and balance. It will allow us to reclaim our Bible and come into a place where a theology of gay liberation evolves from us and around us. . . .

1988 CONGRESS STATEMENT

'The SCM Congress affirms that human sexuality in all its richness is made in the image of God and that, therefore, all committed lesbian, gay and heterosexual relationships are fully compatible with the Christian gospel.

Clause 28 of the Local Government Bill is based on the assumption that lesbian and gay relationships or lifestyles are less valuable than a heterosexual way of life. From a Christian point of view, it implies that lesbians and gay men share less fully than heterosexual people in God-given human dignity and the life of the kingdom. As an attack on the civil liberties of a particular group in society, it is without parallel in the democratic countries of the world. Clause 28 is a human rights issue, with implications for every member of society.

As Christians we are called to build, in a spirit of love and justice, a community which is the image of the kingdom of God. We should be supportive of all relationships that build up the community life through the experience of love given and received. Clause 28, by making ignorance and intolerance of homosexuality acceptable, will encourage distrust and division amongst Christians and in the wider community.

We therefore commit ourselves to supporting lesbians and gay men and to opposing discriminatory practices wherever they occur. We will promote dialogue and education about lesbian and gay issues within the SCM, the churches, and society. We would urge the churches and all Christian organisations to reconsider their policy on lesbian and gay relationships in the light of their responsibilities to all their members and to the Christian community as a whole.'

Just Love: A Resource Book Exploring the Theology of Sexuality, London, SCM, n.d., pp. 17, 18, 39.

(i) *AIDS: the judgement of God?*

If AIDS is only one indication among many, of a society under judgement, why has it been singled out for identification as the judgement of God?

There are four main reasons: One is that AIDS has been the subject of a sensationalist approach by the media (especially the tabloids). It is an infectious, incurable and fatal disease and the impression has been given that it is easy to catch. If one believes this then the fear which has gripped the country is entirely reasonable.

However the premise that it is easy to catch is false and even when people are given those facts about AIDS which are currently available, many persist in their fear, which feeds on the uncertainties surrounding the disease. This irrational, but nonetheless real, fear has driven people to seek an explanation. One possibility is that it is divine judgement.

The second reason is that AIDS has since its appearance in the West been associated with homosexuality. The overlap in this case between the spread of a fatal disease and behaviour that is prohibited in the Bible, and also largely condemned by society has led to the feeling that there is punishment involved here.

Thirdly, there is a residual Christian conscience in Britain and America about the 'permissive society'. As long as people thought that there was no cost to 'free' sex this was repressed, but now that this is no longer so, those who have been either too timid to speak or have enjoyed the permissive society with an uneasy conscience are now speaking up. Another group which is speaking up, though from very different motives, consists of those who, having experienced permissiveness to the full, have discovered it to be a trap and a counterfeit of the richness that can be found in monogamy or celibacy.

Fourthly, there is a sense of 'natural law' in some people's reactions to AIDS. This particular argument states that active homosexuality is against the natural order. AIDS entered the West through homosexuality and now the natural order is fighting back. In the end nature will always have the last word. This particular argument expressed in this way ignores the heterosexual incidence of AIDS in Central Africa, but another form of the argument would state that all promiscuity is against the 'natural order' so that the same would apply.

Roy McCloughry and Carol Bebawi, *Aids: A Christian Response*, Bramcote, Grove, 1987, p. 19.

14

BROADCASTING:
THREE REPORTS

*E*xtracts are printed here from three official reports on broadcasting, from 1949 (a), 1962 (b) and 1977 (c). These serve as something of an epilogue to the book as a whole, reflecting religious changes across the period and also providing a starting point for discussion of the growing role of the media in forming religious attitudes and perceptions.

(a) 1949

246 The treatment of religious questions in British broadcasting is governed by two considerations. The first consideration is that the BBC's highest duty is the search for truth. This was declared in 1947 in explanation of the Governors' decision then that controversial broadcasting should be undertaken. But this decision does not mean that British broadcasting is neutral where Christian values are concerned. 'Of course it is not' declared the Director General of the BBC to the British Council of Churches in November, 1948.

> There are many demands of impartiality laid upon the Corporation but this is not one of them. We are citizens of a Christian country, and the BBC – an institution set up by the State – bases its policy upon a positive attitude towards the Christian values. It seeks to safeguard those values and to foster acceptance of them. The whole preponderant weight of its programmes is directed to this end.

247 Alongside of the first consideration making impartial search for truth the highest duty of the BBC stands a second consideration; that the BBC is an institution set up by the State in a Christian

country. The two considerations are reconciled in practice by having both controversial broadcasting and religious broadcasting as distinct activities of the BBC.

> But it does not seem to me to be an inherent duty of Broadcasting to make people join the Christian faith. By that I mean it is not the duty of the BBC in everything it does. It is the duty of religious broadcasting, of course . . . But there are many other fields of broadcasting in which the duty does not arise. . . .

248 The institution of religious broadcasting, with a special and considerable allocation of programme time, raises the question of which bodies, religious or claiming to be religious, shall be allowed or invited to take part, by conducting services. This question is dealt with by the BBC in accord with a policy decision taken after consultation with the Central Religious Advisory Committee:

> Broadcasts of religious services are generally confined to churches in the main stream of historic Christianity: i.e. to the Church of England, the Church of Scotland, the Roman Catholic Church, and the Free Churches associated in the Free Church Federal Council. The rationale of this ruling is the fact that . . . the message given by preachers from any of those churches is likely to be acceptable to the overwhelming majority of listeners to religious broadcasts, to whatever denomination they belong. (*General Survey*, paragraph 66, printed in Appendix H.)

This likelihood is secured by the understanding on which preachers are invited – that they will not attack controversially the positions held by other churches; with this understanding no censorship of scripts is required.

Report of the Broadcasting Committee, London, HMSO, 1949, p. 63.

(b) 1962

277 The term 'religious broadcasting' includes not only religious services, but also talks of a theological or devotional nature, discussions, and programmes which relate the ideals and practices of

religion to social and moral problems. In principle, the term religious broadcasting need not denote only Christian religious broadcasting. The principle of toleration in matters of religion is so well established in the United Kingdom that any broadcasting organisation with the duty of giving a comprehensive service might be regarded, in theory at any rate, as being responsible for providing religious broadcasting to satisfy the needs of any religious body with enough adherents.

278 But in fact those providing religious broadcasting in the United Kingdom have to take account of two factors. The first is that the United Kingdom is formally a Christian country and that Christians overwhelmingly outnumber the adherents of other religions; the second, that the heavy demands on the limited amount of broadcasting time available make it impossible to attempt to cater for all religions or for all denominations in any one religion. In the result, religious broadcasting is confined, with one exception, to Christian religious broadcasting. Even within the ambit of the Christian religion it is further limited to certain selected churches.

279 The BBC have defined their policy on religious broadcasting as follows:

'The first aim is that it should reflect the worship, thought, and action of those churches which represent the main stream of the Christian tradition in the country. The second is that religious broadcasting should bring before listeners and viewers what is most significant in the relationship between the Christian faith and the modern world. The third aim is that religious broadcasting should seek to reach those on the fringe of the organised life of the churches, or quite outside it.'

We understand that, for independent television, the aims of religious broadcasting are essentially the same as for the BBC. The BBC is advised on religious broadcasting policy by the Central Religious Advisory Committee (CRAC). The ITA is required by statute to appoint or to arrange for the assistance of a religious advisory committee with whose advice the Authority is bound to comply and to secure compliance. The Authority decided not to appoint a committee of its own but arranged for the assistance of CRAC. The churches regarded by the BBC and ITA as constituting the 'main stream' are represented on CRAC. They are: Church of England, Church of Scotland, Methodist, Roman Catholic, Baptist, Congregational and Presbyterian. . . .

281 Our examination of Christian religious broadcasting naturally led to a consideration of the 'main stream' policy. Crucial though the 'main stream' concept is, no one expressly challenged it in principle. The Unitarians, who are excluded from the 'main stream' but who have been given time on occasion by the BBC, agreed – though reluctantly – that the time was not yet ripe for a thorough re-appraisal of the 'main stream' policy. They believed that it was, in any case, eventually bound to become obsolete of its own accord.

282 The concept provides, in our view, a useful practical device; but there is a risk that it will be too narrowly interpreted. Nor can we ignore the fact that the question of what churches are in the 'main stream' is determined by the BBC, and by the ITA, after consultation with CRAC. This leads to the anomaly that responsibility for recommending the continued exclusion of churches seeking admission to the 'main stream' rests with representatives of those churches already included.

283 We were glad to find, however, that the 'main stream' churches were agreed that the concept should be interpreted more liberally, and that they were disposed to accept – and indeed to advocate – that the claims of those not included should be examined in the hope that the answer would be 'Yes', rather than in the expectation that it would be 'No'. It is inherent in the 'main stream' concept that the stream can be widened: the development of religious thought in the United Kingdom shows that some churches which are today among those which 'represent the main stream of the Christian tradition in the country' were not so long ago barely tolerated, if not actually proscribed. It is certainly not part of our task to propose that this or that church should or should not be included in the

'main stream'. But we affirm that the decision whether a church is to be allowed to take part in religious broadcasting must remain a matter for the two public corporations; that is, for the Governors of the BBC and for the Members of the ITA. We note that, in exercising this responsibility, the BBC has thought it right on occasion to broadcast services of excluded churches, as for example the Unitarians. . . .

285 The second of the BBC's aims is that religious broadcasting should bring before listeners and viewers what is most significant in the relationship between the Christian faith and the modern world. This aim is clearly much more difficult to achieve than is the first aim of religious broadcasting. It is easier to 'reflect the worship, thought and action' of the churches, than actively to show a relationship between their faith and the modern world.

286 The third aim of the BBC's policy – that religious broadcasting should seek to reach those on the fringe of the organised life of the churches, or quite outside it – is, we understand, intended to convey that religious broadcasting should not be so narrow in its approach as to appeal only to those who already subscribe to orthodox beliefs. It does not imply that particular churches may pursue a policy of conversion. Generally, the churches considered this interpretation to be right; and there was no suggestion that it was not observed, either in the service of the BBC or in that of independent television.

287 Giving oral evidence, however, the Roman Catholic Church expressed certain reservations about the broadcasters' policy. These were that its effect was to make religious broadcasting so undenominational as to fail to carry conviction; and that, as members of a teaching church, Roman Catholics everywhere believed that their religious broadcasts should teach and expound religious truth as they saw it. Proselytising, to the extent that it might imply attacking other denominations or otherwise taking dishonourable advantage of the opportunities offered by the allocation of broadcasting time, was abhorrent; but denominations should be able to do everything in their power to spread the truth as they saw it.

288 We think it would be unfortunate if religious broadcasting came to be used for proselytisation, but on the other hand the explicit exposition of a doctrinal standpoint must be permitted if religious broadcasting is not to become anaemic. This does not mean, however, that doctrinal differences should be unduly emphasised, and anything like direct disparagement of other faiths should be ruled out. We approve the present policy of the BBC and of independent television, and are satisfied that present practice is a proper realisation of it. . . .

290 As we have already indicated, religious broadcasting need not be restricted to Christian religious broadcasting. The point, however, is not one of great practical importance since – with one important exception mentioned below – the followers in the United Kingdom of non-Christian religions are few and scattered. Where, however, there are in any place enough people of a particular non-Christian faith, local broadcasting, if introduced, may provide opportunities for religious broadcasting for them.

291 The one non-Christian religion represented by significant numbers throughout the United Kingdom is the Jewish faith. No Jewish services are regularly broadcast: the only regular broadcasts for those of the Jewish faith are the two annual BBC broadcasts of short talks on the occasions of the Passover and the Day of Atonement. The Anglo-Jewish Association criticised this allocation, and suggested that some of the other major Jewish religious events should be occasions for regular sound and television programmes. The Board of Deputies of British Jews thought that it was doubtful whether the Jewish Community as a whole would be in favour of broadcasting of religious services, but wanted more time to be devoted to programmes of Jewish interest, including Jewish religion. We make no recommendation; it will be for the representatives of the Jewish faith, when they think fit, to put proposals to the BBC and the ITA.

The Committee on Broadcasting, 1960: Report, London, HMSO, 1962, pp. 88–9, 90–1.

(c) 1977

[W]e next turned for guidance to the body which advises both the BBC and the IBA, the Central Religious Advisory Committee. We asked them about the three aims which the BBC told the Pilkington Committee were the objectives of religious broadcasting. The first was to reflect the worship, thought and action of those churches which represent the mainstream of the Christian tradition in this country. The second was to stress what was most relevant in the Christian faith for the modern world. The third was to try to reach those outside the churches or only loosely attached to them.

20.11 The Central Religious Advisory Committee told us that while these objectives were still valid as a rough working guide, they needed revision and re-interpretation. The new guidelines which they evolved in discussion with the BBC and IBA were the following:

'(i) To seek to reflect the worship, thought and action of the principal religious traditions represented in Britain, recognising that those traditions are mainly, though not exclusively, Christian;

(ii) To seek to present to viewers and listeners those beliefs, ideas, issues and experiences in the contemporary world which are evidently related to a religious interpretation or dimension of life;

(iii) To seek also to meet the religious interests, concerns and needs of those on the fringe of, or outside, the organised life of the Churches.'

20.12 This statement is important because it departs fundamentally from the previous definition of objectives. It recognises that religion in this country is no longer synonymous with Christianity, and it no longer requires broadcasting to pretend that it is. It abandons the notion that broadcasting should reflect only the life of the churches in the mainstream of Britain's Christian tradition. It wants to provide some programmes which would present a religious interpretation of the world rather than specifically a Christian interpretation. It asks broadcasting to cater for the religious needs of people outside the churches, but not to proselytise. This is an important change because it makes clear that even if their religion lays a duty upon believers to proselytise, they must not use broadcasting to fulfil that duty. In other words, religious broadcasting should not be the religious equivalent of party political broadcasts.

20.13 This is the answer which CRAC gave to the first question we put to ourselves: what should be the objectives of religious broadcasting? We accept this answer. The answer is in fact less of a change than at first sight appears and more of a recognition of what religious departments in broadcasting have been moving towards in the last few years. Broadcasting is going to have to reflect the religious experience and faiths of many different denominations and groups including those who through immigration have grown in size. The fourth television channel is a particularly suitable place for programmes designed for the smaller religious groups. Local broadcasting, too, should provide time for some religious group which, though it may *in toto* be small in relation to the nation, is a considerable gathering in the locality. But, this having been said, the life of the principal Christian denominations in their country should have primary place in religious broadcasting.

How should religious broadcasting be presented?

20.14 The second question we put to ourselves was: how should the broadcasters achieve these objectives? There is always a danger that the religious broadcasting departments, their advisers, as well as the admirably concerned who discuss these matters amongst themselves and who react to the theological and social moods of the times, may think more of the message they believe should be communicated and less of the needs of those who will receive it. We detected in the letters which we received disappointment in what people were offered. This was inevitable, because if church goers and non-church goers, believers and agnostics, are all looking to the same programmes for inspiration, quite a number will be disillusioned. Some, particularly the old and housebound, look to broadcasting to recall for them the faith, the hymns and the worship of their childhood days: they want it to sustain them in that faith, and comfort them in their times of trouble. Others expect religious broadcasting to satisfy their desire to understand the creeds, rituals and outlook of other denominations and religions, perhaps because they are in search of a faith, but often out of curiosity and of the pleasure of speculation. Others, among them humanists and athe-ists, expect to be able to listen to programmes in which people of all beliefs discuss moral and social questions in order to distinguish what, if anything, is the value of the specifically Christian, or other religious, approach to these matters.

20.15 Religious programmes can meet all these expectations. But they cannot do so in the same programme. The broadcasters show signs of trying to do so: and the dish served up is a sort of homogen-ised religious mash, in which the sentimental and the weakly reassuring obscure the real discipline and duties of the religious life. In the desire to reach a wide audience, programmes are made to be all things to all men and to cover as many attitudes as possible in one generalised output. But there is another reason for weak programmes which seemed to us to lie at the heart of the matter, a paradox which could not be wholly resolved. A religion must be relevant to the whole of life: anything which claims less is a mere cult. When CRAC came to talk to us, they said that unless there was some overlap between religious broadcasting and current affairs there would be bound to be something wrong with religious broad-casting. It would otherwise become 'a little ghetto within broadcast-ing trying to maintain some kind of conservative propaganda for our own little group of committed Christians'. They must not retire from what they saw as their most important task as religious broad-casters. CRAC wanted to escape from the religious ghetto, engage a wider non-committed audience and attract top-quality producers to make adventurous programmes.

20.16 Who would not sympathise with CRAC's wish to see religious attitudes and thought being brought to bear on moral, ethical and social problems in programmes made to raise such issues?

To many religiously committed people, it is insulting to describe the closed period as the 'God-slot'; to do so is tacitly to assume that religious faith can be compartmentalised, tidied up into religious departments and tucked away on a Sunday. We see no reason why such programmes should be placed only in the shelter of the shortened closed period or relegated to unfavourable places in the schedules. This kind of programme should be intended to attract the attention of a wide audience at a time when people are able and willing to view. Nor need such programmes be shown on Sunday.

20.17 But there are in this policy certain dangers to which we would draw attention. The first is that radio is possibly even more valuable to religious broadcasting than television and we wonder whether the BBC's religious departments recognise this to be so. The second concerns the religious departments themselves. They cannot make a take-over bid for discussion of all the serious issues of our time. Much as we admired the energy and enthusiasm of some of their producers, and in particular some of the productions of BBC's *Anno Domini*, current affairs, documentary and feature departments and groups are as appropriate as religious departments to produce programmes on moral problems. Through no fault of their own, producers in religious departments are locked within a vicious circle. Programme departments generally attract the resources and production skills necessary to make the programmes for which they are responsible. Producers who have the capacity and the yen to make intellectually stimulating programmes which examine moral issues will be tempted to revolt against making the simpler programmes of congregational hymn singing. So religious broadcasting departments will tend to lose producers who show themselves skilled in producing challenging yet comprehensible programmes. Yet, without such producers, they cannot produce such programmes.

Report of the Committee on the Future of Broadcasting, London, HMSO, 1977, pp. 319–21.

INDEX

Leadership,
distrust of, 155
Leeds,
Hindus in, 79
popular opinion of religion in,
159–165
Leisure, 230
Levine, Ephraim, 41
Lewis, C. S., 244
Lewis, Saunders, 223, 224
Liberation theology, 129, 247,
248
Liell, Peter, 264
Life,
inner reality of, 149
meaning of, 69
purpose of, 186
Life after death, 169, 172
Lincoln, Abraham, 245
Liturgical language, 22
as form of action, 277
Liturgy,
black spirituality and, 131
women's, 276
Liverpool,
social divisions in, 237
Local Government Act, 1894, 218
London,
response to churches, 238
social divisions in, 237
synagogue in, 39
working class attitudes to religion,
169–172
London, Green Lanes,
church in, 123
Lord's supper *see Holy*
Communion, Mass

Love, 30, 273, 293, 297, 304
Luton, St. Hugh's, 5

M

McCloughry, Roy, 305
MacLeod of Fuinary, *Lord*, 214,
233
Machine age, 183
Male dominance, 52, 87, 88
Man,
New Age approach to, 150
Rastafarian view of, 134
in society, 121
what is he?, 186
Manchester synagogue, 38
Marcuse, Herbert, 183, 184
Marriage, 300
Charles and Diana, 173
in Hinduism, 90, 94
Jewish, 38, 278
of princes, 174
public commitment of, 301
role of sex in, 288
in Sikhism, 94, 100
Marrinan, Patrick, 229
Mass in Ireland, 34
Mass Observation, 153
Materialism, 42, 79, 107
Matriarchy, 287
Mecca,
pilgrimage to, 58
Medicine, 150
Meditation among Sikhs, 96, 101
Menski, W., 90
Menstruation, 86
Methodism, 121, 167, 169
Minorities *see Ethnic minorities*

New Age, 137, 149–152
  four fields of, 150
  women in, 270, 287
New Religious Movements, 137–145
  causes of worry, 140
  converts to, 139, 140, 141
  families of converts, 145
  parliamentary unease, 141
  problems of, 139
  sinister activities of, 143
  society's response to, 139
Nichiren Shoshu Buddhism, 147
Nielsen, J. S., 59
Nightingale, Florence, 274
Northern Ireland,
  cultural trend in, 225
  loyalism, 227
  Paisley view of, 227
  problems of, 228
  Roman Catholic view of, 227
Nottingham,
  religious experience in, 179
Nuns in Buddhism, 286

O

Obscene Publications Act 1950, 295
Ordination of women, 270, 274, 275, 296
Original sin, 23, 25, 208

P

Paisley, Ian, 214, 225–227
Paisley, Rhonda, 227
Pandya, R., 89
Peace, 204, 273

'Permissiveness', 11, 125, 288, 291, 294, 302, 305
Personal responsibility, 244
Phoenix, Sybil, 128
Pilkington Committee, 312
Politics,
  see also Church and politics
  Jewish view of, 49
  Sikhs and, 106
Poor,
  church's concern for, 220, 235, 236
Pope,
  authority of, 5
  visits, 8, 34
  see also Roman Catholic Church
Pornography, 281, 295
Poverty, 51, 54, 121
  see also Poor
  in Ireland, 34
  in inner cities, 29
  in Third World, 121
Prayer, 20, 21
  in Black Christianity, 120
  at Greenham Common, 277
  in Hinduism, 80, 86, 89, 208
  Jewish women, 281
  Muslim, 57, 58, 60, 61, 63, 65, 199, 259, 269
  for Northern Ireland, 227
  popular opinion of, 170
  in Sikhism, 96, 114, 115
Private Eye, 144
Prophets, Biblical, 49
Prospects for Wales, 31
Punjab, 284
  Hinduism in, 93

Religious doubt, 43
Religious education, 245
  advisory councils, 262, 263
  Birmingham Agreed Syllabus, 251
  collective worship, 260
  content of, 264
  elements of, 255
  future of, 264
  in multi-racial society, 254
  Muslim reservations, 268
  provision of 1944 Act, 249
  right of withdrawal, 256, 261, 269
  school assemblies, 255, 267
  scope of, 253
  syllabus, 250
  world religions in, 252
Religious experience, 178
Religious instruction *see Religious education*
Religious movements, new *see New Religious Movements, and specific groups*
Remarriage, 17
Remembrance Sunday, 177
Responsibility, 244
Rhys, Gethin, 225
Rights and duties, 51
Robinson, John A. T. *Bishop*, 5, 293
  Honest to God, 5, 12–14
Roman Catholic Church, 208
  abortion and, 298
  authority of, 14, 15
  broadcasting and, 310
  contraception and, 5, 16, 300, 301
  dissent in, 5, 14

  evangelical view of, 19
  in Ireland, 33, 227
  Muslims and, 187
  officials' behaviour, 15
  on divorce, 17
  on inter-faith relations, 185, 186
  pastoral letters, 34
  in Scotland, 9, 10
  sex and procreation, 300
  social justice and, 235
Roman Catholic Pastoral Congress, 214
Royal supremacy, 173
Royalty,
  religion and, 172
Rudra, 74
Runcie, Robert, *Archbishop*, 28, 274
Rushdie affair, 56, 68–72, 282, 283, 284

S

Sacraments, 17–18
Sacred, the, 72
Sacrifice among Muslims, 57
Saint Hilda's Community, 276
Salvation, 26, 182, 188, 205, 239
  in non-Christian religions, 189
Samhain, 165
Sanatan dharma, 73, 78
  see also Hinduism
Sarwar, Ghulam, 269
Satan, 26, 70, 189
Schools,
  see also under Education, Religious education
  for ethnic minorities, 256, 259